Joan Abramson

THE
INVISIBLE
WOMAN

Jossey-Bass Publishers

San Francisco · Washington · London · 1975

THE INVISIBLE WOMAN
Discrimination in the Academic Profession
    by Joan Abramson

Copyright © 1975 by: Jossey-Bass, Inc., Publishers
                     615 Montgomery Street
                     San Francisco, California 94111
                     &
                     Jossey-Bass Limited
                     3 Henrietta Street
                     London WC2E 8LU

Library of Congress Catalogue Card Number LC 74-32627

International Standard Book Number ISBN 0-87589-256-6

Manufactured in the United States of America

JACKET DESIGN BY WILLI BAUM

FIRST EDITION

Code 7512

◆◇◆◇◆◇◆◇◆◇◆◇◆◇◆◇◆◇◆◇◆◇◆◇◆◇◆◇◆◇◆◇◆

Preface

◆◇◆◇◆◇◆◇◆◇◆◇◆◇◆◇◆◇◆◇◆◇◆◇◆◇◆◇◆◇◆◇◆

> *"A slow sort of country!"* said the Queen. *"Now,
> here, you see, it takes all the running you can do to
> keep in the same place. If you want to get somewhere
> else, you must run at least twice as fast as that!"*

> Lewis Carroll, *Through the Looking Glass*

Four years ago I was an untenured instructor at the University of
Hawaii. I had been turned down for tenure and could look forward
to one year of "terminal" employment.

Since that time I have filed suit against the university in
state court, filed a sex discrimination complaint with the Department of Health, Education, and Welfare (which resulted in the
temporary withholding of a $2.4 million research grant—my hus-

v

band's—to the University of Hawaii), filed another sex discrimination complaint with the Equal Employment Opportunity Commission, and filed an equal-pay-for-equal-work complaint with the Wage and Hour Division of the Labor Department. And since that time I have received two University of Hawaii research grants and a University Press of Hawaii book contract, taken a 30 percent cut in pay for more responsible work, won a 53 percent raise in pay in the first equal-pay-for-equal-work settlement in the United States for a university woman, been nominated for an excellence-in-teaching award, received three unanimous recommendations for tenure from three faculty review and appeal committees, received a second favorable ruling from the Labor Department, received a finding in my favor from the Equal Employment Opportunity Commission, gained a favorable judgment from a state court, been selected as assistant director of a major university program, been elected director of the same program, seen my program terminated less than two weeks before the start of a school semester, been selected as chairwoman of the University of Hawaii Faculty Senate, and (within the space of one eventful year) been terminated, rehired, fired, rehired, terminated, rehired, and fired—all by the same university. And after years devoted to the advancement of a university career, as this book goes to press I am an untenured—and unemployed—instructor.

When my struggle for academic survival was new and my own level of expectations high, I happened to encounter an official of the American Association of University Professors (AAUP). Impressed by his strong and vocal stance on behalf of faculty rights, I spun out my tale of woe—a tale that had not yet gone through its most fantastic convolutions. My complaint was that I had been denied tenure for one illegitimate and illegal reason: I was a faculty wife, and my department, knowing I could not leave Hawaii, declined tenure with the expectation that I could be hired as a last-minute, semester-by-semester, low-cost lecturer. I had, then, been denied tenure because I am a woman.

How could I file a complaint with the AAUP? How long would such a complaint take to process? Had they taken sex discrimination complaints before?

The official listened sympathetically. But before he would answer any of my questions he wished to ask a few of his own:

"How long have you been at the University of Hawaii?" he asked.

"Four years."

"How old are you?" he asked.

"Thirty-eight."

"What rank were you when you were hired?" he asked.

"Instructor."

"What rank are you now?" he asked.

"Instructor."

The next question was rhetorical:

"Don't you think the fact that, at thirty-eight, and after four years, you are still an instructor is an indication that you are not qualified for either tenure or promotion? Now, perhaps if you had been promoted. . . ."

I realize now what I was too inexperienced to realize at the time: the encounter was a classic one. I was complaining of sex discrimination. The very term, if it has any meaning, means that qualified women are bypassed in favor of less qualified men. Yet, this seemingly sympathetic man insisted that there had to be something wrong with me, not with the system, if after thirty-eight years as a human being, four of them spent at the lowest possible rank of university instructional employment, I was still at that lowest possible rank. Had I been rewarded by the system (and therefore, presumably, not discriminated against), then I might have a legitimate reason to complain of discrimination.

Absurd as it may sound, this handy bit of reasoning pervades our universities today. Complaints of discrimination are met almost inevitably with challenges to the academic credentials of the complainer. As far as the academic establishment is concerned, everyone is rewarded on the basis of merit, and therefore any woman complaining of discrimination is only publicizing her own mediocrity. The arguments in defense of the status quo are endless—and all of them are as insipid and circular as the arguments presented by my friend from the AAUP.

Yet all the arguments, the excuses, the myths, the adamant

refusals to take affirmative action toward establishing equity do not change the fact that sex discrimination is perhaps the most serious problem in higher education today. It is serious because it cuts out or cuts down 50 percent of the potential competition for university jobs and therefore lowers the quality of university teaching and research. In the name of excellence, women are effectively frozen out of higher education. In the name of excellence, it is excellence that suffers. And the students—future university teachers or university trained citizens—are the losers.

There is obvious irony in the indignant refusal of the university establishment to face up to the problem of sex discrimination. Traditional wisdom maintains that, more than any other institution, the institution of higher education is the guardian of independent thinking, of courageous research, of the search for truth. Yet our universities have remained bastions of male self-righteousness. Rather than attempting to analyze the charge that universities discriminate against women, administrators spew forth a veritable geyser of rebuttal. The male higher education establishment reacts with an instinctive fervor more appropriate to religious zealots than to guardians of truth and logic. Certainly this phenomenon is worth exploring because the stakes are high—not just for women but for the quality of education in this country. It was in the hope of contributing to that exploration that I undertook this book.

The thrust of my exploration is threefold.

Part One of *The Invisible Woman* examines in some detail my own case history since it amply illustrates almost every reaction that occurs when a woman complains of discrimination on the basis of sex. The chapters in Part One cover the circumstances that led to my challenge of the university decision not to grant me tenure and to my filing a charge of sex discrimination. They explore the initial indifference to my charge by members of the university faculty and administration and the gradual shift by these persons to increasingly serious harrassment and retaliation. The escalation in retaliation seemed to go hand in hand with an escalation in my own responsibility within the university and continued until I became director of a four-year, degree-granting program and chairwoman of the Faculty Senate—only to be fired once again.

Part Two explores the academic setting and explains how the male academic establishment can proclaim the importance of the pursuit of truth and simultaneously refuse to face the issue of sex discrimination. This part analyzes the major myths of the academic world in relation to women and illustrates the way in which those myths work to exclude women while allowing male academics to believe that merit alone dictates academic success. Part Two also examines the male backlash, which has been surprisingly active in the academic world. It then discusses the academic woman who, even when she has achieved success, may not look upon other women in the academic world with anything other than suspicion and hostility. Last, the role of academic committees is explored, especially in relation to complaints brought by women who suspect that sex discrimination is at the root of their problems. Such committees are unfortunately reluctant to deal with issues of discrimination, thereby forcing women to seek help outside their own campuses.

Part Three takes us off the individual campus and explores the various methods of appeal women may believe are available to them. The logical starting point for off-campus appeal is the American Association of University Professors (AAUP), but that organization, unfortunately, has not been receptive to women who seek aid in resolving discrimination complaints. Government agencies that have been set up for the specific purpose of enforcing antidiscrimination legislation are explored next: The Wage and Hour Division of the Department of Labor, which has had jurisdiction over the equal pay laws for eleven years, still presides over a situation where women earn three-fifths the salary of men in comparable jobs; the Office for Civil Rights of HEW, which has the power to withdraw federal funding from universities that practice discrimination, still seems unable to find discrimination; and the Equal Employment Opportunity Commission (EEOC) is hindered by an enormous case backlog, weak legislation, and lukewarm leadership. Because of weak government enforcement of antidiscrimination laws, women often find that they must go to court. Part Three, then, goes on to examine the risks of legal action.

The final chapter of the book summarizes the current situation and outlines some of the steps that will be necessary if adminis-

trators resolve to attempt voluntary compliance with the antidiscrimination laws.

Experiencing discrimination oneself is an excellent, and perhaps necessary, base from which to examine the extent of its rami-
fications. My experience is atypical only in the variety of government
agencies, university committees, and legal remedies involved. Almost every woman who has experienced discrimination or filed a
complaint of discrimination will be able to add her own anecdotes
to the rapidly growing lore on the subject. But most will recognize
also that the most idiosyncratic twists in the tale are of a recognizable genre. I therefore hope that women will be able to use *The
Invisible Woman* as an affirmation of shared experience and as a
guide both to the workings of the university in relation to discrimination charges and to the workings of the agencies.

I hope that those who have been on the giving end of discriminatory treatment, whether inadvertently or not, can learn
something useful as well. I hope, of course, that what they learn
will be useful in ending discriminatory attitudes rather than tacti-
cally advantageous in continuing the status quo. A common initial
reaction shared by many women who charge discrimination in
academe and by many of the government employees who investigate
such charges is surprise at the vehement anger that descends on
them from male academics. The reaction that follows surprise is,
naturally enough, disappointment, for most of us were naive enough
in the beginning to believe that the institution of higher education
—of all institutions—would react first by questioning and investigating complaints of injustice and then by correcting any injustice
found. Instead, we found anger—not the best starting point for
academic inquiry.

Government agencies have put out manuals and guidebooks
to help university officials achieve equal employment opportunity.
The guidebooks have not produced significant results. And they are
not likely to do so as long as the atmosphere of anger remains. It has
become increasingly clear to me that nothing can be resolved in
such an atmosphere and that government attempts at voluntary
compliance will have little effect while it prevails. What lies ahead,
then, may be years of expensive and embittering court battles, for

it is clear that women have no intention of remaining on the outside any longer.

But there is another way. I continue to hope that among males who have been rewarded by the system there are a number who have preserved enough academic integrity to make a serious effort to understand the problem and to discard discrimination when it can be demonstrated to them that they are practicing it. Only if a concerted effort to understand and to change replaces the current effort at angry self-justification will exhausting court battles be avoided. Not an easy task, to be sure. The changes that will have to be made both in attitudes and in the system through which those attitudes are turned into academic rewards are fundamental and radical. But that task will be rewarding for education as a whole for it may in fact assure an increase in the quality of that education.

I would like to acknowledge my debt to the Hawaii Federation of College Teachers (HFCT), which helped provide legal assistance to me through the years, thereby making it possible for me to pursue both my rights and some vital legal issues in the courts and in research for this book. Thanks are due to John Edmunds, the HFCT attorney, who became my attorney and who has taken the time to understand the issues and to represent them with intelligence and skill; to Bernice Sandler, director of the Project on the Status and Education of Women, and to Representative Patsy Takemoto Mink for their aid and encouragement; to Richard Larson, for demonstrating, over the years, that even full professors can be fair and can change their minds; and to the many women around the country who have supplied me with valuable information for this book. I am also indebted to those United States government officials who made an effort to do an honest and intelligent job of evaluating my case and who maintain a high level of competence despite the shambles that often surround them in the government civil rights enforcement agencies. I am especially grateful to Dorothy Stein for her careful reading and severe but just criticism of several early versions of this book. Acknowledgements are due also to those colleagues, male and female, who can understand political repression on campus even when the issue is equal rights for the campus. I regret that I cannot at this time thank by name the many women

at the University of Hawaii who have helped provide material for
this book, but the battle is far from over. Finally, I would like to
express my warm thanks to the many students who helped make
this book possible by buoying my spirits and steadying my determination over the years.

Honolulu   JOAN ABRAMSON
April 1975

Contents

The Invisible Woman

Discrimination in the Academic Profession

"Oh, you ca'n't help that," said the Cat:
"we're all mad here. I'm mad.
You're mad."
"How do you know I'm mad?" said Alice.
"You must be," said the Cat, "or you wouldn't
have come here."

Lewis Carroll, *Alice in Wonderland*

◆◇◆◇◆◇◆◇◆◇◆◇◆◇◆◇◆◇◆◇◆◇◆◇◆◇◆◇◆◇◆◆◆

1

Toward Tenure Denial

◆◇◆◇◆◇◆◇◆◇◆◇◆◇◆◇◆◇◆◇◆◇◆◇◆◇◆◇◆◇◆◆◆

"When I used to read fairy tales, I fancied that kind of thing never happened, and now here I am in the middle of one!"

Lewis Carroll, *Alice in Wonderland*

In the summer of 1967, I signed a contract that gave me membership in a select group. I became an instructor in the Department of English at the University of Hawaii.

At that time I had no idea that instructors handle a disproportionate share of the undergraduate teaching at most universities. I had no idea that over 40 percent of all university instructors in the United States are women, while women make up only 20 percent of university faculty members as a whole. And I had no idea that, in many instances, instructors are not considered part of the tenurable, permanent faculty of universities.

For me it was enough to cope with the very idea of joining the professorial ranks. I did not stop to analyze. I had been associated with universities since my own student days and had retained that association by marriage. Over the years, my husband slid easily from graduate student to instructor to acting assistant professor to assistant professor, associate professor, professor, and department chairman.

Of course, during my association with universities I had met dozens of men of dubious competence who had attained permanent academic tenure and promotion to the rank of full professor. As a student I had attended innumerable classes that could be described only as an insult to student intelligence. As a reporter I had interviewed professors who left me wondering how any responsible administrator could authorize their salaries. And as a faculty wife (at Stanford, Berkeley, Harvard, and the University of Hawaii) I had entertained and been entertained by a long procession of academics of mixed intellectual abilities. Yet the thought of being employed to teach in an institution of higher education awed me. Like many people, I maintained for a long while that peculiar ability to detach my personal experience from my institutional judgments. It did not occur to me that I might be underrating my own abilities or that the university administrators who hired me might be doing the same thing. And it did not occur to me that the underrating of women by the academic world might be endemic.

The University of Hawaii, in spite of any aura of the exotic that might attach to it because of its locale, is not much different from other land-grant universities in the United States. The State of Hawaii is relatively small, with a population of about 850,000 in 1970. The residents are located mostly on the island of Oahu, where the main four-year and graduate campus of the state system, the University of Hawaii at Manoa, has a student population of close to 25,000 and a faculty of about 1300. The only other four-year campus in the statewide university system is located at Hilo on the island of Hawaii; it is a small institution, with a student population of around 2000. The rest of the state-supported system of higher education is made up of eight small community colleges located on the islands of Hawaii, Maui, Kauai, and Oahu. The few private colleges on the islands are expensive and relatively limited in resources. Travel to mainland universities plus out-of-state tuition for them is beyond the means of a large proportion of island-educated high school graduates. These circumstances make the University of Hawaii at Manoa unique, for it is, realistically, the only university for the majority of college-bound young people, and it is a monopoly employer for most academicians.

Aside from these circumstances—important ones to be sure, for they allow monopolistic practices that contribute to the help-lessness of both island faculty and students—and aside from a noticeable number of palm trees and bare feet on the campus, the University of Hawaii at Manoa exhibits most of the strengths and shortcomings of tax-supported institutions of higher education else-where in the United States.

Like a good many other public institutions, the University of Hawaii benefited significantly from the outpouring of federal funding for research that followed Sputnik. In addition, in the mid-1960s, a popular and capable university president encouraged a willing state legislature to lavish tax money on the university. The mood was right for expansion, newcomers were enticed from main-land institutions, and the campus shared with other state univer-sities that heady sense of finally pushing up into the big leagues.

But the late 1960s were difficult times for university presi-dents. Student unrest and antiwar activity increased, and the turn-over of university presidents increased apace. Once again, the University of Hawaii was no exception, and in 1968 the president resigned over an issue involving a rather outspoken leftwing pro-fessor. The president's replacement, in keeping with a time when expansion gave way to caution in universities, was a cautious man. Trained by Princeton and the State Department, once an assistant to Adlai Stevenson during Stevenson's days as ambassador to the United Nations, straight out of his own uneventful ambassadorship to NATO, Harlan Cleveland arrived in the autumn of 1969 to take over the University of Hawaii presidency. His eastern establishment mannerisms did not make a hit with the largely local, mixed-race legislature. And five years later, with the faculty in a seemingly constant state of turmoil and dissatisfaction, with enormous budget cuts and unplanned cutbacks in personnel, with angry attacks from legislators, and with many students complaining that required courses were so overcrowded that they could not graduate within four or even five years, Cleveland left.

But, again, budget cuts and legislative disenchantment with universities were part of a nationwide pattern during the early 1970s. The presence of a president who did not fit into the local political milieu may have aggravated the situation at the University of Hawaii, but it did not make it different in kind from the situation of most large state universities.

The university's relationship with instructors and its instructor hiring and promotion practices do not differ greatly from the hiring and promotion practices of other universities. In Hawaii, as elsewhere, instructors are, ipso facto, considered less qualified than persons of higher academic rank and, thus, less likely to gain permanent academic tenure. Insularity can magnify the pattern but usually does not change it.

As in most universities, the bulk of the instructional staff at the University of Hawaii is first hired at either instructor or assistant professor rank, though some experienced teachers are hired away from other institutions at either associate professor or full professor rank. Generally all new teachers are hired provisionally. Most are on the tenure track; their positions are full time and in tenurable categories. The probationary period for a new teacher varies from university to university. In some cases, a full professor with a national reputation established at another university may be hired with tenure. At the other extreme, a young instructor may be hired with the expectation of facing a seven-year probationary period before the decision on permanent employment is made. At the University of Hawaii, the rules call for a two-year probationary period for all those hired at associate professor or professor rank and a four-year probationary period for those hired at the two lower ranks.

At the University of Hawaii the tenure decision is a long and involved one that includes a supposedly careful and considered study by an individual's departmental colleagues and a number of reviews by the administration and various faculty committees. The promotion procedure is similar to the tenure procedure, and in many cases the grant of tenure is accompanied by a promotion one step up the ladder.

While the final decision-making power clearly rests with the regents of the University of Hawaii, faculty members jealously guard their right to select their future, permanent colleagues. They take the job of selection (if not always the criteria) quite seriously and often contribute lengthy reports along with their recommendations. The criteria for tenure at the University of Hawaii, as at most universities, are "teaching, research, and service." Where the criteria are taken seriously, each candidate for tenure should be able to present evidence of some success at research (generally measured by publications), superior teaching, and contributions to the university community. Only the first criterion is of real significance in most academic departments.

In Hawaii, as elsewhere, instructors carry a disproportionate share of the undergraduate teaching load. The theory is that the higher ranked professors should teach advanced courses. The advanced courses usually attract fewer students, but they are considered more difficult to teach. Preparation for such teaching is supposed to be more time consuming. Therefore the professors who teach advanced courses should be given more assistance in the form of graduate student help. And these professors should be required to teach fewer classes since the number of hours they put in on each class is increased. In addition, the supervision of graduate students, while it often advances a professor's own research, is likely to be counted as teaching, thus reducing the classroom load of the professor even further. If the higher ranked professors are required to teach fewer classes, someone has to be hired to do the bulk of the teaching. And so we have, in most universities, an enormous number of low-ranked academic employees who average more classroom hours, higher student loads, and far lower salaries than their professorial colleagues.

Albeit unknowingly, I had joined this group of people—a group whose bargaining power is limited by a number of factors. Some are known as ABTs, all-but-thesis graduate students. An instructor appointment might slow their progress in writing the thesis, their only remaining requirement for the Ph.D., but it has compensating attractions in money earned and in professional experience gained. On completing the requirements for the Ph.D., the individual in this position can expect to be automatically promoted or

can find a job at another university. Other instructors may hold
only master's degrees and may be taking a break from study in
order to save money to return to graduate school for work on
their doctorates. Still others may be holders of the Ph.D. who are
bound to a limited geographical area and who obtained their degrees from the universities at which they teach. Many universities
refuse to employ their own graduates in anything but temporary
positions on the assumption that to do so causes serious and deleteri-
ous inbreeding and that inbred departments become stagnant and
void of the new ideas brought in by cross-fertilization from other
universities. The theory is in itself less than sound, for it assumes
that graduates are permanently fixed in their thinking by their
training. The policy has a disparate effect on women since married
women in particular often attend a specific university because it is
within the geographical area in which they must live and seek
employment.

There is also some evidence that this policy is eased more
often for men than for women. My own family provides examples of
this phenomenon. My husband went from graduate student straight
up to associate professor at Stanford. His career was not set back in
the least by the fear of inbreeding. Indeed, the minute he completed his Ph.D. requirements his rank changed from acting assistant professor to assistant professor. In contrast, my sister was told
that UCLA could offer her only a lectureship. Even the lectureship
was available only because she was clearly one of the best qualified
Ph.D.s in her field for some years. She was told that she was lucky
that her department had considered breaking the rules for her and
that the lectureship appointment most likely would not be extended
beyond a single year. A report on the status of university women
released by the Carnegie Commission in 1973 recommended "that
policies which prohibit a department from hiring its own graduate
students be reconsidered since they have often worked to the dis-
advantage of women."

Still other instructors are victims of entry-level discrimination. They may be in disciplines where the Ph.D. is not a requirement for employment or promotion. Art, music, creative writing,
and journalism, for example, all have subcategories of instruction
for which practical experience or artistic achievement substitute for

the Ph.D., and the extent of experience supposedly dictates the initial rank gained. Here, again, is a situation which adversely affects women since professional qualifications and artistic achievement are more often ignored in the female than in the male.

These are but a few of the reasons why people find themselves hired at low ranks in academic institutions. In many cases, obviously, the rank is justified. The position may be viewed by both parties as a stepping stone to something better. But for a large number of women, entry-level assignment to the low ranks is a trap, regardless of the reason for the initial assignment of such ranks. Although I had no way of knowing it at the time—indeed, I was grateful to obtain my job and humble about my qualifications for it —this was exactly my situation.

Over the years I watched two patterns of discrimination develop. Each pattern affected one of my own areas of expertise (journalism and writing). But each can be viewed in a wider context, for each is a pattern that exists at almost every large university.

The first is a pattern of disparate treatment of men and women at the time of hiring: men are often assigned entry-level rank above the entry-level rank assigned to women with the same or superior qualifications. While this is one of the reasons many women work at the rank of instructor, the pattern can occur at higher ranks as well—a woman may be appointed assistant or associate professor with a background that would gain a man an appointment at the full professor level.

The second is a pattern of disparate treatment for men and women of the same rank: the "rules" may state that no one of a certain rank is eligible for tenure or promotion, but the rules may be broken more often for men than for women. This pattern also affects post-tenure employment as well as the chances for gaining tenure in the first place. A woman may have to perform like a virtuoso to gain promotion, while a man may make it to the top by doing little more than staying at one institution for a certain number of years.

In the area of journalism, the first pattern seemed to apply in my case. I had come to Hawaii with considerable experience in newspaper and magazine reporting and with a master's degree in journalism. Over the following three years, the journalism program director hired three men. One had a Ph.D. but no experience in the profession and no publications in English (the director himself later recommended against tenure for him). He was initially hired at the assistant professor level. The second had a master's degree, not in journalism, and no publications. He claimed several years of teaching experience, but I must say "claimed" because much of his long history of practical experience in journalism was reputed to be a cover for government intelligence work—something he openly admitted (after he was granted tenure). He was initially hired at the associate professor rank. The third had only a bachelor's degree (not in the field of journalism) and considerable news magazine reporting experience. In spite of his lack of any graduate degree and minimal publications outside his reporting tasks, he was hired at assistant professor rank. He, too, gained tenure.

In comparison, I was an experienced, practicing journalist with a graduate degree in the field. When I first applied to the University of Hawaii for a teaching position, I wrote to the English Department because journalism was under its administrative jurisdiction. The director of the journalism program interviewed me and told me that he had someone in mind already, but if things did not work out he would want to talk again. He would, said he, keep my file "active." Yet the journalism director later claimed that he had never even considered me for a job in journalism and could not recall that I had applied or that he had interviewed me. By the time this man decided he could not employ me, the hiring of instructors to teach regular English courses was completely closed, and I obtained a job as an instructor in English only because of last-minute illness, which prevented one of the new professors from arriving in Hawaii from the mainland. The fact that I was hired as an English instructor and was not hired to teach journalism was later claimed by the department as a clear indication that I was not a journalist and not qualified to be hired in that field. (The department chairman, years later, was bold enough to state this catch-22 claim in court.)

My qualifications were, of course, not comparable across the board with those of any one of the men hired and tenured in journalism. One-to-one comparisons are rarely possible between university faculty members, which makes it easy to hide patterns of discrimination. The department later treated each of my qualifications in isolation. My master's degree in journalism, for example, was compared unfavorably with one man's Ph.D. in communications. The fact that his teaching was considered to be poor by some of his colleagues and the fact that his publications and journalism experience were negligible were ignored. My experience in journalism was measured against the experience of the twenty-five-year news magazine veteran. His lack of any graduate degree and failure to produce any major publications during his probationary period were not worthy of mention. In fact, a case was made that he had been told *not* to publish but to concentrate on learning how to teach. Prior teaching experience was a point on which I could be compared with the third man, who had taught journalism before coming to the University of Hawaii but who had no publications and whose master's degree was out of the field. By that time, my teaching evaluations had been consistently high, but in the academic world women who teach well are regularly told that universities are places for research anyway, and if they want to teach they should try the junior colleges.

Thus the first pattern—disparate treatment of men and women at the time of initial hiring—had resulted in my employment at instructor rank outside the field for which my background most qualified me. Men with similar backgrounds were hired at higher rank and in their own field.

The second pattern—disparate treatment of men and women at the same rank—can be seen by comparing my situation with that of the men who were granted tenure and promotion in the field of creative writing. I was hired in the fall of 1967 at the rank of instructor in English. Between 1967 and 1974, four men initially hired at the same rank—all of them claiming special competence in creative writing—gained tenure as well as promotion to the rank of assistant professor.

The Department of English at the University of Hawaii openly maintains a policy of not considering instructors for tenure, a policy in conflict with university regulations. The department regulations say that exceptions will be made for persons with special qualifications who can be especially useful to the department. Yet, while the majority of instructors have been women, this chilling fact remains: not one single woman instructor hired by this large department from 1965 to the present gained tenure. The exceptions—those who seem to have a monopoly on special qualifications—are men.

It is time to go back and pick up the thread at the time of my first year as a university instructor. The director of journalism had held my application for six months. When the English Department offered me a job in August, I had little bargaining power. In fact I was told I was lucky that someone had been taken ill. The offer—instructor rank, salary step 2—was made on a take-it-or-leave-it basis.

"Do you mean," I asked, "that all my experience and my master's degree are considered the equivalent of one year past the lowest possible step on the salary scale?" Exactly. After all, I had not taught before, and I should be happy to get even that one step above bottom. Besides, my background in journalism and in writing would make it easier for me to teach: other beginning instructors would have a harder time. I agreed with the administrator making the offer that I had never taught before. And I certainly did appreciate not having to teach three sections of an identical course—the usual boring fate of the beginning instructor. But they were asking me to teach two sections of a freshman course and one of a more advanced class. Wasn't that because of my background, and didn't my background entitle me to a higher step on the salary scale? Nothing doing, I was told. And $6700 was not bad considering I only had to work for nine months of the year and considering that this would be a second income for the family.

I took the job.

Several years later, when my own salary had risen somewhat, I discovered that I was not earning much less than the average for instructors. If I ignored the fact that men with similar backgrounds were taken in at higher rank and if I ignored the fact that my previous professional experience was above average, I could not complain of being paid significantly less than the other instructors.

Nonetheless, the spread of instructor salaries in the Department of English at the University of Hawaii illustrates some fascinating principles of faculty pay. There are twelve possible salaries at instructor rank, and I discovered that the salaries of most of the male instructors in my department were in the upper half of the possible salaries, with no evident correlation between salary and experience or excellence. A few men, however, were earning salaries at the lower end of the scale, and this brought the average salary for male instructors down somewhat. Women were most often earning salaries in the low-middle range. However, there were a few women in the upper range, and they brought the average up so that there was no significant difference overall between the average salaries of men and women. For a long time I wondered what governed the placement of these women at the upper end of the salary scale. Just as with the men, there did not appear to be any correlation between salary and experience or the quality of work. There was, in fact, only one significant correlation—a physical one. All of the women who earned salaries in the upper range for instructors were tall, willowy young women. The rest of us—young, old, petite, dumpy, or whatever—were lumped together in the lower middle range!

At first, the English Department seemed a nice enough place to work. But impressions were slow to form. I was too busy getting the hang of teaching. Like many beginning teachers, I spent enormous amounts of time just planning for those few hours in the classroom. I sped through my first lecture notes—laboriously prepared in a two-hour session—in twenty minutes flat and had to dismiss class early for lack of anything to say. (And I remember experiencing an acute sense of dismay one day early in my teaching career when a student sat in my office and told me of his plans to become a university professor. Since we had to work only six to nine hours a week, said he, he would have plenty of time for surfing.)

Other factors contributed to the slow crystallization of my first impressions about my department. One factor: most new instructors were assigned office space halfway across campus from the building that housed the department office and most of the professors. Our dusty little cottage on the fringe of the campus rarely attracted visitors from the department. Another factor: no one above the rank of instructor introduced any new instructor to other members of the staff.

With students, who are, many people forget, the primary reason for the existence of universities, things went well. I quickly gained confidence in my ability to teach. After awhile I even felt I had something to offer in the way of knowledge.

But with faculty the situation was puzzling. Was I a faculty wife? An intern? A colleague? I was not quite sure. I had never been in such an odd and awkward working situation before. My faculty wife status had already brought me into contact with some of my supposed colleagues. In the role of faculty wife I was treated with casual condescension, chatted with, smiled at, offered drinks, and introduced as "Professor Abramson's wife, he's the computer man." But as a "colleague" I was not treated at all.

New instructors attended special meetings to air teaching problems, chatted in the coffee room with old-timers who never bothered to introduce themselves or ask names, and sat in a small and quiet bunch at departmental meetings—when they were invited. I soon noticed that "old" instructors, those who had been there for a year or two, said little more than we newcomers did. I found it odd that English professors took so long to warm up. And gradually I realized that we were not colleagues at all: it was something of a shock. But most instructors caught on quickly enough. They taught their three classes, held office hours, conversed casually with the real faculty members, and formed friendships with fellow instructors.

I rationalized at times, given my dual role as faculty wife (who could obviously see things from *their* point of view) and English instructor (who was in daily contact with other instructors). I rationalized that we were not treated as colleagues because some of us did not act responsibly the way colleagues should act. On a visit to the women's room one day I had seen a young instructor crying. She had just broken off with her fiancé and insisted that she could not be expected to go out there and teach. Being the mature young woman the department thought I was (someone had penned that comment in the margin of my application letter, though I did not know that at the time of this incident), I was struck by the unique idea that "the show must go on" and if instructors behaved irresponsibly then it was no wonder that they were not accepted wholeheartedly as colleagues. But a few years later I watched a full professor drink himself to death in the hallways—it took almost two years at full pay—while his colleagues covered for him in the classrooms. Responsibility, it seems, has little to do with collegial treatment.

At the end of that first year I could not help but realize the source of the division: most instructors in English, like enlisted men in the army, were—and are—temporary employees at the University of Hawaii. After three years in one location they must move on. Small wonder, then, that they form a separate but not quite equal category of faculty. And small wonder that they rarely achieve the status of friend and colleague.

In the news business there is a kind of collegiality between reporters and editors. At least I had the feeling that I was of the same cut as my coworkers, whether they were editors, bureau chiefs, or publishers. But the collegiality of the newsroom was missing in the college, in spite of the disclaimers of presidents, department chairmen, and professors.

The English Department housed faculty members and faculty members. The real faculty members were hired with tenure track appointments. They were generally hired at assistant professor rank, and, during their fourth year, they were considered for tenure, which a remarkably high percentage of them received. The other faculty members were also hired with tenure track appointments. They were generally hired at instructor rank, and, after their second year, they were given terminal contracts and removed from the tenure track. They were never seriously evaluated and never considered eligible for tenure. Whether good, bad, or indifferent, they remained for three years—no more, no less. After that time they were let go to avoid the necessity, dictated by the rules governing the faculty, of considering them for tenure.

One instructor challenged the procedure during my second year on the staff. He received a letter from the American Association of University Professors (AAUP), the prestigious organization that supposedly dictates professional standards in universities. The letter indicated that the academic world did not look with favor on dual-track employment systems. But the English Department praised the system loudly, claiming that it was the only system through which lower division courses could be staffed and that it exposed Hawaii students to fresh, young, and enthusiastic teachers. No one who touted the system ever drew one logical implication of this particular argument: that the tired, old, tenured faculty must be somewhat lacking in enthusiasm and uninspired in the classroom.

Still, the problem was not immediate for me. I was a successful teacher. I wrote, either for the Time-Life book division or for myself, and I gained some publishing success. During my first year as an instructor a coauthored novel was published. During my second year two nonfiction books were accepted for publication.

Year two went by without any great upheavals. One instructor, a married woman, had completed her third year at about that time. Minor rumblings spread through the ranks of instructors because the woman was rehired on a piece-rate basis. She was told she was so good that the department wished to keep her teaching. However, she was also told that there was no point in her coming up for tenure since she would not get it. Therefore, the only job she could be offered was a lectureship—an arrangement by which the faculty member is paid for each course or semester hour taught, and also an arrangement by which the faculty member is not considered to be a faculty member. Thus, with the same duties she had performed the year before, she would receive a salary reduced by $3000 and a position with no security from semester to semester. This was her reward for being so good that the department wished to retain her. Others, not so favored, were sent away after their three-year tour of duty. It became obvious to me that the only person who might be forced into such a position was a woman tied to Hawaii by marriage. Her choice of university teaching positions was simply nonexistent. She could take the lectureship or leave it. The terms and conditions were fixed. She had no bargaining power.

The woman took that job, and I realized that I might find myself in a similar position a year later. Only my publications would save me, I thought. I was still not convinced that the problem affected women instructors as a class since it was obvious to me that not all women instructors were prepared to do the research and to produce the publications which seemed an expected part of university professional activity. However, I was becoming increasingly aware of the fact that not all men—not even those with tenure and full professor status—were capable of these functions either.

After their three-year tour in Hawaii, most instructors returned to graduate school to obtain what they called union cards (Ph.D.s) or found teaching jobs at colleges on the mainland. But most of the married women stayed on—some finding jobs in two-year community colleges, where the teaching load is higher and the pay lower, and a few working on a last-minute basis as lecturers, picking up a class or two when registration for basic courses surpassed the number of sections available.

Other events, as well, helped rock my confidence in the ultimate wisdom of my "colleagues." One was the biannual meeting in the hallway with the director of the journalism program. These chance meetings were flattering at first, then annoying. They were always the same. The director sometimes came across me as he flitted from mailroom or men's room to classroom. He began each conversation casually: "Say, Joan, we may be shorthanded next semester. Do you think you could fill in on one of our journalism courses?"

I was willing enough. But the opportunity never seemed to materialize. And after a few such meetings I began to realize that I was, as far as he was concerned, nothing more than a security blanket. Just as my application for employment had been an insurance policy in case he could not fill a faculty slot with a friend or a friend of a friend (and possibly lose a faculty position forever if it remained unfilled too long), my presence in the department now was a hedge in case one of his regular staff members wanted a leave or a teaching reduction. If things got too tight, he knew he had a competent journalism teacher on hand. At the same time, he had no need to make a commitment to me. He could still retain the freedom to bring in new journalism faculty members whenever he was able to gain an additional faculty position.

The second series of events that helped to sour me on the departmental system of hiring was the biannual meeting in the hallway with the director of the writing program. These meetings had a genesis slightly different from the journalism meetings. Halfway through my first semester of teaching I found a mimeographed notice in my mailbox. It asked me to state, in order of preference, the courses I would like to teach the following semester. What a novel idea: I had a choice in course assignments! I eagerly thumbed through the catalog of course offerings. By that time I had discov-

ered that teaching was thoroughly enjoyable and that I could handle
it easily. My initial modest proposal to the English Department,
back when I had first applied for the job, was that I could probably handle beginning courses as well as the next person. I had
found, during that first semester, that I could also easily handle my
more advanced writing course. And now, confronted by this invita-
tion to select my own courses and spurred by my success in the
classroom, I recalled my training and professional experience, and I
saw no reason to resist trying my hand at a few other course offerings.
I found a course in nonfiction writing—perfect! I put it down as
first choice. Form and theory in fiction—why not? Beginning creative writing and advanced creative writing—they sounded good,
and, after all, I had a coauthored novel in galley proofs. I listed
them all. And for good measure I listed a few other upper-division
writing courses, some sophomore literature courses, and then the
obligatory freshman English course last since I hoped to minimize
repeat assignments.

My course preference list was ignored. I received the same
two sections of freshman English and one of written communications that I had been assigned during my first semester.

By my third semester I had branched out into one section
of sophomore literature, one of written communications, and one of
freshman English. And by semester four I was never again assigned
a freshman course.

My first teaching choices, repeated each semester on the
mimeographed request form, were always creative writing courses.
And during those chance meetings in the hallway, the director of
the creative writing program began telling me that he certainly
wished he could find a way to give me one of those classes and he
sure would try to do something soon.

During my second and third years, with my first novel published, I began taking his word seriously. And I began to take a
closer look at the people who were gaining assignments in creative
writing.

I noticed the obvious first. With the exception of the departmental poet, they were all men. It took a little longer for me to
realize that not all of them had published.

One morning during my second year, a first-year instructor

wandered into my office, an office I shared with two other female instructors. He was "just looking" at available office space. He complained that it was impossible for him to get his novel written while he was forced to share an office with another instructor.

He got his private office. And during his second year (my third) he got his assignment teaching creative writing. From my vantage point in my three-person office I was impressed. Somebody important, I thought. Probably a young whiz kid who published early and had significant work to do. In my mind he walked around with a "do not disturb" sign permanently affixed to his thoughtful brow.

It turned out that he had a master of fine arts degree in writing. But he had not published yet, and he was only a few years younger than I. Publication, it appeared, was not as important as the nature of the degree for those who taught creative writing. But publication by me was apparently embarassing enough so that the director of the creative writing program, who did not have the master of fine arts degree but was the proud author of several published novels for the teenaged reader, continued to "hope" that he could find a place for me.

During that second year another "writer" was up for tenure and promotion, both of which he got. He, too, had a master of fine arts degree. His publishing record was a little more beefy than his aspiring novelist colleague: three short stories in such journals as *Carolina Quarterly* and *December*—in seven years' time.

Since discrimination was not yet an issue in my mind, his tenure and promotion did give me hope of continued employment. First, he had no Ph.D. A Ph.D., then, for writers and journalists at least, was not a necessary requirement for promotion or tenure. And of all the writers and journalists in the department, I was the only one who could claim some training or experience in both areas. Second, he had begun his career at the University of Hawaii as an instructor. If he could gain tenure with his degree, three published stories, and a middling teaching reputation, there was a chance for me.

During my third year at the University of Hawaii, the 1969/70 academic year, several instructors became rebellious. Why, they asked, did the department insist on a three-year policy for instructors? Instructors were perfectly willing to be scrutinized for excellence. They were perfectly willing to put their chances in a system of review for a fourth year. A fourth year, after all, did not mean lifetime tenure. And, furthermore, they resented the paternalistic reasoning that told them that it was better for them to get back to school and obtain their Ph.D.s. There were Ph.D.s going unemployed just then. Certainly it might be better for some people to return to school, but not all.

The English Department bent slightly. Two female instructors received offers for a fourth year of employment. I was one of them.

The offer was made grudgingly. The department chairman requested that the terminal clauses be removed from our contracts and that we be offered a fourth year without designating that year as terminal. He stated, however, that the department would be unlikely to grant tenure to "either of these ladies since neither has the terminal degree." In my case the argument later proved to be specious: the department has tenured six males without doctorates in my areas of competence since I was hired. But the chairman asked that the fourth year be left nonterminal since "if they are reviewed for tenure and turned down, we will be able to use them for a fifth year," the mandatory year offered after a denial of tenure.

Both of us received fourth-year contracts. Both of us were asked whether we wished to come up for tenure. Both of us said we did. But both of our contracts for that fourth year (though we did not know it) were already marked "not eligible for tenure." Apparently the decision had been made even before tenure consideration was offered.

Both of us were turned down for tenure. I vividly recall being asked to come into the chairman's office a day before Christmas vacation in 1970. I recall the chairman's casual tone as he announced that the department had decided not to grant tenure—he announced it as though I should have expected the decision. And I am sure he did think I expected it. I am sure he thought I would be grateful for receiving a mandatory terminal fifth year, which I could not have received except through the clever device of bringing me up for tenure and turning me down. Under university rules, tenure consideration is mandatory during the fourth year of employment at instructor rank unless the department has already decided that tenure is out of the question and has informed the individual that the fourth year will be the last. Thus, the department apparently had decided that going through the motions of tenure consideration, with a foregone negative conclusion, was a nice way to get five years of service out of me and offer me five years of employment without any serious obligation.

The department chairman, a man of quiet mannerisms, softened the blow. He told me that the department wanted to have me continue teaching and that something would be worked out so that I could do so. That "something" could only be one of those low-paid, last-minute, no-security lectureships I had seen assigned to other former instructors.

I believe the professors who run the English Department expected me to be grateful. That is undoubtedly one reason why my reaction surprised and angered them.

Exactly how did I feel? Disappointed. Bitterly disappointed. I was too shocked to say much of anything that day the announcement was made. I went home, and over Christmas vacation I did a great deal of thinking. Just what had I expected? Certainly the signals from the department were mixed. On the one hand, most instructors were not retained. And I was an instructor. But, on the other hand, I had been retained an extra year—an exception had been made for me that led me to believe I was considered well above the average. And I had already seen one male instructor obtain tenure with few publications. I had also watched as several other male instructors were primed for tenure consideration by being assigned a variety of writing courses—courses I had asked to teach and was qualified to teach. And I had seen men hired in journalism, without the Ph.D. and in one case without even a master's degree, at assistant and associate professor rank. In those ranks serious tenure consideration was almost automatic.

Most important, I had been told I would be considered for tenure. I had thought consideration would be real. I prepared my dossier, quite seriously. I gathered written and published material for colleagues to read, quite seriously. I had my classes videotaped so that colleagues could view them at their convenience, quite seriously. I was naive enough to take the whole thing quite seriously.

And now the department chairman was making it as clear as possible that tenure had never even been a viable option. The whole thing was a device for keeping me on for one more year!

Every single memo written by the department since that time for the purpose of justifying the tenure decision in my case emphasizes this point: instructors are not tenurable for the most part, and tenure consideration was the only way graciously to allow me an extra year. I should have known tenure was not possible. Could the department be blamed for my failure to understand? One more year was all that was ever intended. Yet I had been expected to submit to a nervewracking tenure consideration, and I was professionally judged not worthy of tenure, even though that judgment was not based on qualifications. The written recommendation against tenure emphasized the excellence of my qualifications. It was just a matter of need. I was not needed. My abilities in journalism and writing, where I had been deliberately excluded and where five men obtained tenure (and presumably were needed) in the three years following the negative decision on me, were called "peripheral." That "peer judgment" would stick with me regardless of its basis. And I was expected to be grateful.

I expected fair and honest consideration. I had not received it, and I was not grateful.

A few weeks later the fact that my faculty wife status had played a role in the decision was confirmed. I learned that the members of the departmental Personnel Committee, the committee that makes the first major decision on tenure, had discussed that status and had considered the notion that there was no need to give me tenure in order to retain me. Since I was tied to the islands (and the university) by marriage, I could always be hired as a last-minute lecturer.

That discussion was later demoted to the status of a joke— and perhaps that is the status it deserves, for the decision not to grant me tenure was probably made long before the Personnel Committee met. But faculty wife status, while it may have been a joke in the committee, is one important reason for my not receiving serious consideration for tenure. That status was immediately noted on my initial letter of application in 1967—not by me, but in a marginal note penned by the department chairman. It played a role in assigning both my low rank and my low salary. After all, where else could I look for work? And, in the same way, it played a role in the decision to turn me down for permanent tenure.

I had a lot of time to think about the situation over that Christmas vacation. When the departmental tenure decision was made in December 1970, I had three and one half years behind me as a fairly quiet instructor. I did not have a reputation as a fighter of causes. My years of training and practice as a journalist had shaped me into what I thought was the stance of a permanent observer. I figured that an appeal of the departmental recommendation—so obviously based on improper considerations—would probably take a long and grueling six months. I decided that it was worth it and that I could not live quietly with myself if I let the departmental judgment rest unchallenged.

I returned from Christmas vacation in January 1971 ready to protest the recommendation. I could hardly have realized at that time just how long the protest would take, just how convoluted and absurd it would sometimes seem, or just how enlightening and educational it might become.

It has been all of that and more.

But most important, what might appear to be a quixotic pursuit of justice has helped me to retain my self-respect—and I feel good about that.

2

First Protests

*"I don't think they can hear me," she went on, as
she put her head closer down, "and I'm nearly sure
they ca'n't see me. I feel somehow as if I was getting
invisible."*

Lewis Carroll, *Through the Looking Glass*

I know of few topics that are sure to raise the ire of male academics
more than the topic of sex discrimination. Avoidance, denial, wrath—
all the defense mechanisms of injured pride seem to be triggered by
a charge of sex discrimination. The result is that fighting to support
one's charge or even to obtain a hearing on it is like wading through
a huge vat of oatmeal mush: one just never manages to leave much
of a footprint.

My own progress through the University of Hawaii appeal
process was first marked by the mechanism of avoidance. Time after

time I tried to impress deans and committees with the importance of investigating my charge of discrimination. Time after time I was ignored. Decisions were made, but always on some basis other than the charge. One way or another, the preference of the predominantly male academic establishment was to avoid dealing with the issue.

In 1967, our university was attempting to quiet a major political uproar over the failure of the administration to grant tenure to Oliver Lee, a member of the Political Science Department who had been recommended for tenure by his colleagues. The man had gained public attention, and some public disfavor, because of his leftwing political beliefs, and the university regents would have gladly dumped him if they could have. However, the 1960s provided a friendly climate for demonstrations and sit-ins. It did not take long for the university administration to back down. The president and a dean resigned over the issue, and the professor received tenure.

As a result of that case, for five years the University of Hawaii was blessed with an unpopular president, a new dean, and a legendary incident involving student and faculty power with which to compare all similar or potentially similar incidents. Every year there are a certain number of potential hiring, tenure, or promotion scandals on the campus. And every year I hear the same reaction from faculty members. Even with the knowledge that the mass demonstration era of the 1960s is over, they claim, "This is the next Oliver Lee case."

No one (with the exception of my perennially optimistic husband) has ever claimed such university-shaking import for my own case. Yet I was denied tenure in the face of major procedural irregularities, not to mention violations of federal law. I was fired—more than once—in the face of failure to observe academic due process. Indeed, a whole program was destroyed in what many people, including United States government investigators, have charged was an effort to get rid of me. By themselves, each and every one of these breaches of ordinary academic due process would have led to disconcerting controversies—potential Oliver Lee cases— had I been a man. With the possible exception of administrators in some rural church colleges, university administrators just cannot do things to men like the things done to me, at least not without hearing considerable fuss about the rights and privileges of faculty members. But if the victim is a woman and if the woman not only refuses to remain silent but also raises the embarrassing spectre of sex discrimination, an attempt is automatically made to sweep the whole mess under the rug. Somehow such a victim and such a charge are not serious. Or perhaps they are too serious. If they are not looked at or dealt with, the attitude seems to be, perhaps they will go away.

Avoidance, then, was the most immediate and striking reaction I encountered. I registered my complaint at all the proper levels of university review and decision-making—in some instances more than once. The almost unanimous reaction on campus was to pretend the complaint had not been made and either to do nothing or to sidestep it.

My first move, after deciding not to accept the negative departmental tenure recommendation, was to make an appointment with the dean. The legislature of Hawaii passed a law several years ago that encouraged all state employees to form collective bargaining units and select collective bargaining representatives. At the time I decided to pursue the tenure issue several unions were vying for the right to represent the university faculty. I had joined the Hawaii Federation of College Teachers, and I asked the executive secretary of that union to visit the dean with me.

Dean David Contois was a nervous and soft-spoken man when I first met him. (I believe he is a lot more nervous and soft spoken now—but he has had to spend a great deal of his time since then dealing with me!) Our first meeting was not terribly helpful. I went through the details of my grievance and asked exactly what procedure I should follow to correct the various injustices that seemed all too apparent in the case. I told the dean that I felt review committees, which normally scrutinize all departmental recommendations, should be alerted to the fact that there were problems in my case.

The dean did not see fit to inform the executive secretary or me as to when such committees might be considering the case or how I could go about conveying my feelings to them. Instead, he assured us that I had not been denied tenure. The decision would not be made until May or June, said he. And until the regents announced that decision there was no reason to worry and no point in protesting. At that time, if I wished to appeal, there were appropriate channels.

Both of us realized that this was nonsense, that the time to make a meaningful appeal was immediately, while the recommendations leading to the regents' decision were still in process. What we did not know, what the dean refrained from telling us, and what almost every administrator on campus seemed to want kept secret was the route through which such decisions passed.

I have since found out, through a process of blundering, that the steps in the tenure process and the promotion process are fairly numerous but fairly simple. They begin early in the fall semester during the year of tenure or promotion consideration. A departmental personnel committee scrutinizes dossiers and makes a recommendation. The department chairman then adds his own recommendation, which may or may not agree with the committee's. Both recommendations are sent to the dean for transmittal to the College Personnel Committee—another faculty committee, but one made up mostly of professors outside one's own department. This committee adds its own recommendation, as does the dean. All four recommendations are then sent to the Manoa Faculty Personnel Committee, a campuswide committee composed only of full professors, which adds its recommendation. Next the chancellor makes a recommendation. The whole stack of recommendations then goes to the president, who adds his recommendation and passes the collection on to the regents.

When I set out to appeal the tenure decision in February 1971 I did not understand the official procedures. But after years of attempting to discover and then to use them, I learned they are not always followed.

The union executive followed up on our meeting with the dean by writing a lengthy letter detailing my complaints, including the complaint of sex discrimination. The dean responded with a letter of his own, once again insisting that "Mrs. Abramson has not been denied tenure. No decision on her case has been made nor will one be made until May or June." But he did not limit himself to repeating the unhelpful advice he had given at our meeting. He went on to insist, in no uncertain terms, that "any complaint or appeal she may wish to make must be initiated by me." And he added that if I wished, I could take up the matter with the members of one or the other of the faculty committees that existed to review departmental recommendations and make recommendations of their own.

The dean failed to point out that the College Personnel Committee had already rubber-stamped the departmental decision in a two-sentence report written a full two weeks before my visit to his office: "The College Personnel Committee agreed with both the Department Personnel Committee and department chairman in the recommendation *against tenure* for Miss Abramson. The vote was five against, one abstaining, and two absent." He failed to point out that a senior member of my own department—a man who had opposed tenure for me—served on that committee. He failed to point out that he himself had sustained the departmental recommendation just one day before I met with him. His one-sentence report: "I see no reason to go against the departmental and College Personnel Committee recommendations." And he failed to mention the fact that I could also initiate complaints.

I wrote him a short memo asking that the union executive's letter be placed in my file for forwarding to the Manoa Faculty Personnel Committee. In checking that file one year later I discovered that the letter and my memo were missing. But the letter from the dean was there. It had been slightly corrected from the copy I had received. It read: "Any complaint or appeal she may wish to make must be initiated by her." My attorney later asked about that while the dean was under oath. The dean admitted that he saw no need to send me a corrected copy—his original, which clearly said "Any complaint she may wish to make must be initiated by me," contained only a small and obviously insignificant typographical error. Apparently his meaning was not clear enough for the administration files, which needed correcting. It was clear enough for me!

Luckily, the dean's unwillingness to help left me suspicious enough to ignore his advice. I did write to the Manoa Faculty Personnel Committee and asked that they check into the case carefully since, I pointed out, tenure appeared to be denied because of my faculty wife status and the consequent possibility that the department could continue to hire me at low pay and without tenure.

My letter to the Manoa Faculty Personnel Committee uncovered three things. First, as expected, the letter alerted the committee members to the peculiarities in the departmental decision. For the first time since the decision left the department, it was not merely rubber stamped. Instead, this prestigious committee, elected by the entire faculty and made up only of tenured full professors, recommended unanimously for tenure: "While granting that any department must retain considerable authority over its tenure decisions, the university Faculty Personnel Committee finds that it must oppose the English Department in this case. We do not believe that Mrs. Abramson's outstanding competence, which is acknowledged by all, can be readily replaced or increased by another, even another with a Ph.D. We believe that demonstrated excellence in lower division teaching must be retained and rewarded for the good of the university as a whole if not for the department. In short, if 'Mrs. Abramson's achievements and qualities are admirable,' as the chairman states, we think that her department is in error to 'see no secure permanent place for her.' "

Second, the committee demonstrated that it had faith in the professional judgment of the department. They merely came to an opposite conclusion based on the same judgment. At that point, even the department had not questioned my merit, although that merit had been arbitrarily limited to a rather narrow area of teaching. The committee blindly accepted the departmental representation that I was primarily a lower division teacher. I was later forced to spend a great deal of time attempting to challenge this notion. One third of my teaching assignments had been in upper division courses. But, more important, it seemed to me that any individual who is seriously considered for tenure should be allowed to teach in his or her area of specialization before being judged. Certainly this had been the rule with everyone in my department who was seriously considered. But I was not allowed to teach one single class in journalism or creative writing until after the tenure decision was made, when I was no longer a danger to the men competing for the limited creative writing and journalism slots. Yet the Manoa

Faculty Personnel Committee accepted the departmental judgment that required courses for freshmen, which I had not taught for two and a half years, and sophomores were my only area of competence.

Third, the committee demonstrated the male academic's penchant for avoiding issues of sex discrimination. In spite of the fact that this had been the main issue raised in my letter to them, they carefully avoided any mention of it.

All in all, the Manoa Faculty Personnel Committee, with its unanimous vote for tenure, ended up doing the right thing for what were to me the wrong reasons. Nonetheless, the decision of that committee seemed at the time to be a major victory.

"Aha," said my husband, "you'll get tenure."

His opinion was not uninformed. That very year he had served as chairman of the personnel committee in his own department. Both his committee and the department chairman had recommended unanimously against tenure for two people: one, they claimed, was a mediocre teacher with few publications and the second was a poor teacher with a publication record below average for the department. The Manoa Faculty Personnel Committee had asked for reconsideration in both cases. The dean, in both cases, reversed his recommendation and asked for tenure, even though the departmental committee and chairman remained unanimously opposed. Both these people received tenure. I did not. Both are men.

The positive committee recommendation was passed on to President Cleveland, who proceeded to ignore it and proceeded, as well, to ignore university regulations calling for tenure decisions to be made by the regents. Instead, Cleveland viewed it as his role to make all negative decisions himself and to pass on only positive recommendations for action by the regents. This procedure caused him some difficulties in a subsequent suit on procedural irregularities brought in state court.

I was informed officially of Cleveland's negative decision in late May 1971. I was entitled to a terminal year of employment, and during that year I was entitled to appeal the decision to a committee of the Faculty Senate established to hear tenure and promotion disputes. The Faculty Senate at the University of Hawaii, like similar bodies at other institutions, is set up in the belief that faculty members will have an impact on university decision-making. Faculty members are elected to the senate, which votes on major curricular and personnel issues and passes on recommendations to the university administration. Such recommendations are usually the product of senate committees, which often work long and hard to turn them out. Whether the effort is worth the faculty time devoted to it varies from university to university. At the University of Hawaii, during the five-year presidency of Cleveland, the effort was not worth much—the president, for the most part, gave little weight to faculty opinion and preferred to go his own way. But at the time I had no idea that faculty committees were held in such low esteem by the administration, and I submitted my appeal to the Faculty Senate Privilege and Tenure Committee.

I discovered that the same avoidance mechanism for sex discrimination charges used by the Manoa Faculty Personnel Committee operated in the Privilege and Tenure Committee. By the time that committee was ready to discuss my case, I was in my terminal year of employment at the university. And in spite of repeated efforts to call the issue of discrimination to the attention of the administration and the faculty, no one had bothered to examine that issue. "The Privilege and Tenure Committee declines to involve itself in the question of what bearing the appellant's sex has on the denial of tenure." Their excuse was that the Department of Health, Education, and Welfare (HEW), which was investigating the case, "will be better able to effect a determination than this committee."

Nonetheless, using much the same reasoning that the Personnel Committee used, the Privilege and Tenure Committee unanimously recommended that I be granted tenure: "The Privilege and Tenure Committee recommends, in the interest of excellent teaching of composition at the freshman and sophomore levels for students in the various schools and colleges of the university, and because there were procedural irregularities in the administrative handling of the case, that tenure be granted to Joan Abramson."

Once again a committee did the right thing for the wrong reasons. And, in the bargain, they reinforced the Faculty Personnel Committee label, a label I hardly deserved since by that time I had not taught freshman or sophomore courses in composition for three years. Their acceptance of this view of my area of teaching competence had come straight from the English Department. The committee members had called in the department chairman to testify. They had not felt the need to hear testimony from me.

I certainly have no desire to appear ungrateful, and it was nice to have another unanimous positive recommendation. But the limitations of the recommendation were obvious, and it was equally obvious that if I pointed out the limitations, I thereby called the conclusion into question.

Once more it had been demonstrated that faculty committees do not consider the issue of sex discrimination particularly relevant. The issue was simply shunted aside as the province of a government agency, and the decision was made independently of the issue.

Two unanimous decisions from two important committees did seem promising, even though the basic issue remained untouched. "Aha," said my husband for the second time, "now you'll get tenure." But for the second time the recommendation of a supposedly important committee was ignored.

On the basis of these two, major, unanimous decisions, I asked the English Department to reconsider the case. I asked, also, for consideration for promotion since I had reached the top salary step of instructor rank. I felt my grounds for reconsideration went well beyond the two committee decisions. I had another book in print by that time and a third ready to come off the presses within two months. I had also received a university research grant for work on yet another book. And I had accrued a number of other normally significant honors: membership in the Faculty Senate, which indicated some recognition of my abilities by my colleagues, I thought; selection as a member of the leadership of New College, an experimental undergraduate program within the university system; selection, at long last, to teach a journalism course and a course in creative writing; and selection by my writing colleagues as a faculty member for a proposed graduate program in creative writing.

But the department chairman huffily replied to my request by informing me that he had not received a copy of the Privilege and Tenure Committee decision. I certainly could not receive consideration for promotion—consideration that is normally mandatory when one has reached the top of rank—since, said he, I was on a terminal contract. As to the tenure reconsideration, the department saw no need to act until it had seen and considered the report of the Privilege and Tenure Committee.

The department saw that report a few days later. But it only elicited an even higher level of departmental anger. None of my additional academic accomplishments seemed to matter. I was informed, rather tersely, that "the Department of English Promotion and Tenure Committee does not at this time find reason to re-open the tenure case of Joan Abramson. And be it further resolved that therefore she not be considered for promotion."

The ultimate offense had been charging the English Department with sex discrimination. My lack of gratitude for five years of low-paid employment was measured by the number of disappearing figures in the hallways. As I went about the building from mailroom to classroom, men, in unexplained droves, ducked into offices and restrooms at my approach or bent over water fountains to quench sudden thirsts. The avoidance was so obvious that one friend constructed and slipped under my door an "advertising brochure" offering paid companionship for the lonely. It occurred to me at one point that the ancients were kind to insist that lepers wear bells as a distant early warning system. It certainly saved them the discomfort of seeing people flee immediately before them.

The departmental reply to my charge of discrimination was (and is) to point to the many females on the faculty. Given the fact that 40 to 50 percent of the faculty members of this large department were women, one was not supposed to inquire further. The fact that all but a handful of these women were hired as temporary instructors was apparently not relevant. And the fact that no woman had received tenure for several years while a steady stream of men was considered and tenured was also beside the point. Indeed, it appeared that many tenured faculty members viewed the employment of women as temporary instructors as some kind of charity. The chairman at one time complained that perhaps a "committee on the status of men" should be formed since relatively few men were given this golden opportunity.

I had only one remaining avenue of action within the university. The chancellor also received a copy of the Privilege and Tenure Committee report. Normally, reports from that committee recommended specific action. In my case, tenure was recommended, but no particular procedure for granting it was specified. The failure to specify a procedure was probably the result of a case the committee had handled a year before: a woman was turned down for tenure by the English Department, and the committee recommended reconsideration by the department. A cursory "reconsideration" rapidly legitimized the original negative decision. Thus the recommendation of the Privilege and Tenure Committee was followed to the letter, but to no avail. Since no specific mechanism was recommended in my case, either departmental action or administrative action could have solved the problem. Some response was in order from the chancellor's office.

I waited for that response. I waited through November. Then through December. In January, I called the chancellor. I discovered that I was not important enough to get through to him. Instead, I talked with one of his assistants. I was told that the matter was still under discussion and that I would hear within a few days.

A week later I called again. The same assistant now told me that he had nothing to do with the matter and I should talk with someone else about it. When I asked who that might be, he pondered for a moment and told me he had no idea.

Once again I tried to get through to the chancellor. I finally did manage to reach his personal secretary. She told me she would check to see whether he was in, left me hanging on the phone for a few minutes, and returned to inform me that he was, indeed, in his office, but he had nothing to say to me. I confess that a little smoke must have been transmitted through the wires at that point. I wrote to the president.

The Privilege and Tenure Committee decision had been rendered in mid-October and transmitted to the chancellor in early November. I wrote to the president in late January. Three months, it seemed, was enough time to study, debate, and resolve far weightier issues than mine. Could I, therefore, request a meeting with the president, a reconsideration of the tenure decision, and, most important, "that further actions in this matter be handled by the university administration with reasonable dispatch and reasonable civility?"

The answer this time was prompt but hardly useful. It came from the vice-president for academic affairs, another of the many bureaucrats who make one wonder exactly what universities are in business to do. The chancellor, he informed me, was taking care of the matter. If I was not satisfied, then in good time I could take it up with the president. That, of course, was exactly what I had in mind when I wrote!

Late in February, the chancellor finally decided to meet with me. He saw no reason, said he, to reverse the departmental decision. He freely admitted that he had done nothing about my complaint of sex discrimination. He confirmed this in a memo a few days later: "The issue of sex discrimination was not covered in this review." Sex discrimination was out of his area, he said. I could take it up with the newly appointed campus equal employment opportunity (EEO) coordinator—a woman. The subject was simply not substantial enough for serious men to bother with.

To the chancellor, the issue was something quite distinct from the merits of the case. The merits of the case convinced him that there was no reason to overrule the department (even though the department vote was split) in favor of two review committees (even though their votes were unanimous). And discrimination, proven, or not, was totally immaterial.

I did take up the issue with the EEO coordinator. She was beginning a one-semester, half-time term, and, admittedly, she was not yet sure of her role. Interestingly enough, she was the first and for several years the last person to receive an honest salary for performance of equal employment opportunity tasks on our campus. Half her pay that semester was supposed to cover her EEO duties. Even with half time, she found the job overwhelming. Yet, after one semester, she was reassigned. It was another three years before the administration saw the need for a paid equal employment officer.

The EEO coordinator readily admitted that there was no procedure on campus to handle matters of sex discrimination, in spite of the fact that the president had ordered chancellors and deans a year earlier to set up a peer hearing procedure for such cases. But the coordinator would not go any further. She even wrote to HEW and told civil rights officials there that since they were investi-

gating the case, it would be "inappropriate" for anyone on campus
to do anything about it!

In March 1972 I once again wrote to the president and
asked him to reconsider the case. By the time he decided to meet
with me in April, I had received the backing of the grievance chief
of the local chapter of the AAUP, who had written an academic
amicus brief on my behalf. I had also received support from HEW
in the form of a letter to President Cleveland requesting that the
peer hearing procedure be tested with my case. Although HEW
officials did not know it, that procedure was still nonexistent, though
it had been promised by Cleveland in February 1971.

My meeting with Cleveland did not start in a reassuring
fashion. He began with a hard line: he saw no reason to overrule
the department or the chancellor. In fact, he argued strongly that
departmental decisions should remain of primary importance. The
argument did not wash well since I had with me the person (my
"advisor on university administrative practices," who is also my husband) who had been chairman of a departmental committee that
was twice overruled by the president. But after awhile Cleveland
speculated on the possibility of allowing his own, hand-picked Commission on the Status of Women to investigate the case. After an
hour of argument, during which the usually calm and expressionless
face of our chief executive became progressively more red and
rattled looking, we both agreed to allow his commission to investigate. I agreed to forgo immediate court action on the issue so that
it could be handled by his commission.

Several weeks later my *husband* received a short memo confirming the investigation: "I mentioned during our recent meeting
that the university would be investigating Joan Abramson's charge
of sex discrimination. This investigation has already been initiated."
I happened to see the note because my husband happened to show
it to me. Cleveland did not even bother to send me a copy, though
he sent copies to four other people. Nor did he acknowledge in the
note he sent to my husband that I had been at that meeting and my
charge of sex discrimination had been the only topic of conversation.
Indeed, my husband came along, as did my attorney and a representative of the AAUP, because of Cleveland's State Department
habit of trying to gain a psychological advantage in two-sided

meetings by outnumbering the other side. (This particular meeting was a standoff, with four of them and four of us.)

A few days later, I wrote a short note to Cleveland's wife, asking her to advise her husband that I had learned he was having my complaint investigated and asking her to pass on my thanks to him. I never received an acknowledgement.

Cleveland's Commission on the Status of Women began its investigation of my charge of sex discrimination in April 1972. Considering all that had gone before and considering Cleveland's State Department background, it seemed likely that he was looking for a face-saving exit from a deteriorating position. It seemed likely that he wanted to accept a finding of sex discrimination from his commission and to use it as the excuse for reversing his previous decision—an act he knew would antagonize some members of the English Department. Yet I admit to being uneasy about the investigation since the commission members had all been selected by Cleveland himself. Nonetheless, the results were gratifying. The commission members investigated my charges and found unanimously in my favor. They recommended that the unusual treatment of instructors by the Department of English be ended and that the department be made to follow university personnel regulations. The commission also recommended that the president "take appropriate action to remedy the injustice done to Joan Abramson in her application for tenure because tenure appears to have been denied resulting from discernible sex discrimination." But this time the favorable committee decision did not move my husband to say, "Aha, you have tenure." We would celebrate when the president acted.

But Cleveland rejected the report of his commission—which made me wonder why he had asked them to investigate in the first place. On May 2, 1972, he released a "Memorandum for the Record" that was notable only for its verbosity. In the main, the memorandum rehashed the old excuses for not granting tenure. It pointed out the importance of departmental decision-making, dismissed the work of the Faculty Personnel Committee and the Privilege and Tenure Committee as sloppy, and otherwise totally avoided any genuine inquiry into my qualifications or the merits of granting me tenure.

The most interesting section of this long memo dealt with

the report of the Commission on the Status of Women and Cleveland's reaction to it. He pointed out that there was no need to do anything because "there is no evident solution under existing tenure arrangements—except to discriminate in favor of faculty wives." In other words, no solution for discrimination exists except reverse discrimination! A most interesting excuse. Somehow, our president never thought to seek a simple solution such as equity. Fair and equitable decision-making based on individual qualifications rather than marriage relationships seemed not to occur to him.

Cleveland had perfectly applied a technique he himself has labeled "creative ambiguity." He had met with me, agreed to have his commission look into my case, left me thinking we had both agreed to accept the findings of that commission—and ended up by doing exactly nothing. I discovered only later that Cleveland made quite a study of the use of creative ambiguity in management, writing a book with the idea as one of his central themes. As far as I can make out, creative ambiguity means nothing more nor less than the ability to commit oneself with such vagueness that one is never committed at all and therefore never caught holding the bag or taking the blame. Cleveland's position shows the grossest failure to understand the meaning of sex discrimination, which is precisely that qualified women are being bypassed for less qualified men.

I wrote to Cleveland again, and I admit that my intentions were somewhat sullied by my feelings about the man. He had rejected unanimous decisions by three faculty committees. Two committees had said that there was sufficient justification to grant tenure even without looking into the matter of sex discrimination. The third, Cleveland's own hand-picked commission, investigating the case at his own request, had found discrimination. I asked, then, if he intended to set up the peer hearing procedure that had been promised to HEW so that he could have yet another committee finding to ignore. He replied humorlessly that he already conveyed materials to me that "adequately cover my position in your case." He softened the blow somewhat by hand writing "Joan" across the formal salutation and by signing "Harlan." In the face of my unemployment, I suppose he felt a chummy tone could not hurt him.

For fifteen months I had persistently attempted to gain a hearing on the issue of sex discrimination within the University of

Hawaii. I had written the dean, the Manoa Faculty Personnel Committee, the chancellor, the Privilege and Tenure Committee, the president's Commission on the Status of Women, the equal employment opportunity officer, the Senate Executive Committee, and the president. Finally, the issue of discrimination had been faced by one committee, and avoidance slid into indifference. The university had investigated my charge, found it accurate, and ignored the findings. If I had been discriminated against, it did not matter anyway—and now would I please just go home and leave them all to their duties?

3

The University Reacts

◆◇◆◇◆◇◆◇◆◇◆◇◆◇◆◇◆◇◆◇◆◇◆◇◆◇◆◇◆◇◆

> *"Were you ever punished?"*
> *"Only for faults," said Alice.*
> *"And you were all the better for it, I know!" the Queen said triumphantly.*
> *"Yes, but then I had done the things I was punished for," said Alice: "That makes all the difference."*
> *"But if you hadn't done them," the Queen said, "that would have been better still; better, and better, and better!"*
>
> Lewis Carroll, *Through the Looking Glass*

What happens after indifference? At the time I had no idea. But university officials quickly educated me.

The English Department had not had the foresight to offer me a leper's bell. The foresight of the administration was no better.

38

Bureaucracies employ subtler means of conveying the message. The message, however, was becoming plain. I was an embarrassment to the university. Because I gained rulings in my favor, I had expected action in my favor. And, if avoidance and indifference did not make me understand that such action was not a possibility, then more active means would have to be used.

I was about to discover that one of the conditions under which sex discrimination becomes more than an apparently insignificant and annoying charge against the university is success. When the individual making the charge persists in obtaining ever more responsible jobs or when outside agencies confirm the discrimination charge, administrators find it difficult to explain away the initial charge. They still however need not face the charge, investigate it, and seek an equitable solution to the problem. They need only step up the pace of activity against the individual who has filed the charge. Because I had accepted another job within the university, I could now be labeled a "confrontational" personality. I was, said the administration, using my new position to get back at the university.

Here I must backtrack a little, for the new phase of accusation and active resistance on the part of administrators somewhat overlapped the phase in which the issues were ignored. In September 1970 a new program began at the University of Hawaii. Like a good many programs at other universities, New College was mandated to attempt to overcome some of the problems recognized in the 1960s—an ossified and irrelevant curriculum taught within a too large, too impersonal, and too technically oriented university.

The first faculty of New College had been carefully picked by the founder and first director, history professor Richard Rapson. Students and faculty together then decided to attempt a full democracy that would include student participation in the selection of future members of the faculty. Applications for positions on the second-year faculty were solicited in October 1970. Intensive interviews of applicants were carried out in November and December. About ninety people applied and about twenty were selected. I was one of the twenty.

The first year of my association with New College (1971) was supposed to be my terminal academic year at the University of

Hawaii. I was given a split-appointment contract for that year with two thirds of my time supposedly spent in the English Department and one third spent at New College. New College, however, turned out to be the more demanding job. In the English Department, I was merely putting in time. Administrators and professors did not in the least care whether I participated in committee work, researched and wrote books, or kept office hours for students. At New College I was expected to remain a contributing member of an educational community.

Halfway through my first semester in the program, the director announced his own gradual disengagement. He intended to go on sabbatical leave during the fall semester of 1972, return for the spring semester of 1973, and then step down permanently as director. The college would have to choose an acting director to take over during his sabbatical and then a new, permanent director to take over beginning with the fall semester of the 1973/74 academic year.

But New College students rarely settled on the simplest way out. They decided to try a new directorship: a three-person group that eventually became known as the troika. Two faculty members and one student were selected to take part in this probably unworkable arrangement, and the assistant director was asked to continue, but as assistant director to a troika. I was elected a member of that three-person directorship. With one semester remaining before his sabbatical, Rapson decided it would be useful for the troika members to begin training by doing the day-to-day work of managing and administering the program on top of our other, full-time duties, with Rapson keeping final control over policy.

Our new duties had hardly begun when Rapson decided that I was a potential embarrassment to the program. He had talked with President Harlan Cleveland, Rapson said, and Cleveland wanted "one man" who would be responsible for what went on at New College. That man could hardly be our student troika member—after all, one of the duties of the job was signing employment forms for faculty members. The other faculty troika member, Arnold Edelstein, was a "regular," if untenured, assistant professor in the English Department. Since I did not even know whether my case would be settled or whether the university would authorize a position for me for the 1972/73 academic year, Rapson implied, wouldn't it be wiser to have Edelstein, in the good graces of the administration, be the outside spokesman? We could still take equal roles in the internal management of the program. It was clear to me, at least, that the person who signed the forms and met with the administration was, in fact, the director. I did not much like sharing the work without sharing the authority, but it seemed I had no other choice.

A few weeks after that decision was made, my role in the administration of the program shifted once again. There had been growing dissatisfaction with the work of Reynold Feldman, the New College assistant director, whose job required that he authorize credit for third- and fourth-year students working on independent study projects. A kind-hearted man, he had repeatedly approved inferior work and late work for full academic credit—a performance not doing our reputation much good with an already skeptical administration. More important, students were not gaining the opportunity to confront standards of excellence. It was decided (not very openly for a program that valued openness) that the assistant director would return to more teaching while I took over his tasks. A month later, he decided to resign at the end of that academic year. I was selected to replace him.

I had a job for the 1972/73 academic year. The only question remaining was whether the university administration would authorize a salary to cover that job. The assistant director's contract ended on June 30, 1972. The college obviously needed a replacement for him, and the dean had already authorized a sufficient number of positions to cover a full-time replacement. There was no question that the position could be filled—but by me?

The dean delayed. In early March he informed the outgoing and incoming directors of New College that a faculty position for me would be out of the question. He acknowledged, however, that it would be difficult to turn down a request for a lectureship for me if New College recommended it. Since lecturers are paid by the course or by the credit hour, they are not considered genuine members of the faculty. Thus the idea of assigning a lectureship to someone who would be taking on a heavy load of student advising and administration in addition to classroom teaching was something of an anomaly.

I do not believe that Rapson made much of a fight of it. I think I was becoming as much of an embarrassment to him as to the administrators further up in the hierarchy. Soon he made it clear that he felt he could not fight, that in spite of my qualifications it was apparent to him that the dean would never authorize a regular instructional position for me, that the only possibility for employment was a lectureship.

Looking back, I realize that Rapson did not act responsibly. At the least he should have taken a stand in favor of an appointment he had approved. He should have informed the dean that a lectureship offer was discriminatory; he had, after all, continually claimed that I was the best qualified person for that job. In fact he had claimed that Edelstein and I were equally qualified to be director of New College, except that Edelstein was more acceptable to the administration.

Even the modest proposal for a lectureship had rough sailing however. In September 1972, when I had already been working for more than two months, my employment forms were returned by the administration to the New College office. Someone had typed in a few extra conditions: my job was described as one that was not eligible for tenure and as one with rather limited duties. A note was attached to the forms: "It appears imperative that we obtain Joan's signature on this 5B form before we proceed further, i.e., evidence that she agrees to the statements presented thereon." Several university administrators had told me that they had no intention of being "blackjacked" into granting me tenure. This concern, which apparently stemmed from the notion that I engaged in coercion, did not stop them from demanding that if I wished to continue working, I would have to sign a document intended to prove I had not gained tenure. The note was probably not intended for my eyes, but, luckily, someone in the dean's office forwarded it to me.

On September 14, I returned the form—signed. I did not have much choice. If I refused to sign I would not have a job. But I did attach a memo to the form, and I signed subject to that memo. My memo made two points: first, a clarification of my job responsibilities; second, my belief that I was eligible for tenure and that the matter might be decided by the courts. Apparently the employment form and my memo met with no objections—I would find it hard to believe that the dean did not scrutinize them with great care—and they were sent to the faculty records office for filing.

But the issue of my employment for the year was hardly dead. On September 18, 1972, I filed an equal-pay-for-equal-work complaint with the United States Department of Labor. The complaint was simple enough: When the previous assistant director had taken over the job, he had moved from a nine-month to an eleven-month on-duty period. His salary had increased from just over $13,000 to $16,000. When I took over the same job, I, too, was expected to be on duty for eleven months of the year. My salary moved from just under $10,000 to $7700.

Early in the negotiations for my 1972/73 job, I had asked both the outgoing and incoming directors of New College to be sure they were not responsible for my not obtaining an instructional position and a decent salary. I had wanted to make sure that New College could not be accused of discrimination. Upon receiving their assurances, I was satisfied that it was the dean who had insisted that a lectureship was all that would be available to me, and therefore my complaint to the Labor Department was against the dean.

On Tuesday morning, September 26, a week after I filed my complaint, a Labor Department investigator came to the university to talk with Dean David Contois. Edelstein was summoned to the dean's office that afternoon to "get our stories straight" on the Abramson complaint. Edelstein returned from that meeting and informed me that the dean had considered three methods of handling my complaint: First, he could give me a salary equivalent to that of my predecessor—buy me off, the dean had apparently said. Second, he could insist that my duties were different from those of my predecessor and trust that the Labor Department would become hopelessly confused. Third, he could fire me.

On Friday afternoon, September 29, he fired me. He sent Edelstein a memo telling him, "I think it is necessary that you relieve her of all duties at once." He sent me a letter that stated, in part, that "as matters now stand, it is my unpleasant duty to inform you that you cannot be employed by New College. Further, the university's counsel advises me that you are unauthorized to function in any capacity in any of the university's programs."

Firing an academic employee after the beginning of a term of appointment is almost unheard of. At most institutions, breaking a contract in the middle of an appointment period must be preceded by a statement of charges by the administration and a full academic hearing on those charges, unless the teacher presents an immediate danger to students. Moreover, the Labor Department could choose to view my firing as retaliation against me and retaliation is, if anything, a more serious offense than an initial act of discrimination.

The dean claimed that I had never been hired—a story he still insists is true. However, he never bothered to explain why his letter to me stated that he was removing me from my duties. I could hardly have had duties at the university if I had not been hired. I had not been hired, said he, because I had added unacceptable "stipulations" to my contract in my memo. Yet that memo had crossed his desk two weeks earlier and he had not objected to it. And, if the memo was really the source of difficulty, it seemed to me that a reasonable person would sit down and discuss terms and conditions with me rather than unilaterally proclaiming that after three months on the job I would no longer be allowed to "function in any capacity in any of the university's programs." Nevertheless, the administration had cleverly placed me in a defensive position by insisting that I had added unacceptable "stipulations" to my contract. They naturally ignored their own belated stipulations, which had launched the entire contract episode.

Inside the university, the Faculty Senate Committee on Academic Freedom began investigating. Outside, the Labor Department stepped up its efforts. The chief of the Honolulu office of the Wage and Hour Division of the Labor Department called me several times a week during my month of enforced retirement. Each time he advised me to take it easy, go to the beach, not worry— I would get pay for that period anyway. But I have seldom gone through a month where I had to work harder. The Committee on Academic Freedom requested a continuous flow of information and documentation. Reporters called to find out what was happening.

Faculty members, by ones and in groups, wanted to be supplied with information to ascertain whether they could support me. My New College students decided they would rather hold classes at my home than be forced to pick up new classes with other instructors. And the Equal Employment Opportunity Commission (EEOC), which had accepted my complaint of discrimination three months earlier, decided that my situation was urgent enough to send an investigator to Hawaii immediately. I thus had to prepare additional information relevant to my EEOC charge.

At that point I was not without political support. A collective-bargaining election was scheduled for the campus in October. The AAUP was attempting to become the agent, as was my own union, the American Federation of College Teachers (AFCT). The western regional director of the AAUP, who had avoided dealing with my complaint until that time, called to inform me that the memo I had added to my contract appeared to be perfectly legitimate and that I had been illegally dismissed. He wired the chancellor, suggesting that I be reinstated and that the administration state its charges against me and hold a full hearing if there was a need to dismiss me before the end of my contract term.

Still other support came from a group of faculty members who circulated a petition on campus demanding my reinstatement. The New College faculty wrote its own petition and sent it off to the dean. And another petition was sent by New College students.

The university administration caved in almost immediately and began negotiating my contract terms with the Labor Department. Nevertheless, it took a month for the negotiations to produce an acceptable contract. On October 16, the dean agreed to meet with me. Kenneth Lau, the university counsel, was present, and I had brought along my husband as my counsel and witness. It was not a pleasant meeting. Dean Contois was technically in charge but seemingly out of control. His normally shaky hand shook more than usual, and he did not look me in the eye. He asked what I wanted. I told him I wanted my job back: the same full-time job I had held on September 29, before his letter arrived at New College. He insisted that I had never held a full-time job and could not hold one now. But he admitted that my job was the same as the full-time job my predecessor had held. He then began the whole routine again, asking me what it was that I wanted. Through it all, Lau sat and laughed. A strange meeting.

But a day after that meeting, I received a call from the dean's office asking me to stop by to pick up a new employment contract. The contract contained the same old offer—$7700 for the year—but in new trappings: The attachments were acceptable and consisted of nothing more than a disclaimer that appeared to protect both my legal rights and the rights of the university.

I was tempted to accept. The Labor Department had informed me that the investigation of my equal-pay-for-equal-work complaint would continue, even if I accepted the low pay offer. And the pressure to return to New College was growing. My work had been shouldered by others who already had enough work of their own to do.

Luckily, I waited two days. On October 19, the acting director of New College received a memo from the dean asking that my duties be reduced: "It is my understanding that Joan's duties will consist of class instruction in NC 240 and coordination and advising of upper-division students working on individual projects. These duties apparently are similar to those performed by Reynold Feldman last spring. However, you'll recall that Feldman was full time on an eleven-month contract. Since Joan's appointment would be less than full-time-equivalence, her assigned work load should be adjusted accordingly." But the one thing I had insisted upon with the dean all along was that I be returned to the duties I had left on September 29. And the cover letter that accompanied the new contract offer seemed to acknowledge that request. It read, in part, "I hope that you can accept this offer and return immediately to your duties in New College." Not some of my duties—just my duties.

Having seen the memo to Edelstein I could hardly sign the contract. I returned it unsigned and attempted to explain to the dean, once again, that my duties were the same as those of my predecessor. I also informed him that I did not appreciate his extending me an offer "to return to your duties" at the same time that he was writing to Edelstein to request that he "adjust" my duties.

Six days later the dean made a second offer. It carried the same disclaimer and the same statement that the principal purpose of the contract was to return me to my duties. It was, however, for 91.667 percent of full time as an instructor with an eleven-month contract retroactive to July 1.

91.667 percent?

Since the Labor Department investigator, Thomas Moriki, was named as a participant in shaping the contract, I contacted him immediately to ask why the duties my predecessor performed for full-time compensation were mine to do at 91.667 percent compensation. He claimed that he had no control over any terms other than salary, and he promised to return to the dean's office to negotiate a full-time salary. In the meantime, he advised me to send this second contract back to the dean unsigned. I did, with the following letter:

Dear Dave,

On the advice of Tom Moriki I am returning, unsigned, the 5B form you proposed to get me back to work at New College. As you know, I wish to be returned to the same job from which I was dismissed on September 29. I do not wish to be returned to a different, less responsible position.

Furthermore, I fail to understand the peculiar formulation of 91.667 percent of a full-time job. Your proposal leads me to entertain a number of interesting speculations: Am I to refuse to see every twelfth student who walks through my door? Should I work 45.8335 hours per week as opposed to the more than 50 hours per week I put in before? Should I perhaps work only 26.-58343 days per month as compared to the 29 days 1 worked in September? Maybe I should lop off the last 8.333 percent of the days at the end of the 170 or so working days between now and commencement and leave my job at the end of April? Has the job to be done at New College shrunk to 91.667 percent of its former size? Or am I 8.33 percent more efficient than Reynold Feldman, who performed the same duties last year?

Let me urge that we get together one more time with Tom Moriki and work this out. I think we all agree on the importance of getting me back to my responsibil-

ities as soon as possible. We seem so close now that with
a little extra effort and a little goodwill this whole matter
can be resolved.

I had more to say but my time does not cover
writing the other 8.33 percent of this letter.

91.667 percent Sincerely,
Joan

The question of what a reduction of duties meant still remains unanswered. The 91.667 percent of full time had but one
purpose. University regulations clearly state that any full-time instructional employee who works more than five full-time years is
automatically tenured. By the transparent device of offering me a
less than full-time contract for a full-time job, the university administration hoped to be able to prove later that I was not entitled
to tenure.

I should point out that most universities still limit tenure to
full-time employees. I should also point out that the percentage of
women employed in part-time instructional jobs at American universities is far higher than the percentage of women employed in
full-time instructional jobs. The conclusion is obvious: Arguments
about family obligations notwithstanding (and such arguments
most often come from males in administrative jobs rather than from
females seeking academic employment), the part-time employment
of women in the academic world has been a useful device in keeping that world masculine.

The university administration eventually did offer the full-
time salary required by the Labor Department while limiting me
to a supposedly less than full-time job. They started with my 1971/
72 salary as a base, moved three steps up on the salary scale (one
a year is normal), and then reduced the dollar figure by 8.333 percent. I was to receive 91.667 percent of a salary that was two steps
too high. That way, my salary was not very different from what it
would have been had I continued on a full-time contract and merely
gained an ordinary annual increment. But my contract read 91.667
percent of full time and I had gained three annual increments! I
had full-time pay for full-time work (at a rate I was still protesting

since I claimed that I had been offered too low an entry salary), and the administrators had a paper they could use to claim I was not working full time and was therefore not eligible for tenure.

The Labor Department negotiator said he could do no more. He advised me to accept the offer. My attorney also advised me to accept: both of us found it difficult to believe that a judge would view the contract as proof that I was only working part time.

I signed. And on November 5, I wrote to inform Dean Contois that I would be most pleased to return to the same job I had been forced to leave on September 29. The press acclaimed the settlement. Headlines let the local community know about the victory: "UH Instructor Wins Job Back, Raise," and "Annual Pay Upped $4330—Woman Reinstated at UH."

People marveled at my 53 percent pay hike, believing I had gone from the lectureship fee back to the instructor pay scale. I had never, of course, received a paycheck at the lecturer rate. But it looked good in the newspapers. Unfortunately, a few people considered the whole equal-pay complaint somewhat tacky. To them I had revealed a grubby, grasping quality that showed I was beneath the dignity they expected of university professors or, for that matter, of females, who are not supposed to be so basely mercenary. Months later one student came into my office to tell me that she had supported me until she had found out that I was fighting for money rather than principles.

But, for the most part, I listened to a series of congratulatory statements. For weeks—and months—I could not push a shopping cart through the supermarket without being told how fine it was that I had won and that the whole thing was over. For a while I tried to point out to my congratulators that I had won a year's contract and nothing more, that my salary was still $4000 below that of my predecessor (a man I had replaced because he was not doing an adequate job), that my rank remained unchanged, and that, most likely, the next year would bring another attempt to end my employment. People did not want to hear that. They did not want to be reminded that several years before I had been an untenured instructor, supposedly on the tenure track and with a full-time appointment, and that I now was still an untenured instructor, definitely off the tenure track and with a 91.667 percent appointment.

And so I quickly gave up explanations. I smiled at my congratulators and thanked them for their good wishes, even when the congratulations were offered six weeks after I returned to work. But six weeks after I returned to work I once again received a notice informing me that my job would be terminated.

◇◇◇◇◇◇◇◇◇◇◇◇◇◇◇◇◇◇◇◇◇◇◇◇◇◇◇◇◇◇◇◇◇◇◇◇◇◇

4

Up and Out

◆◇◆◇◆◇◆◇◆◇◆◇◆◇◆◇◆◇◆◇◆◇◆◇◆◇◆◇◆◇◆◇◆◇◆◇◆◇

*Alice began to feel very uneasy: to be sure, she
had not as yet had any dispute with the Queen, but
she knew that it might happen any minute. "And
then," thought she, "what would become of me?
They're dreadfully fond of beheading people here; the
great wonder is, that there's any one left alive!"*

Lewis Carroll, *Alice in Wonderland*

On September 29, 1972, a week before my fortieth birthday, I had
been fired. It was a new experience for me. But over the following
year the experience became commonplace.

Indeed, my final year at the University of Hawaii was
marked by two trends: first, a rapid increase in my responsibilities
and second, the equally rapid acceleration of administrative attempts to rid the university of my presence. These two trends

51

affected both my position at New College and my position in the
Faculty Senate.

In the early spring of 1973, I was elected to succeed Richard
Rapson as director of New College. The selection process had been a
long and complicated one. First, the college had conducted a
nationwide search. But administrators, who originally had encouraged such a search, later backed off, and it became clear that the
college would have to find a new director from within the university.

The college founder, Richard Rapson, opposed my selection.
His opposition arose, he said, not out of any lack of confidence in
my qualifications but out of his keen, if somewhat cynical, per-
ception of how the university functioned. Quite simply, he believed
that the administration would discontinue the program if I were
elected its director.

The situation is not atypical for a woman who finds herself
identified with the cause of equal employment opportunity. One of
the administrative assistants at New College put it to me this way:
"I know you are qualified, but the administration opposes you. Why
can't you wait until the situation resolves itself and *then* become
director? There will be other chances when all this blows over."
And while the director selection debate was going on, Harlan Cleveland gave an accurate insight into the thinking of the male academic establishment with his theories of "horizontal management"
in an address to a group of women educators. Back in the old days,
according to Cleveland, men dominated executive positions since
the style of management was vertical and called for a strong and
forceful hand at the top. Back then, he explained, a woman would
not be found at the top of any organization. Why, even technology
did not support women: one could hardly expect a woman to make
a speech in the agora since her voice, without benefit of electronic
amplification, would be shrill and unpleasant. But now that we
have such electronic amplification a woman can, for the first time,
be heard without sounding unpleasant to the ear. And now that
administration is changing from a vertical to a horizontal style (the
mental images run rampant!), we can expect to see more women
entering the ranks of the administrators.

We all know, he told his audience of more or less liberated

women, that women by nature are more skilled at interpersonal relations. And we all know how good women are at low-key, consultative styles of management. (The hostility level in the room was rising, although Cleveland did not seem to notice.) Because of these factors, undoubtedly we would begin to see more female administrators and executives.

I submitted a written question, both to test how far he would carry his theory and to explore his possible reaction to me as a candidate for the directorship of New College. Suppose a woman is otherwise qualified for an administrative job but has been active on behalf of equal employment opportunity for women. Would her activism disqualify her from holding that administrative job? Cleveland assured the audience that no "political" activity should disqualify anyone from any job. However, said he, this particular kind of activity would certainly indicate that the woman in question was not the low-key, horizontal type of executive he would be looking for.

Back at New College, the selection committee debated the relative merits of the candidates. When the decision was finally made, the issues seemed clearly drawn. My point of view was simply that morally and legally the college should select the person it felt most qualified to do the job. Rapson insisted that qualifications were not alone important, that we had to take into consideration the fact that the administration would almost surely do away with the program if I was proposed as director. To do so would, of course, be illegal. Federal antidiscrimination laws expressly insist on job selection based on qualifications and expressly forbid retaliation of the sort Rapson feared. Furthermore, the college had no tangible evidence, beyond Rapson's personal insistence, that this might happen.

The issues were aired carefully and openly. The decision was not made casually. If any mistake was made, it was not in misunderstanding the basis of the choice. It was, rather, in assuming that administrators would treat the question of director selection overtly rather than covertly. In spite of Rapson's warnings, it did not seem possible that educational administrators would disregard the welfare of close to three hundred students in order to deal with one bothersome faculty member.

It should be clear that the program was already on somewhat shaky ground for reasons that went far beyond the presence of one faculty member who had fallen from grace. For the most part, college faculty members, administrators, and regents tend to look with suspicion on any program that smacks of innovation. The very plea for change carries with it an implied criticism of the way those same faculty members, administrators, and regents are running things. In a sense, then, New College had been in trouble from the moment it was opened. Early discussions about the program in faculty review committees revealed seeds of resentment. Over and over again one came across faculty comment on how in "our department we are innovating all the time so I can't understand why we have to have a special program to do it." The attacks on our faculty and program were not unexpected.

The administration remained silent following my selection as director: my nomination papers as director of New College and my employment forms for the 1973/74 academic year were received by the dean but not acknowledged. But the clouds for New College were not on the horizon, they were overhead and threatening.

A few days before Christmas vacation in 1972 (just six weeks after I had returned to work from my first experience at being fired), I had received a letter notifying me that my employment would be terminated as of June 30, 1973, "with thanks for your services and best wishes for the future." Identical Christmas presents had been sent to all faculty members who had been hired exclusively in innovative programs. Even when the reason—or alleged reason—for the letters was spelled out, it did not make sense. One of the many central administration bureaucrats, a vice-president for academic affairs, had issued a new policy memo affecting employment in so-called experimental programs.

There are a number of people who still claim they never did understand the new policy. Small wonder. The memo announcing it was a classic of academic obfuscation. It read, in part:

> The problem is that these three special academic
> programs are provisional and that part-time appointment
> to them of faculty at these (instructional) ranks who do
> not hold appointment elsewhere in academic departments

of the university imply a status which neither the programs nor the appointees have. . . . It is these academic ranks which when the appointment is full time place a faculty member on the tenure track. They therefore have implications for tenure; that is, for the ranks at which it would be appropriate to reappoint to a full-time position and for the standards of recruitment and election appropriate to tenure track appointments.

The logic is not easy to grasp. Apparently, *if* these people were in full-time positions (which they were not) and *if* they were in traditional departments (which they were not), they would be on the tenure track since they had been assigned professorial ranks. However, since they were neither full time nor in traditional departments, their positions did not have tenure implications. But, just to make doubly sure, they should be made low-paid lecturers. The vice-president then went on to question their competence, ignoring the fact that all of them were required to undergo the identical set of tests faced by appointees of traditional departments, including a careful scrutiny of their records by the dean of the graduate division. And, to heap insult on injury, he accused the appointees themselves (as if they had made job offers to themselves at the highest possible rank and salary) of circumventing "the lecturers' pay scale in order to perform tasks which are those of a lecturer."

Stuart M. Brown, the vice-president who developed the policy, had a hard time explaining it when later required to do so in a hearing before a state labor board. It wasn't really a new policy, said he, but a reiteration of a long-standing policy of the Board of Regents. Then why had he written a policy memo stating that people who *were* hired at instructional rank would, in future, only be eligible for lectureships? And why had the regents approved appointments for those people in the past? Well, said he, some people had violated the policy in the past because they had not known that it existed. Apparently no one had bothered to announce it or write it down before. And why was his memo rescinded just a few months after it was circulated? Well, it never had been rescinded, really, but just recalled, though the policy remained in effect, since the policy could be handled in another way. Part-time status was enough to keep these people from accruing time toward tenure; it was not necessary to make them lecturers as well. Why, then, were people terminated with specific reference to the policy in that memo, and why were those people never reinstated when the memo was terminated? They were not really terminated, it seemed, since notices of that sort were fairly standard and were sent out to instructors in experimental programs every year. But had those people been rehired at rank in the past? Yes, that was true enough. But with the memo recalled, or rescinded, or whatever, why were those people still terminated? It seemed that while the memo was in circulation, the chancellor had put a freeze on all the positions and all of those who were sent letters under the policy were now frozen out, even though the policy had been declared nonexistent!

In May 1973, those of us who had been "terminated" under a nonexistent policy remained terminated. We were told that if the budget loosened up and if positions were unfrozen, we might be considered for jobs, not as continuing employees but as *new employees.*

There is a high probability that this puzzling situation was nothing more than the result of incredible ineptitude. But it is also possible that the ineptitude merely served as a convenient cover for a political move to get rid of a number of controversial faculty members. I was one of those. Among the others were some Hawaiian brown power advocates who had been hired by an experimental ethnic studies program, an environmental activist who had made life uncomfortable for a number of local politicians, and a former head of the public defender's office who had made the mistake of winning most of his cases against the state attorney general. (He was so successful, in fact, that the state abolished the office of public defender—and then reestablished it, with a new and less embarrassing incumbent.)

When the smoke settled in May, the experimental programs had lost most of their faculty members and a budgetary freeze foreclosed the possibility of rehiring. New College, a program that had serviced close to three hundred students and maintained a position count of about twelve (which enabled us to hire around twenty-four people on a part-time basis), was left with 40 percent of one faculty member from the Political Science Department, a secretary, and two half-time administrative assistants. All of our New College-based employees had been told that, policy rescinding or no, they had been terminated and would remain terminated.

Our faculty was not the only thing under attack. In November of 1972, the Board of Regents decided, in a closed subcommittee session, to terminate three of the four experimental programs at the University of Hawaii. The regents came under heavy fire for interfering with curricular matters and almost immediately backed down and released instead a request that "students, faculty, and administrators" review three of the innovative programs to determine how they could be absorbed into the College of Arts and Sciences.

The seven-person subcommittee set up to review New College under the regents' order had an interesting composition: two students, one associate dean who worked directly for Contois, a faculty member from the East Asian Literature Department who also happened to be married to a professor from the English Department, and, finally, two professors from the English Department, one of them my old friend, the director of the creative writing program. One of the student members later told a government investigator that the review committee, from the start, seemed to be in business for one purpose only: to get Joan Abramson. While this may be partially true (and perversely flattering), I am sure I was not the only object of their resentment. But their first report did not neglect this goal. The initial draft contained a series of ultimata, including the demand that the college pick someone else as director if it wished to continue in operation.

It was New College students who helped turn the tide, along with the basic fairmindedness of one of the committee members, Professor Richard Larson from the English Department. The students prevailed on Larson to discuss in detail some of the distortions they felt were present in the report. While some of the review committee members complained that it was too late to change the report, Larson simply asked for additional documentation. Then he took the time to read it.

Larson also took the time to talk with students about the director selection process. They carefully detailed the entire process and left him thoroughly impressed with the standards New College had set for itself and with the care with which students and faculty alike had gone about meeting those standards.

The effort to reevaluate could not have been easy for Larson. He had opposed tenure for me in the English Department on the grounds that I was much like other instructors and that tenure for me would open the floodgates to unqualified instructors seeking permanent positions. Yet it was largely due to Larson that the derogatory references to me were taken out of the report and the ultimatum to drop me or have the program dropped was deleted.

The "final, revised" report of the review committee came out just two days before the College Senate was to meet and vote on continuance of the program. The report recommended that New College be continued. The recommendation was adopted unanimously by the College Senate, endorsed by the dean and the chancellor, and sent to the central administration for forwarding to the regents.

Walking back from that May 1973 meeting of the College Senate, Richard Rapson told me that he thought the worst was over. We had won. There was nothing that could change things now. No administrator would dare overturn a unanimous recommendation of a faculty senate on a curricular matter. And, in fact, the administration was already accepting new students into the program.

I had too many such moments behind me, and I could not share his sense of confidence. I thought back to the time a year earlier when the regents were presented with another review of the New College program and when Rapson had assured us that we had made it into permanent status. He had even organized a special celebration for the New College faculty, an eleven-course Chinese dinner, to honor our new permanent status. It was a fine celebration, but only later did the faculty discover that the regents had not even voted on the program. Trusting Rapson's new assessment of our situation did not seem warranted. But I prayed that this time he was right.

Only a few days after the College Senate meeting I was selected to serve as chairwoman of the Faculty Senate Executive Committee. My term of office was to begin on June 1, 1973, a month before I was to take over as director of New College. The selection did not pose any problem, since each of the positions was viewed as half time.

The position of senate chairperson had carried a half-time

salary with it for the three years before my selection. The chairperson simply arranged a workload reduction in his or her department and carried out the numerous duties of heading the Faculty Senate under a split-appointment arrangement with half the salary for the year paid directly from the senate budget and half paid by the department.

I was selected as senate chairwoman on May 22, 1973. The decision was announced to the chancellor and a number of his associates on the same day. The next day it was announced to most of the members of the Board of Regents and to a number of officers from the central administration, including the president of the university. On May 28 the announcement of my selection was carried in the Manoa campus faculty and staff bulletin.

The reaction of the administration to my selection as head of the Faculty Senate differed markedly from their reaction to the New College directorship. No meaningful silence greeted the new contract forms that had to be submitted to cover the split appointment. No one demanded a review of the senate or questioned the way it utilized the time and energy of its members.

Instead, the senate office received a memo outlining the senate budget for the coming year. The half-time position for the senate chairperson was crossed out in red ink. Typed at the bottom of the page was the following notation: "Red-lined positions were deleted by the legislature. The revised position count for this program is 1.0—Stenographer III." There were some who considered the deletion an act of deliberate retaliation. Others, including one investigator from the HEW Office for Civil Rights, simply called it an "incredible coincidence."

For a number of weeks after my election the Senate Executive Committee and the administration debated the propriety of that deletion. Administrators in the chancellor's office blamed it on administrators in the president's office, and administrators in the president's office said that they were truly sorry since the job was certainly essential to the faculty, but they could hardly be expected to contradict the legislature. In spite of all the debate, there was no real evidence that the legislature had been responsible for cutting that specific half-time position from the budget. The state budget certainly did not show the deletion.

Finally, one of the many assistant bureaucrats from the office of the vice-president for academic affairs produced a document. It was a yellow sheet of paper on which a felt-tipped pen had been used to jot down a number of deletions. The yellow sheet, said he, was a legislative worksheet and clearly indicated the intent of the legislators. However, he did admit, when pressed, that the sheet did not really come from any legislative committee—the committee members would not allow him to take their worksheets from the room. But a clerk had allowed him to copy deletions from those worksheets and that was what he had done on his yellow scratch pad.

I was not overly impressed: the sheet also listed "sabbaticals," a deletion that was noted as saving the university hundreds of thousands of dollars. Some legislators, it is true, had discussed getting rid of sabbaticals, but sabbaticals had not been deleted, nor had a number of other items listed on that yellow sheet. That sheet was hardly evidence that the legislature had deleted the senate position.

I officially took over as senate chairwoman on June 1, 1973. And after three more weeks of buck-passing between the chancellor and the president, the chancellor informed me that my split-appointment contract would be approved: half time as director of New College and half time as senate chairwoman. Indeed, the vice-chancellor signed my contract the very next day. But an error was then discovered in the contract form, and his signature was carefully covered up. Yet another bureaucrat, the assistant vice-chancellor for faculty affairs, took charge of straightening out the technicalities.

In a long telephone conversation, he and I reviewed the problems in the contract and he instructed me on how to fill in the forms properly. As with my previous contract, the administration was worried about giving me automatic tenure (though this would be my seventh consecutive year of full-time employment!). Nonetheless, as long as I agreed to a mutual demurrer that left the tenure issue to the courts, the administration had no objections to the full-time appointment: half as New College director and half as senate chairwoman. Following that conversation, the assistant vice-chancellor, whose official responsibility was to handle faculty personnel matters, sent me a memo confirming the details for filling in the new contract forms. In court several months later the administration claimed that the memo was merely the work of a kind man who was helping me to properly fill out a job application!

In early July, yet another administrator, the vice-president for business affairs, wrote a last memo to dispose of the issue of legislative intent. It was his opinion that the legislature had never meant to delete the salary for the faculty senate chairperson but preferred that the position be funded through the instructional rather than the administrative budget. And in early July, the administration, in exchange for the release of $2.4 million of NASA funds that were being withheld from the university, promised officials from the HEW Office for Civil Rights that I could keep my tenuous position.

The matter of my employment for the 1973/74 academic year seemed resolved. I met with administrators and received correspondence from them. I was called by the chancellor to attend meetings of his advisory council and his budget committee. In fact the chancellor told me that his secretary often told people that he was not in but I would always be able to get through to him, since he considered it important to listen to the senate representative. And over the summer my file cabinet grew full with memos and letters from presidents, regents, chancellors, and others addressed to me as chairwoman of the senate and as director of New College.

But for New College the alarms grew louder. Our review was due at the regents' office on June 1. On June 13, I attended a meeting of the regents and discovered, much to my surprise, that the innovative program reviews were not on the agenda for the month. The regents were not planning to meet again until August 9, just ten days before the beginning of advising for the fall semester. The August meeting would be crucial for us since both our program reviews and our faculty recommendations would be before the regents.

It was almost impossible to believe that the Board of Regents would kill a program ten days before the start of a semester. Nonetheless, it was an anxious time for students and faculty alike. I would be six weeks into my contract when the regents met, and it would be difficult not to honor it, especially since the common practice at the university was for people to begin jobs before they had gained the pro forma approval of the regents. The university could not have functioned if all contract forms had to be approved by the regents first—too many classes had to be staffed at the last minute, and the instructors hired to staff them usually worked for five or six weeks before they received the authorization of the regents. Then, too, administrators had promised HEW that I would remain employed. But the rest of our faculty faced a serious problem. They would have no way of knowing, until August 9, whether or not they would have jobs on August 20. It was possible for the regents, if they terminated New College, to refuse to hire them since they had not yet begun work.

As senate chairwoman, I received materials for the regents' meetings several days early. When I received the agenda for the August 9 meeting, I discovered that there were no innovative program faculty members on the list of new appointees. And even though I had been working with the knowledge, consent, and even cooperation of the administration for six weeks of a new contract period, my own name was also missing from the appointment list. Our low-keyed anxiety became high-pitched alarm.

The chancellor's office assured us smoothly that there was no need for worry, since it was possible to work under special letters from the president until the regents approved the contracts. And a negative vote on our program seemed improbable. How could the regents terminate an academic program less than two weeks before the start of advising for the fall term? And how could they justify terminating a program that had been approved at every step of the review process on the Manoa campus?

Impossible? Not at all.

On August 1, the regents' subcommittee on academic affairs met to discuss the reviews of three innovative programs. When the meeting was over, the subcommittee members refused to drop any hints as to our fate. Back at the college, our elder statesman, Arthur Goodfriend, called a meeting. It seemed apparent to him that I was the problem. If only the college would get rid of me, the regents would refrain from getting rid of the college. Goodfriend had come to me with a proposal that I graciously resign. I thought about it for awhile and told him I felt it was too late to affect the regents' decision. I added that I could not imagine any kind of resignation letter, and I suggested that he might try writing one for me if he still felt I should resign.

On August 7, two days before the regents were set to meet, Goodfriend obliged. He sat down and drafted a diplomatic masterpiece:

> The Board of Regents will shortly announce its decision on the future of New College. Believing deeply in the purposes of an experiment that has demonstrated to all informed individuals and Review Committees its right to survive, my desire is to contribute all I can to a positive decision. To ensure that my own difficulties with the University's administration do not adversely influence this decision, I withdraw from the Directorship of New College, and pledge that any action by the Board of Regents in respect to New College will not be used by me, legally or otherwise, in pursuing the personal and separate matters in which the University and I are involved.

Goodfriend's effort was hardly surprising. The tendency of members of the male academic establishment is to blame the victims of the system rather than the system. That this was done in the name of a belief in "the purposes of an experiment" one of whose major goals was democratic process is no more surprising. I did not sign his letter.

On August 8, the informal (closed) meeting that then preceded every formal (public) meeting of the Board of Regents took place. Several New College students were allowed time to discuss the program. They spent two hours with the regents, and they took their responsibility quite seriously. But the next morning, when we entered the room where the regents were to hold their formal meeting, the report of the regents' committee on academic affairs was handed to us. It was dated August 7. Our students had wasted their time and their breath. The decision had been made already. On August 7, it had been too late to appease the regents with a sacrificial offering and on August 8, too late for student persuasion. The regents had callously allowed students to plead for continuation of their program, with the report already written and the negative decision apparently made.

Seven regents voted to terminate the program. One voted against termination. The vote was followed by an emotional statement by one of our dispossessed students that left even the newspaper and television reporters in tears.

And after the meeting, the chairman of the Board of Regents told me that he did not believe that the program was too expensive or that it had major weaknesses. Incredibly, he had voted against continuing the program because it was *too successful.* If the hallmark of the program was its tutorial system for upper division students, said he, it was undemocratic and unfair to the rest of the students to offer that system to only a few!

Every element of the university community had supported continuance of the program. The student body president spoke out, the Faculty Senate pointed out the dangers of regent decision-making on curricular matters. Members of the review committee wrote to reemphasize their belief that the program had corrected most of its internal problems long before the review was conducted. The AAUP quoted doctrine about faculty control of curricular matters and warned the regents not to reverse unanimous decisions of the faculty and the Manoa administration. The union warned of the danger of breaking the collective-bargaining law by making major policy changes ten days before the beginning of a semester and without consulting union representatives. The local press lauded the program and pleaded for keeping alternative forms of education open to local students. But on the basis of confused and uninformed opinions, the regents were able to overlook all the advice and admonitions and to carelessly do away with the work of two years of planning and three years of experimenting, not to mention the jobs of a number of faculty members at a time when it was too late in the year for them to relocate. And, worst of all, they banished a program in which over two hundred and fifty students had planned to continue or begin their academic work in ten days.

Rapson was bitter. In spite of his later optimism, his early prediction that the administration would discontinue the college if I was selected as its director had been terrifyingly accurate. When his prediction was realized, his reactions were understandable, if unfortunate. After insisting that I was no longer to consider myself director of the program, he met with the chancellor and then fired off an angry note to me:

I have just concluded a conference with Chancellor Gorter. They have checked all records to find some indication of the letter you described yesterday or any evidence that you have been appointed director of New College. They have found none, and from the point of view of the administration of the University of Hawaii, I am—for what it's worth!—still director of the program until the beginning of my leave of absence on August 31, 1973. While I appreciate that you should like to assert your claims within the program, the immediate consequences of this determination by the administration are, from my point of view: (a) that you may not use the title of director of New College for yourself either within the college or outside, and that should you insist on so doing, legal action against you may follow; and (b) that the office staff, being responsible chiefly to me, is free to decide whether or not to do work requested by you.

I have no objection to your use of the title director-designate of New College, or to you initiating measures in that capacity which you believe to be in the best interests of the students and faculty of the program. Within this framework I hope we can brings [sic] things within the program and within our relationship to a peaceful conclusion, free of rancor and confrontation. I can see no value in further tumult to anyone—students, faculty, staff, you, me. I suggest we both practice restraint and give Time a chance to heal the wounds.

And two days after the program was killed, an interview with Rapson appeared in one of the local papers. It began:

New College was killed in part by the University of Hawaii administration and regents because of "issues surrounding" Joan Abramson, who was elected director last spring by New College faculty and students, Dr. Richard L. Rapson conjectured yesterday. Rapson is the man most responsible for the birth and three-year life of the innovative program.

Rapson went on:

> Whenever curriculum was discussed with the fac-
> ulty review committee, the administration and the regents,
> it was as though it didn't matter. There was always
> something lurking beneath the surface of things, revealed
> by a shrug of the shoulders or a nervous laugh or an
> exchange of glances whenever the issue of Joan was
> raised [Evinger, 1973].

Had I gone home when the administration first told me to, I might
have won a reputation for congeniality. Instead, the very fact that I
gained increasingly responsible positions gained me a confrontational
label. "This year," Rapson continued in his interview, "in choosing
Joan—who is competent—the program committed itself by inference
to an adversary relationship" (Evinger, 1973).

The university administration eventually found something,
even small parts of jobs, for all but two of our male faculty members. Indeed, there was considerable expression of concern by administrators that something be found for them. None of the women
was placed (although one retained a low-paying lectureship she had
held in another program).

The most interesting placement was the job found for Arthur
Goodfriend, the man who had drafted a letter of resignation for me.
During the previous spring semester I had written a memorandum
to the dean, pleading with him to allow Goodfriend to work for one
more year, even though he would be past the mandatory retirement
age. An associate dean had informed me that hiring Goodfriend
was questionable and that his course could be dropped without
harm to New College. After the termination of New College, however, Goodfriend was hired as the "New College historian." When
questioned later by an HEW investigator, administrators claimed
that Goodfriend was in a neutral position, and since I was too involved in the story, I could not be counted on to write it well.

A few loose ends remained to my summer. In a situation
almost identical to that of a year before, the administration claimed
I had never been hired—thus I was not being fired. The summer
stack of memos, addressed to me by administrators as director of

New College and as chairwoman of the Faculty Senate, apparently had been forgotten. The signed contract that had been unilaterally voided by the vice-chancellor and the verbal contract agreement with the assistant vice-chancellor along with the memo that confirmed it had vanished as far as the administration was concerned. The meetings I attended had never occurred, at least not that anyone could remember. The promise to HEW had been forgotten. Retroactively, I had been made invisible.

My invisible status was further confirmed a few weeks later, once again in a series of actions that almost directly paralleled the actions of the previous year's firing. On September 6, the chancellor wrote to the Faculty Senate Executive Committee (thereby confirming my nonperson status quite thoroughly) to inform them: "Since Ms. Joan Abramson is not a member of the faculty, I must, in fairness to all concerned, inform you that at this time the administration can see no basis for recognizing her as chairperson of the committee."

To acknowledge that I had been working all summer was to acknowledge that I had a valid contract and could not be fired. The administration preferred to take another route. I simply had not been there all summer, and if I thought I was, it was not their fault that I was not smart enough to know I was unemployed.

My nonperson status remains, now, confirmed by the administration. It has traveled full circle. I filed a complaint and was studiously ignored. When that did not work, a vigorous effort was made to rid the university of my presence. Then it was time to ignore me once again.

Students, however, ignored the official edicts. The members of a seminar I conducted in the spring of 1973 decided, at semester's end, that there was more work to do. The group, somewhat expanded in size, continued to meet through the summer and fall and into December, almost a year after the seminar began. And one morning, several months after New College closed, I awoke to find a familiar sign from our old quarters over my bedroom door. A student had managed to come in during the night and quietly tack it in place. It read: ADMINISTRATION—NEW COLLEGE

5

Merit and Other Myths

Alice laughed. "There's no use trying," she said, "one ca'n't believe impossible things."

"I daresay you haven't had much practice," said the Queen. "When I was your age, I always did it for half-an-hour a day. Why, sometimes I've believed as many as six impossible things before breakfast."

Lewis Carroll, *Through the Looking Glass*

Several years ago I had occasion to sit in on the final oral examination of a New College senior. She had completed two years of independent study under the supervision of a psychologist who specializes in the study of sexual behavior and sex differences, a man who kept a cast of an erect penis on his desk.

The student's tutor praised her work and insisted that she was doing as well as some of his Ph.D. students. I asked him what he thought of her chances of obtaining an academic post if she went on to complete a Ph.D. in psychology. He smiled, assured me of his empathy, and explained that one had to take into account the individual productivity of faculty or potential faculty.

"And if you have a man with thirty-two publications and a woman who has only eight, well, who would you choose?" The question was rhetorical. He went on to insist that women, with their very natural outside interests in home and family, were just not as productive as men in academic life and probably not as capable of being productive.

In the space of a two-minute conversation the psychologist had addressed himself to the nature of the academic advancement game and to the two major myths concerning women in that game. He had revealed that publication is the yardstick of academic fitness. (Teaching was not even granted a small aside in the conversation.) And he had repeated the two myths: (1) women do not take themselves as seriously professionally as do men, and (2) they lack professional commitment and ability.

His comments indicated an unfailing grasp of the way things are, according to academic men, and a belief that this was also the way things ought to be. The combination—an academic yardstick where productivity is the key to success and a firm belief in the low productivity of women as a class—has served well to keep women from achieving success in the academic world. It has an admirable symmetry: each side supports the other and works to keep the academic world male-dominated.

This circular combination of standards and myths presents a number of obvious advantages for men. First, it serves to reduce by almost 50 percent the potential competition for jobs. This may not be the overt motivation for the combination of notions that tend to exclude women from the academic world. But it is clearly an effect of those notions.

Second, while reducing competition, it serves to preserve the *idea* of competition through merit. If access to the academic world and to advancement in that world are based on objective criteria of productivity, then those who have gained access can believe that they have done so through their own merit in open competition with others.

Third, it serves to reinforce the liberal self-image of the male academic. In a system so admirably based on merit, no one can be accused of prejudice or discrimination. Those terms are reserved for redneck Southern sheriffs whose weapons are billy clubs, fire hoses, and police dogs.

A very convenient piece of packaging.

However, it is not without flaws. The idea that productivity can be measured by number of publications and that productivity is the sole yardstick of academic competence is highly vulnerable. And the myths of female lack of professional commitment and lack of productivity are, if anything, even more suspect.

In this chapter, each part of the package will be examined in turn. There are flaws in each part, and they are substantial enough to demand the kind of honest questioning that is supposed to be the hallmark of academic endeavor. I do not pretend to know all the answers. But I do suggest that those who push pat standards and unexamined myths have not even begun to ask the right questions.

The argument that shores up the use of number of publications as the yardstick for academic advancement seems, at first glance, both rational and fair. Universities are, ideally, places where new knowledge is created, explored, and transmitted and where the tools of exploration and creation are passed on to new generations of scholars. Following this logic, it makes sense that the best professors are not engaged in transmitting the same tired body of knowledge they picked up from their professors twenty or thirty years ago. They can themselves explore and speculate and perhaps infect others with the excitement of exploration and speculation. Therefore, the best professors are themselves deeply immersed in research and are committed to sharing the results with their colleagues, their students, and indeed the rest of the world through their publications. Ideally, these people make the best teachers, for they will never allow themselves to be bored with what they teach.

In the abstract, the idea is appealing. Teaching becomes a taken-for-granted byproduct of research. Research occupies the principal position. And it follows that the rewards of academe— tenure, promotion, increased salary, sabbaticals, research grants, travel, peer recognition—are reserved for those who can demonstrate a fairly high rate of research production through the visible and measurable result: publication.

But, in the concrete, there are cracks.

The first crack is obvious. If good teaching and good research went hand in hand, one would expect good research to be rewarded by both more research opportunity and more teaching opportunity. Instead, assignment to teaching is treated as a form of punishment, or at best as an onerous task, one of the unpleasant duties one must put up with if one wishes to partake of the many rewards of academic life.

And almost anyone who has attended a major university knows of award-winning researchers who could not relate a murder mystery without putting half their students to sleep. In fact, most universities take this reality into consideration when they *reduce* teaching loads for their best researchers (or for senior people who are *supposed* to be engaged in research).

Of course, by reducing teaching for some, universities add to the teaching load of others—often part-time or low-ranked women employees. And the very fact that some must carry a heavier teaching load has its obvious consequence: those who carry the heavier load will have correspondingly less time available for research.

The second crack in the rationale is in the nature of publication itself. Ideally, publication means publication of research of good quality. And ideally, universities measure the quality of the work by which men acquire more and more of the rewards of their profession.

But even the best of universities fall into the quantity trap. The excuse offered is that nowadays, with so many esoteric subfields growing up, it is virtually impossible for anyone to evaluate the work of anyone else who is even slightly outside the field of interest. Therefore, the mere *fact* of publication in the more reputable journals of one's field may be used as an indication that the publication must be good.

A number of feminists have argued against the productivity yardstick and have pointed out the very real dangers of it: ". . . if there is any institution in modern society that should place quality above quantity, it should be the university. . . . I suggest the university should push and push hard to assess quality, not merely quantity. One fine article can often equal a dozen mediocre ones, or one book surpass three" (Rossi, 1970, p. 926). Unfortunately, it is not just the second-rate universities that have fallen into the trap of measuring productivity by sheer volume of publication. Several years ago, an acquaintance was denied tenure in one of the scientific departments of Harvard. Shortly before the tenure decision was made, he had published a book that was highly acclaimed by colleagues in his field. However, he had no other publications. From his new job in industry, he reflected that he had not had the good sense to take the book apart and publish it, chapter by chapter, as a series of journal articles rather than as a single book. That, he said, would have given him fifteen publications instead of one. "Deans can't read," he complained, "they can only count."

And, absurd though this may be, it is often the prevailing logic in academe.

A third crack is the failure of institutions to apply the publication yardstick uniformly. If the key to achieving the rewards of academic life is publication, why is it that there are so many men who have *not* published and who are enjoying those rewards? And why is it that there are so many women who *have* published and who are still on the outside looking in or at the bottom of the ladder looking up?

In spite of these major cracks, the logic of publish or perish prevails in the academic world, and everywhere academic men continue to argue that only through scholarly productivity is it possible to separate the men from the boys and make adequate judgments on retention and advancement.

But assume, for the moment, that there are *no* cracks and that the basic yardstick of productivity is as fair as any other possible yardstick for academic advancement. Even if this were the case, the acceptance of the two basic myths about women in academe would work to severely limit the way in which the yardstick is applied to women. Again, those myths are that women lack professional ability and commitment, and that women are not as productive as men.

If these are not myths but realities, if men are both more productive and their products are of higher quality, then (so the argument goes) men *are* worth more in the academic marketplace.

Men fresh out of graduate school *are* better risks than women fresh out of graduate school. Men will advance more rapidly than women. And there will naturally be more men than women in academic work, now and forever.

This argument, of course, overlooks the obvious fact that, even if there were such group differences, there also would be large group overlaps: even if women as a group were by nature less able and less productive than men as a group, enormous individual differences would exist and discrimination against productive individual female scholars could still be very real.

Although the two myths interact dynamically, examining them separately might be enlightening.

Most women in the academic world (or those barred from the academic world) must find it rather tiresome by now to be continually reminded by those who believe in the first myth that they are not as serious about their professions or as skilled in them as are their male colleagues. This myth is qualitative in nature. It argues that women, because of biological or natural differences from men, do not have the same commitment to their professions as do men. Outside interests such as home, husband, and children naturally take first place in their lives. Their primary satisfactions come from aspects of their lives outside their professional work while, for men, the primary satisfactions are found in their professional work. The myth has probably followed academic women since the moment they entered college, if not before. And whether it is true or not, most women are treated *as if* they were not taking their own academic lives seriously. But they may in fact be more serious than men, since they have faced more obstacles in getting there.

The road to an academic career is most difficult for a woman. Years ago, the girls in my high school graduation class who did not yet have engagement rings were teased that they were going to college to obtain their "Mrs." degree. Later, and conversely, women who were married and working while their husbands went to school were told they should be very proud to be getting their "PhT" degree—putting husband through! Whether a woman is actively going to school or actively working to support a husband who is going to school, the reason attributed to the activity is the same: advancing oneself and thereby identifying oneself through a man.

Because of societal pressure to fulfill goals through a man, many young women are discouraged from considering entering the arena. Others are actively barred. At some schools, even publicly supported universities, admission to undergraduate status is more selective for female students than for male students. The admissions policy of the University of North Carolina, for example, was openly discriminatory a few years ago: "Admission of women on the freshman level will be restricted to those who are especially well qualified." And in 1970 the freshman class consisted of 1893 men and only 426 women (Sandler, 1970, p. 298). The American Council on Education reported that freshmen who entered four-year colleges in 1968 had widely divergent high school grades: more than 40 percent of the girls had averages of B+ or better but only 18 percent of the boys could boast of the same (Hole and Levine, 1971, p. 318).

The attitude of some male alumni certainly indicates that they would find nothing at all strange in having disparate admission standards: In congressional testimony in 1970, Ann Sutherland Harris reported the following: "At Yale, when the new women undergraduates protested the quota on women and made the modest demand for fifty more women undergraduates the coming year at an alumni dinner, an alumnus was cheered when he said: 'We're all for women, but we can't deny a Yale education to a man.'" And when Harris was questioned by Congressman William D. Hathaway of Maine on school admission policies, the same bias became apparent: "Mr. Hathaway: If you take the college administration and they have just so many kids that they can take into school and they know that 90 percent of the men, for example, in our society have to get a job and, say, only 50 percent of the women are going to have to get it, and they have a limited number they will take in, aren't they warranted in taking nine out of ten men and fewer girls?" (Green, 1970, p. 293).

Disparate standards for men and women, standards that obviously cut down the number of females who might otherwise compete in the job market, do not seem to bother the Yale alumni or the congressman from Maine in the slightest.

Once enrolled as undergraduates, young women cannot

always expect to receive the same treatment as their male colleagues. At the University of Hawaii several years ago, for example, some young women were barred from a course that was partially supported by federal funds, in spite of the fact that discrimination in such directly funded programs is explicitly forbidden by federal law. It may have been mere coincidence that the course was considered valuable as background for one of the university's graduate programs.

A strikingly similar incident was reported in December 1973 in *On Campus with Women:* "A group of women at the University of Michigan in Flint have used state and federal civil rights law, as well as the university's own bylaws, to gain entry to an experimental criminology course restricted to 'men only.' Women students were denied admission to the federally funded course (which included work with inmates from the Department of Corrections Honor Camp) because of 'some undefined security-contraband risks.' "

The bias against women in education continues into graduate school. An Iowa State administrator wrote the following in 1970:

> Too many young women are casually enrolling in graduate schools across the country without seriously considering the obligations which they are assuming by requesting that such an expenditure be made for them. And they are not alone to blame. Equally at fault are two groups of faculty—undergraduate instructors who encourage their woman students to apply to graduate school without helping them consider the commitment that such an act implies and graduate admissions counselors who blithely admit girls with impressive academic records without looking for other evidence that the applicant has made a sincere commitment to graduate study [Harris, 1971, p. 244].

Yet despite the prevalence of this attitude, there is evidence that women are quite serious about their graduate training and tend to make good use of it. Helen Astin, for example, has surveyed women doctorates and found that of 2000 questioned ten years after the completion of their degrees, 91 percent were working (1969, p. 249). Moreover, there is ample evidence that the bias against the admission of women at all levels of higher education tends to ensure the excellence of those women persistent enough to gain admission. Work done by Jessie Bernard indicates that women who are accepted to graduate schools have higher IQs than do men accepted to graduate schools (1964, p. 80).

In admission to graduate school, nothing much has changed since I applied twenty years ago. Young women are still told that offering them a slot would be a waste, since they will probably get married anyway and not make use of their education. Or they are told that graduate slots for men take precedence, since men have more years in which to be productive—being women, they will undoubtedly take time out to have babies. Yet a study by the American Council on Education refutes this hard-dying myth: "The [American Council on Education] study released last summer found that only 20 percent of women faculty members had interrupted their careers for nonacademic reasons, compared with 25 percent for men" (*Newsweek,* Dec. 10, 1973, p. 123).

On the other hand, women who were discouraged from continuing their education years ago and attempt to reenter academic life after raising a family are just as often told that they could have obtained admission when they were younger but they waited too long and are too old. One of my former students was recently denied admission to a graduate program in speech therapy for just that reason.

When I was interviewed years ago at the UCLA graduate school of journalism, I was asked why on earth I had chosen journalism: didn't I know that the only careers in journalism open to women were on the society pages of papers and did I really want to do *that?* No, I did not, I told them. Then what was I doing there, I was asked.

Our graduate class had almost thirty students. Only five women were admitted. Three were single, and two of us were married. And both of us were pregnant but had the good sense to keep our mouths shut when we were interviewed. Three babies were born to students in the program that year—my friend had twins. And the two of us had the highest grade-point averages of the class. Had either of us admitted that we were pregnant, our graduate school days would have been over before they had begun. And we both took jobs for which we could not have qualified had we not been permitted to study for the journalism degree.

The welcome into graduate school is not exactly exuberant for those women who do gain admission. They are apt to learn rather quickly that they must fend off remarks such as, "You're really not serious about the degree, are you?" or "Well, it doesn't matter if you finish your thesis this year, you probably won't use it for much anyway." Unmarried women are often viewed with even more suspicion than married women: there is sometimes an unspoken assumption that they are there only because they have been slow to find mates or because they are seeking husbands within a group that is apt to produce higher-than-average income or social status.

In spite of the persistence of the notion that women are not serious, the statistics show the contrary to be true. A 1970 University of Chicago report on the status of women, one of the first studies to include student attrition rates, shows only a slightly higher rate for women than men, about 2 percent more at the undergraduate level and 5 percent more in graduate schools (Neugarten and others, 1970, pp. 806–807). In view of the persistent myth of lack of commitment and the overtly cursory treatment accorded women as a result of the myth, it is surprising that these attrition rates are not higher.

One factor which might be expected to account for even higher attrition rates for female students is the difference in financial aid provided. At the University of Hawaii, officials have long insisted that there is no student pay differential based on sex. What they neglect to point out, however, is that there are pay differentials based on type of job. Clerical tasks receive little more than the minimum wage, and tasks requiring manual or technical skills receive higher rates of pay. Female students are invariably steered to the clerical jobs, while males do the manual and technical jobs such as mowing lawns, raking leaves, wiring computer circuits.

On the graduate level, men are more apt to receive financial support than are women. A 1970 Berkeley study on status of academic women reveals the following:

> Ignoring those fields where there are almost no women, there is evidence that women doctorates are more likely to have received *no* teaching assistantship and also more likely to have received *no* support of any kind. The overall percentage of men who received no support as a teaching assistant is 33 percent, the corresponding percentage for women is 44 percent, which is 11 percentage points worse. The percentage who received no support of any type is 9 percent for men and 15 percent for women, a large difference [Colson, 1970, p. 1188].

It is important to point out that these figures are for men and women who completed their doctoral work. Those students who may have dropped out because they obtained no financial support are not included.

If a woman does make it through graduate school, her chances of gaining a good academic job are lessened by the same, persistent myth of her lack of commitment. Her male advisors and her department chairman may be less apt to recommend her for vacant posts at distant universities than her male colleagues. Such vacancies are generally filled by the "old-boy" method. Professor X will contact his old graduate school or convention buddy, Professor Y, and ask if there are any "bright young men" available in the new crop of Ph.D.s. Even the government's recent insistence on widespread job advertising for openings does not change the picture much. It may increase the number of unsolicited applications for a job, but the "bright young man" will still have the inside track. Indeed, the major effect of this government requirement (intended to promote equal employment opportunity) may be merely to provide departments with "proof" that they have searched for qualified women, obtained numerous female applicants, but found their male choice to be most qualified after all. Thus, they may be able to demonstrate to the government their "good faith efforts" without changing their employment situation in the least.

When Professor X does call, it is possible that Professor Y might even think of a bright young woman. But Professor Y, out of paternalistic kindness shaped by his own adherence to the same myth, may refrain from submitting her name. He may recall that a woman student has other obligations—perhaps she has a boyfriend who is still in graduate school or a husband who works in the vicinity or even an elderly mother who is dependent on her. Surely (he may assume) she would not want to leave town. It may not be conscious, but Professor Y will be limiting the opportunities available to his female students far more than he would ever limit them for his male students by simply assuming that the females are more concerned about their outside lives and obligations—women do not take their professional work as seriously as do men.

And so, often because of someone else's misguided consideration for her welfare, a woman student may not even be permitted to make the choice for herself. Such considerations would rarely get in the way of recommending bright young men. Obviously they are serious about their careers and can be depended on to put career first. They do not need to have their responses predicted by someone else nor do they need to be protected from the temptation of potential job offers that might interfere with their personal lives.

In cases where women *are* recommended for jobs, the recommendations are often far from academic. The following comments are from letters of recommendation for women seeking academic jobs:

> While ——— probably doesn't have the stamina for independent scholarly work, she loves big parties and mixes well.

> ——— is a large broad-boned somewhat awkward young woman who must be close to six feet in height.

> If she has any faults, they are those that usually accompany the ambitious woman of her age [Hoffman, 1972, pp. 5–6].

One rarely finds equivalent remarks in letters of recommendation sent on behalf of male candidates.

Since women are so often overlooked and, when not overlooked, are often honored with recommendations that provide extraneous, silly, or degrading information, they may find that they receive fewer jobs offers than do men. They will, then, have little bargaining power in relation to rank and salary, since bargaining power is highly dependent on the number of offers one has received and the prestige of the universities from which those offers come.

The notion that, for women, outside interests interfere with professional interests continues to affect women further along in their careers. Long after graduate school has been left behind, creeping paternalism may dictate decisions without the knowledge of the woman concerned. Recently, the faculty of a major West Coast university department, realizing that there was an embarrassing shortage of women in the department, discussed the possibility of interviewing a woman from the Midwest who was well-established in the field. The discussion did not, however, center on the woman's qualifications or even her possible willingness to leave her present job. It centered on finding a job for her husband, a less prestigious scholar from the same field. Department members pondered long and hard about ways to convince *other* universities in the vicinity to offer the man a job. Finally they gave up in despair, and the woman was not offered a job or even brought to the university for an interview. Since no job could be found for her husband, she was denied the opportunity to make up her own mind. Such thoughtfulness is almost never found in reverse. At Columbia, Ann Harris reports the following:

> A brilliant European couple were invited to teach in one department, for they specialized in different areas. He did not have a Ph.D.; she did. He had not published a book; she had. He was hired as a visiting associate professor; she, after considerable hassle, as a visiting assistant professor. Throughout the negotiations, they were told that the nepotism rule would prevent Columbia's offering her a full-time position in the same department as her husband, although in reply to a questionnaire circulated by the AAUW a few years ago, Columbia declared that it did not have any nepotism rules. Clearly Columbia does not think that it should have any nepotism rules. The couple concerned have since returned to Europe, where she has just been given a distinguished appointment at a rank above that of her husband, an appointment to which her academic achievements clearly entitle her. She

has told me that she does not think a married woman
will receive such fair treatment in America for many
years [Harris, 1970, pp. 254–255].

Academic men frequently receive job offers from other universities without the slightest effort being made to place their academic wives. In these cases, one often hears that the woman has
to make it on her own and cannot expect special treatment. Certainly
she would make it on her own if she had any merit. A man was
recently hired by one University of Hawaii department and his wife
had the bad taste to inquire of another department (in her field) if
there were any openings. She was promptly informed that it was
rather gauche and unprofessional to simply wait until her husband
was committed to coming to Hawaii and then expect the university to look into hiring her. Of course, the University of Hawaii has
a monopoly on university-level jobs in the state and, short of a very
tiresome commute, there is little hope for that woman's professional
career while her husband stays in Hawaii and she stays with her
husband.

When the partners in a marriage take jobs in distant towns
and must take on long-distance commuting as a way of life, prevailing opinion will generally find it absurd for a man to put up
with the situation. His wife should obviously move and, if she must,
take a job closer to his work. However, by the same logic, she will be
accused of lack of professional commitment when she does just this.
If, on the other hand, it is the husband who seeks a job closer to his
wife's work, knowing eyebrows will be lifted: the man may be
considered henpecked (*not* unprofessional) for letting his wife (*not*
his lack of professional commitment) interfere with a promising
career. Since, according to the myth, women academics lack commitment and place other factors above their careers, it is quite
natural to assume that a woman would not accept a better job offer
out of town unless her husband first found a job and wished to
move—so there is no need to extend such an offer to a woman.
But, if her husband has accepted a job elsewhere and moved, she
demonstrates her "lack of commitment" by moving with him when
she has no job. Women seem to be damned either way.

Even teaching activities, supposedly preferred by women, are not immune from the belief in sex roles. In my former department, a woman with an excellent teaching reputation proposed some changes in the required reading list for a sophomore literature course. The professor in charge of the course, a man who did not have an outstanding teaching reputation, responded with a negative tirade that closed, "Let me end with a nasty assumption of my own. Anyone who can't captivate classes with the greatest writers in the language—Chaucer, Shakespeare, and Milton—ought to give up and go into home economics."

Indeed.

Given the pervasiveness of the myth that women lack aptitude and commitment when it comes to scholarly endeavors, the pervasiveness of the myth that women do not produce as much scholarly work as do men is not surprising. It is amazing to note how many men and women alike have accepted this myth without the least effort to study actual sex differences in academic productivity.

Even feminists, in arguing against mere quantity of publication and in favor of quality, have apparently accepted the basic assumption that women publish less than men and have moved on to rationalize that failing: "Married academic women may indeed write and publish less often than their male colleagues. Since many women are supplementary rather than exclusive breadwinners, they have had the luxury of avoiding the trap of publish-or-perish thinking. Before we push women into such a competitive race, we should be sure it is a race either sex should be in" (Rossi, 1970, p. 926).

Economics professor Juanita Kreps asks questions stemming from this same assumption: "To say that women seem to prefer colleges to universities, teaching to research, continued work in one institution to moving around does not of course tell us why" (Kreps, 1971). But to ask why women are more interested in the less rewarding academic activities is to assume that indeed they *are*. It is to assume, for whatever genetic or environmental reasons, that women like teaching better than research (and perhaps even that they like the lower pay and lower prestige that comes with such a job). Making such assumptions oversimplifies the problem and narrows the job equity solution to two possible alternatives. The first would be to assume that the preference is natural to women and work to alter the rewards offered. The second would be to discover why women have such a preference and work to alter the preference. Neither is an acceptable solution, because both assume that there is no problem outside of woman herself: either she must assert the value of what she does most naturally, or she must learn to do better what is naturally valued.

The more immediate questions—the proper questions—are not why do women prefer teaching to research or why are women less productive, but do women prefer teaching to research and are women less productive than men. I do not have the answers to these questions, but I suggest that there is sufficient evidence available to make the questions appropriate ones for study.

For example, work done by Jane Loeb and Marianne Ferber (1972) indicates that female faculty members are as productive as their male colleagues. Further, a 1967 study of female Ph.D.s by Rita Simon, Shirley Clark, and Kathleen Galeway states that despite equal productivity, academic women (both married and single) earn less than academic men and gain lower academic rank.

A number of other studies, particularly single discipline studies conducted by commissions and caucus groups on the status of women, give support to these findings. One such report on the status of women in sociology reveals that sociology departments with graduate schools had a national total of 12 percent women faculty members in 1972. During the same period 12.8 percent of the authors in the two major journals of sociology were women (Hughes, 1973, p. 10, 44). While the figures are not directly comparable, they do give some indication that women in sociology *may* be holding their own in the two major journals in their field. Little has been done in the way of carefully controlled study, but there is evidence that women may be publishing as much as men, in spite of the fact that they are generally found in positions where research and publication can only be more difficult to produce. There is no conclusive evidence to support the myth that men publish more.

The myth of male productivity gains support from several factors that demand more critical exploration. These factors all concern the problem of access. First, the necessary conditions for research: do women have access to sufficient time in which to conduct research and writing activities? Second, the necessary tools for research: do women have access to sufficient means of support for research? Third, the necessary means of display of research: do women have access to sufficient means of exhibiting the results of their research and writing?

There are several aspects to the question of access to time. One centers on the actual locations where women find college-level work. Statistics for 1973 from the Department of Labor show that women are more often found in small colleges and that the small percentage of women found in larger universities generally can be found in the lower ranks. This evidence is often used to support the contention that women *prefer* teaching. After all, if they did not, why would they be attracted to the small colleges where teaching activities are primary, where teaching loads are heavier, and where the resources for academic research—laboratories, libraries, sufficient mass of colleagues with whom to exchange ideas—are not readily available. The fact that women in most universities are massed at the lower ranks is often used to illustrate the same point. That they have not moved up through the ranks is taken as evidence that they have preferred to concentrate on teaching, an activity seldom rewarded by promotion.

But the same set of facts could (and should) be turned around and used as an explanation of why women publish less (if indeed they do) rather than being used as a demonstration of lack of inclination to publish, which is the explanation being assumed. It is quite possible that women are not drawn to teaching more than to research but that they find themselves in jobs where teaching is emphasized because those are the jobs where they meet the least employment resistance. And once in those jobs, the simple fact is that the time available for activities other than teaching is severely limited. Small colleges generally assign heavier teaching schedules than do major universities, and major universities often assign heavier teaching loads at the lower ranks. The rationale is that the professors need more time for research and even for class preparation (since they generally get their pick of smaller graduate-level seminars while lecturers and instructors and assistant professors often teach the large, mandatory undergraduate courses).

Furthermore, the research that full professors do may sometimes be credited to them as teaching, thus lowering their classroom teaching load even more. This can occur when the load includes supervision of graduate students who, like professors' wives, may perform a good deal of the drudgery involved in research. Thus, the (usually male) senior professor receives at least double credit for his time—no wonder he is paid at twice (or more) the rate of most women! His supervision of graduate students may count as teaching, while the graduate students advance the professor's own research.

Interestingly enough, time sometimes works to increase the individual productivity of men to unbelievable rates, rates that help boost the average productivity of male academics. For there is a surprisingly common phenomenon in American universities that can double the available working hours for men. The phenomenon has been labeled the two-person single career by Hanna Papanek:

> Colleges and universities, large private foundations, the U.S. government (particularly the armed forces and the foreign service), and similar institutions all develop their own version of the two-person career pattern among their employees. They all communicate certain expectations to the wives of their employees. These expectations serve the dual function of reinforcing the husband's commitment to the institution and of demanding certain types of role performance from the wife which benefit the institution in a number of ways [Papanek, 1973, p. 858].

In universities, such a career—almost always a male career—often finds the marriage partner spending enormous amounts of time researching, editing, and helping to write the grant proposals, articles, and books of the other partner. This situation is sometimes abetted or produced by antinepotism rules or other barriers that prevent the wife from obtaining a paying job of her own at her husband's university.

Several years ago, I grew increasingly curious about the amazing number of books turned out by a male colleague at the University of Hawaii. As a professor, his teaching load is light, he is entitled to paid sabbaticals, and he has a good chance of obtaining study and research grants. But in spite of all these factors I still found his output of books unbelievably and enviably high, until I realized that he was able to invest in his career twice the number of hours each week that I could invest. His wife (and former secretary) is an excellent researcher. Every morning she goes to whatever library or archive needs exploring. Every evening she comes home to organize the results of her day's work or type up the manuscripts that come out of her research. With the exception of one short newspaper article (rather more like a long letter to the editor), I have not come across any book or article that has included her name as joint author. Papanek has taken note of this aspect of the two-person career situation: "It is probably correct to say that openly acknowledged collaboration, in the context of a two-person career, is not very frequent. This ambivalence surrounding the wife's contribution suggests that many institutions, again particularly in the academic world, recognize the fragility of male self-esteem in American society and have adopted a number of ways of safeguarding it" (1973, p. 862).

A rarely mentioned side effect of this kind of situation is that it allows a wife to gain knowledge and expertise in her husband's field that eventually may exceed the expertise gained by a graduate student at the time he or she gains the Ph.D. degree. Yet the wife cannot translate her education into a paying career of her own, since her Ph.D. level of competence was not attained in the ordinary way. Her expertise is, therefore, committed all the more firmly to the furtherance of her husband's career.

The two-person career can also be found in professional associations that are made up, for the most part, of university professors and researchers. Mindless praise of it, such as that found in an editorial in the November 1973 edition of *Computer,* is not infrequent:

> "Nobody said anything specifically about a package deal," says Edith Hayman, wife of Computer Society Executive Secretary Harry Hayman, "but when Harry went to work for the Society that's the way it worked out."
>
> Edith, who accompanies her husband to about a half-dozen conferences a year, has become a Society regular—operating membership booths, helping handle

sales of conference digests and proceedings, and providing general, part-time clerical support to Harry—all as an unpaid volunteer. The net effect may be the only husband-wife team in all the IEEE. It is without question the only two-for-one package in the Computer Society.

I know of no women who are blessed with full time secretary-research associates by marriage. The only example I can think of where both partners are at work on the wife's career is not from academic life but from sports—Billie Jean King. And there is a difference: Larry King is paid (rather than kept) to manage the King enterprise.

Time is an important factor in any accurate study of the relative productivity of men and women academics. The plain fact is that on the average women academics, for whatever reason, do not have as much time for research and writing as do most men. Yet no serious study has been made of the relationship of such factors as time to productivity. This lack of such scholarly investigation has not stopped many supposed scholars from all too eagerly concluding that women do not produce academically. In drawing this conclusion they have bypassed the evidence that might make the pattern and the reasons for it a little less clear but a little more accurate.

Access to the means of support for research is the second important factor. A simple rule of thumb exists in gaining research support: the less secure your academic position, the lower your chances for gaining such support. The converse also applies, much to the benefit of academic men. Like bank loans and credit, those who have can always get more.

The major source of financial support for the research of college professors comes from outside the university, from government agencies or private foundations. Most grant-giving organizations maintain systems that have a built in catch-22: all grant applications must be funneled through the institution that employs the individual seeking the grant. Granting organizations expect all applications to be approved by these institutions, and they also expect the institutions to contribute something toward the maintenance of the grantee. Usually this takes the form of continued

salary. For low-ranked women in untenured positions, this requirement imposes two burdens that are not imposed on tenured faculty
members when they apply for grants. The institution itself might
object to the grant application, since it contains an implied commitment to continue the grantee's salary. And grant-giving institutions
are often reluctant to give money to low-ranked, unproven faculty
members who, they reason, might not be around long enough to see
their research through to completion.

Department chairmen and research directors on campus
have been known to require that younger women, especially untenured ones, not use their own names as principal investigators on
research proposals. If proposals are accepted under the names of
senior professors with tenure, it is reasoned, the disappearance of the
junior faculty member from the campus would not affect the income to the institution.

Like most of the arguments used to exclude women, this
argument is flawed. First, in most cases the senior faculty member is
only vaguely interested or completely uninterested in the project.
He would, therefore, have no use for the grant if the real researcher
left. In fact, it might prove something of a bother—he would have
to find someone else who was interested in doing the work, convince
the granting agency to apply the funds to other work, or return the
grant. Second, the rule is applied unequally to men and women. I
know of a man, for example, who was allowed to submit his name
as principal investigator on a grant proposal even though he was
untenured and considered an unlikely candidate for a permanent
position. He was turned down for tenure while his proposal was
under consideration. The proposal went through, and the administration then reversed itself on tenure rather than lose the grant!
In contrast, I know of a woman who put together a research
proposal and won preliminary backing from the National Science
Foundation. Her university's research director then refused to
authorize the proposal. His refusal was based on the fact that the
woman was not tenured. He would, however, allow her to submit
the proposal if she would agree to have someone else with proper
credentials sign on as a coprincipal investigator. Eventually, the
research director himself took on the task, though his field is
linguistics and the project was in the natural sciences. In other
instances women have been denied even a shared principal investi-

gator status and forced to take a subordinate role, even though they originated the research idea. Yet most universities view principal investigator status as a clear indication of productive research.

Added to intrauniversity considerations is the fact that grant proposals submitted by women are bound to be judged by male readers outside the university who have thoroughly internalized the myth that women are less committed to their career work than are men. The smallest reason to suspect that a woman cannot be trusted to give her all to the work, when added to such factors as low rank and tenuous employment, might well tip the scales against a research proposal submitted by a woman.

Access to support for research covers more than funding from outside agencies. It includes the use of research laboratories, laboratories often jealously guarded by their male occupants. An acquaintance who does not have access to such facilities and needs them for her work recently approached a male colleague about to go on sabbatical. She explained her needs and the thrust of her research and asked if she could use his laboratory facilities during his sabbatical year. He listened politely and then, ignoring her work completely, suggested that during his sabbatical year she might be interested in using his laboratory facilities to continue his project in his absence.

Research support also covers such simple things as the availability of colleagues with whom one can discuss research ideas. Yet many women, especially when they are still in the lower ranks, exhibit exasperation at the unwillingness of male colleagues to hold serious discussions. They are often treated with condescension or their ideas are treated as a form of entertainment for which the appropriate response seems to fall into the category of cocktail party repartee. Or through politeness or dependence on the good will of male colleagues for future employment they may submit to long and simplistic explanations of material they already know because their male colleagues assume they know nothing.

Even the simplest forms of support that may be taken for granted for men can become barriers for women. A state university department that employs six lecturers (all but one female) recently announced that since lecturers were hired to teach and not to conduct research they would not be allowed to use xeroxing facilities in the department for their papers. One of the lecturers received over twenty requests for a paper she presented at a conference. Distribution of such papers is, of course, a necessary part of professional advancement (not to mention of securing anything other than a lectureship position in the future). She was told that she would have to petition the department's executive committee for special permission to xerox her paper.

The third factor in achieving productivity that can be measured by departmental colleagues is access to the means of displaying the results of research. Traditionally, this access is through publications (books, monographs, articles in journals, and conference proceedings) and through presentation of papers at scholarly conferences. Most academic disciplines have scholarly national or international professional organizations that sponsor professional conferences and journals. Decisions to accept or reject papers for these conferences and journals are generally made by professors from the relevant field of study. Thus persons in the discipline serve a screening function, and they tend to have strong preferences for their friends and for male colleagues whose work they are much inclined to respect. And they are, for the most part, men who have absorbed the very same set of myths that will cause them to view material submitted by a woman in a different, less serious light than material submitted by their male friends.

Another factor should not be overlooked: circumstances more often force women to work outside their primary field of training. They therefore publish more frequently in interdisciplinary or out-of-field journals. Such publication is not given as much weight as publication in recognized in-field journals, and colleagues are often right in there among the deans in their inability or unwillingness to read. "Quality" publication often is defined only by the name of the journal.

Once it has passed the many barriers to publication, the work of women is still not treated in the same manner as the work of men. Let me cite a book review in the November 5, 1973 issue of *Time* (emphasis added):

> As current biographers go, Lady Antonia Fraser
> is not necessarily the best, but she is certainly the prettiest.

It is a title she would not relish, for she is to scholarship
born and bred. Her father, the Earl of Longford, a
sometime leader of the House of Lords, is also the author
of a number of books on topics that range from banking
to philosophy. Her mother Elizabeth is a distinguished
biographer of Queen Victoria and the Duke of Wellington.
One sister is a novelist; another turns out textbooks. A
younger brother is a historian.

Still, for years her British compatriots have known
her chiefly as one of the most beautiful of the Beautiful
People, wife of the rich M.P. Sir Hugh Fraser, and
mother of six. Then, *to the astonishment of nearly every-
body*, at age 37, she produced a massive, readable,
academically respectable biography of Mary Queen of
Scots. Now, nearly five years later, *as if intent on proving
that her first* success was no accident, the lady has delivered a fatter and more scholarly study of Oliver Crom-
well, the florid, slovenly country gentleman who became
Britain's first Lord Protector.

What her age and looks, her father, mother, siblings, husband, and
children, her wealth and her jet-set connections have to do with
anything is a puzzle. The only insight one gets from the entire
introductory section of the review that may be of any value in
assessing the quality of the work being reviewed is that it is "more
scholarly" than her previous "academically respectable" book. The
fact that the first book was produced is merely an "astonishment."
And, with her second book, she is accused of being "intent on
proving" that her first book was no mere accident—seriousness
about her endeavor has, apparently, nothing to do with the case.

A number of male academics, confronted by this kind of
evidence, ask why women are so offended by having their looks or
their connections mentioned. Perhaps they are correct and there is
nothing wrong with these inclusions. However, it is peculiar that
reviewers avoid the same kinds of information in reviews of the work
of men. Indeed, a biographical novel is reviewed in the very same
issue of *Time*. It does point out that people may envy and hate the
author, Gore Vidal, for his newest success, and it alludes to Vidal's
use of characters who are developed out of the novelist's own
public and political connections. But it is a book review and so
there is, apparently, no need to mention unrelated personal and

private circumstances. Such circumstances only seem to occur to reviewers as appropriate when they are discussing a female author.

The myth of female lack of scholarly commitment operates to diminish access to the tools for achieving scholarly production. Time, support for research, and display of research are simply not as readily available to women as they are to men. In spite of this there is evidence that women are at least holding their own. Yet, if careful study did confirm the available evidence, the argument backed by the myths might easily be switched to quality of publication. The myth of female lack of professional commitment and ability leads naturally to the belief that the scholarly work done by women is not of the same excellence as the work done by men.

Jo Freeman discovered some striking patterns in the employment of women on the social science faculties at the University of Chicago. Most striking of all, no woman who became a full professor had come up through the ranks in the department of her discipline since the university opened in 1892. All female full professors either had been promoted in "women's departments" such as household administration or home economics, or had been brought in after attaining full professor rank at another institution. Most of these women were exceptional by any standards. Men, on the other hand, had risen through the ranks in their own departments. Freeman points out that "qualified" means something very different for men and for women: "In conversations with (male) faculty members one is given the impression that qualified for a woman means only the best in the field." Freeman concludes: "It cannot be said that women are judged equally with men until ordinary women and ordinary men are judged by the same standards. As long as all the women are judged by the standards of the extraordinary few, women will continue to believe that they are inferior, and the University of Chicago will be able smugly to reassure itself that it has an equalitarian policy" (1970, p. 998).

If women must be better trained and more persistent to get into graduate schools, if they are given less financial assistance in getting through them and less advice and assistance in finding good jobs, if they are consistently treated as if they are not serious about their work, and if they are consistently granted fewer of the aids to achieving productivity, it defies logic to state that those who persist are not gaining the rewards because they are not as qualified as their male colleagues. Yet this smug and offensive rationalization for the underrepresentation of women in academe is still offered at every opportunity.

At the beginning of this chapter, I described an incident with a psychologist who could not even imagine that a woman might produce as much or as well as a man. At the University of Hawaii our chancellor displayed the same limited imagination when he wrote in his cover letter to the university affirmative action plan. ". . . we are not required to hire women to the exclusion of better qualified male candidates. This is illegal as specifically pointed out in Order 11246, by being in itself discriminatory." It did not occur to him that the issue of "qualifications" might better be phrased in reverse: "we are not required to hire men to the exclusion of better qualified female candidates. This is illegal, as specifically pointed out in Order 11246, by being in itself discriminatory." Yet this is exactly the situation that exists, and it is the very situation the executive order was intended to correct.

One can readily anticipate that with all these limited imaginations at work there will be a frantic search for "qualified" women, a search preordained to produce no results. One way or another, the male academic establishment seems to prefer its myths to the less secure possibility of facts and open-minded study. It makes one think again of the benefits conferred by those myths. The myths allow academic men to believe in their liberality, equality, and fairness. And more important, they allow academic men to smugly assure themselves that they are successful competitors in a merit system while actually reducing the competition they must face by almost 50 percent.

In view of the shifting percentage of those of college age in the population of the United States, this factor cannot be lightly dismissed. Educational institutions expanded rapidly in the last decade in an effort to accommodate an enormous jump in population among the young (52 percent growth in the fourteen to twenty-four age group in the 1960s). During that time no thought was given to equal employment opportunity in rapidly expanding university faculties. Now, just as laws demanding equal employment opportunity are finally beginning to be talked about and just as large numbers of women are beginning to make demands, expansion has slowed markedly. Competition for limited job openings is bound to become more frenzied. The time is not exactly opportune for stripping off the comfortable old rationalizations.

Indeed, the prospect of potentially doubling competition at the same time that the job market is closing up might be thoroughly frightening to the academic male and to his hopes for his sons and surrogate sons (male graduate students). Even the modest government demand that universities establish goals in line with currently available women doctorates is appalling to male academics, who readily scream "quotas" and complain that "standards" will be lowered by allowing women to be represented in proportion to their numbers in the doctoral pool. Imagine how much more frightening it would be to open competition even further by bringing up our daughters to consider the same range of possibilities our sons consider and by allowing them equal access to the training needed to engage those possibilities.

For those whose sex has automatically placed them on the inside, that closed circle of beliefs has distinct economic advantages, whether they are acknowledged or not. It is hardly surprising, then, that those beliefs are so unshakeable. And it is hardly surprising, when there is faith in the standards and belief in the myths, how difficult it is to find "qualified" women.

"Qualified" men on the other hand . . .

6

The White Male Backlash

"Contrariwise," continued *Tweedledee, "if it was so*
it might be; and if it were so, it would be; but as it
isn't, it ain't. That's logic."

Lewis Carroll, *Through the Looking Glass*

One of the most immediate results of the first tentative government attempts at enforcing regulations prohibiting discrimination in higher education was an enormous outcry on the part of male academics. An outpouring of magazine articles and speeches raised the specter of undemocratic quota systems and the fear of a take-over of higher education by people of mediocre ability whose only qualification for their jobs would be the fact that they were black or female or both.

Advocates of this argument insisted that the issue was one of meritocracy versus bureaucracy and that agencies such as the HEW Office for Civil Rights has no business going into universities to scrutinize hiring, tenure, and promotion practices. They objected to government demands for affirmative action, a term that covers agency efforts to get universities to analyze their own employment situations, examine the available pool of qualified women and minority group members, broaden their personnel search procedures to encompass previously excluded groups, and set reasonable hiring goals.

As viewed by the U.S. Civil Rights Commission in a 1972 statement, affirmative action seems harmless enough. In a discussion of long-standing systemic discrimination the commission said: ". . . affirmative action programs are designed not to establish preferential treatment for minorities and women. Rather, the purpose of such programs is to eliminate the institutional barriers that minorities and women now encounter in seeking employment and thereby to redress the historic imbalance favoring white males in the job market." The protestors, however, raised the alarm, claiming that affirmative action was nothing more than the imposition of absolute quotas for the hiring of blacks and women. If universities caved in on this issue, they claimed, it would be the end of quality higher education in the United States.

Berkeley political science professor Paul Seabury soon distinguished himself as one of the virtuoso performers in the fight against equal employment opportunity. His argument carefully lays down the basic rationale of the entire movement by male academics to undercut affirmative action. Seabury aired a good deal of his argument in the pages of *Commentary*. In one article in the February 1972 issue, he lodged a grumpy disclaimer of university responsibility for injustice: "As universities climb out of the rubble of campus disorders of the 1960s, beset by harsh budgetary reverses, they now are required to redress national social injustices within their walls at their own expense" (p. 38). He goes on to a romantic discussion of the rise of a democracy of excellence in American universities, a phenomenon that, according to Seabury, has quite naturally resulted in uneven representation of certain groups: "And it is interesting to note that the quest for professional excellence in some respects has mitigated against the achievement of group parities: among those women's colleges which had obtained by the 1950s an enviable academic status as being more than *apartheid* seminaries, one apparent 'price' of scholarly excellence was the rapid infusion of male faculty" (p. 41).

Seabury goes on to bemoan what he calls "preferential hiring." By preferential hiring he does not mean, as one might expect, the current old-boy system: "If departments abandon the practice of looking to the best pools from which they can hope to draw, then quality must in fact be jeopardized. To comply with HEW orders, every department must come up not with the *best* candidate, but with the best-qualified *woman* or *nonwhite* candidate. For when a male or a white candidate is actually selected or recommended, it is now incumbent on both department and university to *prove* that no qualified woman or nonwhite was found available" (p. 42). Again, the specter of mediocrity is raised. Again an end to the meritocracy seems to be the fear. But nowhere in this long complaint does Seabury bother to inform us of the nature of merit or of the substance of excellence, those wonderful qualities that led so directly (he would have us believe) to the predominance of the white male on the university campus; that led, even, to the "rapid infusion of male faculty" in the woman's colleges as the price of "scholarly excellence."

In an article published in December 1972 in the same magazine, Seabury does attempt to define merit: "Let us consider the idea of merit. As a conception of justice, it means 'to each according to his abilities,' or in another and closely related sense, 'to each according to his works.' In these two combined senses merit advances and rewards according to ability and accomplishment, rather than according to status, preferment, or chance" (p. 41). An unstated assumption in this and in the rest of Seabury's article is that the system has in fact been working without regard to "status, preferment, or chance." Without missing a beat Seabury moves on to distort the intent of affirmative action: "But we are now told by the critics of merit that either its standards are themselves unfair and discriminatory, or that the fair and uniform employment of such standards leads to unequal and unjust results" (p. 41). Again, the assumption is that the standards are employed in a "fair and uniform" way and that the advocates of affirmative action are opposed to merit and are whining about not coming in among the

winners. In a classic rhetorical twist Seabury carefully explores the
difference between equal opportunity and equality of results. Equal
results, he explains, do not derive from equal opportunity: the
unequal representation of certain groups among the meritocracy is
the expected result of equal opportunity. Thus, anyone arguing for
some semblance of equal representation in the meritocracy must
unquestionably be arguing against equal opportunity:

> Yet even in the fairest of all procedures, where
> arbitrariness has been banished, and where steps have
> been taken to overcome the effects of inherited disadvan-
> tage of every kind, equal opportunity will all too often
> fail to produce the equality of results some would wish.
> The consequence is that those who value equality of re-
> sults over equal opportunity, and over the principle that
> all men should be judged and treated according to their
> individual merits, are attempting to lead us into a new
> era of discrimination on the basis of race, creed, and
> color (p. 44).

Seabury takes a long and rather circuitous route to arrive at
the notion that merit, not bias, is the prevailing state of affairs in
American universities and that the white male, given equal opportunity, will show his superiority by oozing to the top like pallid
cream on the milk. The real issue, however, does peak through the
emotional pleas for maintaining the excellent state of affairs: "But
someone *will* pay: namely very large numbers of white males who
are among those distinguishable as 'best qualified' and who will be
shunted aside in the frantic quest for 'disadvantaged qualifiables.'
. . . Large numbers of highly-qualified scholars will pay with their
careers simply because they are male and white" (Seabury, Feb.
1972, p. 44). The real issue is not fear of mediocrity or the potential
destruction of the so-called merit system. The real issue is fear that
white males will go jobless.

It was pressure from groups of white males, including the
Anti-Defamation League of B'nai B'rith, that was responsible for
the establishment of the office of ombudsman within the Higher
Education Division of the HEW Office for Civil Rights several years
ago. The same groups were responsible for the abolition of that

office recently. The ombudsman was originally viewed as a means for the rapid processing of complaints of reverse discrimination. It was somehow assumed that such complaints deserved more immediate attention than complaints of discrimination against protected classes of people such as women and blacks.

According to one HEW official, most of the complaints of reverse discrimination have been frivolous, and almost none required any real investigation. In some cases, department chairmen had, indeed, misinterpreted the law and refused to hire white males. They had assumed that affirmative action meant the exclusion of white males until the proportion of women and blacks had been increased. Ironically, this false impression may have been encouraged by the distorted view of affirmative action spread by Seabury and others who share his views. Ironically, it became the job of the HEW ombudsman to straighten these few department heads out and assure them that they did not have to refrain from hiring qualified white males. But in even more cases, the complaints of reverse discrimination proved to be misleading. Often a department chairman merely used affirmative action as a convenient excuse for refusing to hire a white male he did not wish to hire in the first place.

Thus the *Carnegie Quarterly* could report in the fall of 1973: "It is easy to understand how one might get the idea that less qualified females and minorities are being given preference. For instance, one department chairman who turned down four white, male job applicants, using the excuse that 'the university was under pressure to hire women and minorities,' then went out and hired the white male he wanted all along." I wonder if the department chairmen who use this technique of putting off white males ever stop to consider the real damage they are doing to the cause of equal employment. I can well imagine the genuine resentment among young white male academics that must stem from the conviction that they cannot get jobs because universities are being forced to hire women and blacks, regardless of qualifications. The anger of male academics who believed the unfounded horror stories is still with us today.

In the spring of 1974, the office of HEW ombudsman was abolished, not because the flow of reverse discrimination complaints had dried up but because ADL and other groups that had lobbied for its establishment were not satisfied with its achievements. It seemed to them that far too many complaints were found invalid.

The ADL also has been responsible for bringing a number of reverse discrimination cases in the courts. The one that gained the most notoriety was the case of *DeFunis* v. *Odegaard*. When the U.S. Supreme Court agreed to hear the case in March 1974, its importance was underscored. "The Court's decision, which is expected in a month or two, stands to have a profound effect on the job market. It will affect every white who believes that a black was given a racial preference in getting a job or a promotion—and every man who thinks that he was unfairly passed over in favor of a woman. The DeFunis suit could prove a direct challenge to the 'affirmative action' concept outlined in the 1964 Civil Rights Act to increase the employment of minorities in almost every segment of American industry" (Footlick, 1974, p. 61).

The plaintiff in the case was Marco DeFunis, a young man who was denied admission to the University of Washington law school and who claimed that affirmative admission policies favored blacks and other minorities who were less qualified than he for admission. The University of Washington agreed that DeFunis had scored higher on the Law School Admission Tests than had thirty-six minority students who were admitted. He also had scored higher than thirty-eight white students who were admitted. But law school officials pointed out that twenty-nine white students with even higher scores than those achieved by DeFunis were rejected. Law School Admission Test scores, said they, were not the only measure by which students were accepted or rejected. Other factors, including the student's extracurricular activities, personal recommendations, and place of origin were taken into account.

Indeed, these kinds of factors have been an accepted part of admission policies at most universities for decades. Some schools seek geographical balance, while others grant first preference to residents of the home state. Some grant preference to sons and daughters of alumni or to individuals who will bolster the athletic teams. Such special considerations have long been a part of the American college and, regardless of their merit as a means of selecting students, it is unlikely that the backers of DeFunis really had in mind their destruction. Yet it was just such special considerations that were the heart of the legal case.

Even though DeFunis subsequently was granted admission to the University of Washington Law School (under court order), the case proceeded through the courts. The Anti-Defamation League backed DeFunis with funds and expertise, and on the other side, a number of black and women's rights organizations allied themselves with the University of Washington. By the time the issue reached the Supreme Court, twenty-six organizations had submitted amicus briefs. By a vote of five to four, the Supreme Court justices decided to sidestep the issue on the grounds that the appeal was moot. The refusal to rule was a major disappointment for both sides.

Justice William J. Brennan, Jr., writing for the minority, pointed out, "Few constitutional questions in recent history have stirred as much debate." The issues, said Brennan, "will not disappear" simply because the court has refused to rule (Mathews, 1974). Clearly, the same issues would have to come before the court again, after long delay and great expense. And Justice William O. Douglas, in an independent dissenting opinion, faced the issues quite directly. "The equal protection clause commands the elimination of racial barriers, not their creation in order to satisfy our theory as to how society ought to be organized," said Douglas, thereby rejecting the notion that any special race- or sex-based criteria for admission would be valid. Douglas, in fact, pointed out that assigning special places to be filled only by blacks was akin to stating that blacks could not make it and were inferior to whites in their qualifications. But Douglas went on to point out that tests, such as the Law School Admission Test, were in themselves racially biased and "do not have the value that their deceptively precise scoring system suggests" (Hechinger, 1974, p. 51). A ghetto-raised black who had pulled himself up through night school or junior college might not score as well on the Law School Admission Test as the scion of a wealthy family who had made it with ease through Harvard, but he might have more of the qualities that make for excellence in an attorney than the Harvard son. Thus, Justice Douglas made it clear that special consideration on the basis of race, sex, or ethnicity was repugnant to the American constitution, but the tests themselves may grant such special consideration to the privileged. The criteria for admission, then, while they cannot be based on such illegal considerations as race, must be flexible and human and must have as their goal the ability to consider individual human beings "in a racially neutral way" (Hechinger, 1974, p. 52). The proponents of real affirmative action would have been happy with the Douglas decision, had it been the decision of the majority. In spite of "reverse discrimination" propaganda, they have been insisting all along that the current system has a built-in bias in favor of white males and that changes must be made to facilitate equal employment for those currently screened out solely because of their race or their sex.

Some disappointed (and perhaps misguided) supporters of a supreme court decision pointed out that "reverse discrimination" was a necessary step in the eventual achievement of equality. Such ideas even made their way into the editorial pages, where they undoubtedly contributed to the resentment quotient of white males. A *Honolulu Advertiser* editorial on April 24, 1974, took the following ill-considered stand: "On the negative side, affirmative actions often do amount to reverse discrimination. But the overriding point is that women and racial minorities deserve a fairer opportunity to compete. Extending that opportunity sometimes results in penalizing others equally, or even better, qualified. That is not easy to accept. Yet the alternative is to further delay fairer treatment to those who have long been discriminated against. That would be even harder to accept."

But others, perhaps with more sense, point out that such a notion implies the inferiority of all but the white male. They point out that the white male preferences current in graduate student admission and in employment are not based so simply and so purely on any fact of white male superiority (albeit gained by centuries of discriminatory favoritism). Such preference might be aided and abetted by institutional blindness (perhaps built in by that same system of discriminatory favoritism) that manifests itself in the inability to perceive merit in the nonwhite and the nonmale: women and blacks, ipso facto, are of inferior ability. If one believes that this is so, then obviously it would take reverse discrimination—favoritism to the incompetent and the underqualified—to overcome disproportionate representation. If one follows this logic, one has the choice of favoring such reverse discrimination or of pointing out that such discrimination is repugnant and insisting that the blacks and the women ought to get on with it, gain competence, and stop complaining. The argument, of course, fails to explain the incompetent and underqualified white males who abound in graduate schools and on university faculties. It is, in fact, one more device for putting the burden right back on the classes of people who have suffered discrimination while maintaining the old and undefined concept of merit.

The white male assault on affirmative action has not been limited to lobbying inside HEW or to the press and the courts. It has made itself felt within the universities. Several years ago, a rumor circulated in academic circles that a New Orleans meeting of presidents of land-grant colleges and universities had produced a secret agreement that all would deliberately utilize delaying tactics as a weapon against government agencies seeking to enforce the law. While the truth is probably much less conspiratorial in nature, the recent events at the University of California at Berkeley, where years of delay resulted in a compromise plan between university officials and HEW to allow further delay, indicate that such tactics can pay off. (The Berkeley story is discussed in more detail in chapter eleven.) And a 1973 report to the American Association of Presidents of Independent Colleges and Universities states that affirmative action was "lowering the standards for both faculty and students . . . producing serious discrimination-in-reverse . . . and . . . assaulting the integrity of educational institutions, largely through pressure in the area of federal funding" (Roche, 1973, p. 11).

Most recently, the effort has moved from actively resisting implementation of the law to an active effort to have the law rescinded. Lobbying in Washington by male academics is directed at eliminating the need to keep statistics on university hiring, eliminating the possibility of class complaints of discrimination, and shifting the burden of proof in discrimination complaints onto the individual.

One HEW official has explained the resistance this way: "The fact of the matter is that almost all colleges that are federal contractors are still run by white males and affirmative action is an invasion of their empires—it means sharing the wealth." But the irrational anger with which many male academics resist affirmative action requires further explanation if for no other reason than the simple fact that equal opportunity traditionally has been a goal, at least a stated if not actual goal, of education in the United States.

The fact that men react with such vociferous anger to the subject of sex discrimination in higher education can be placed in perspective by examining the treatment accorded to the traditional male campus radical. In chapter two I discussed the Oliver Lee case at the University of Hawaii. I suspect that almost every American campus has its Oliver Lee, its male academic who espouses an unpopular racial cause and is penalized by denial of tenure or promotion or by attempted dismissal. In almost every such case a number of male academics will rally to the support of the victim, even male academics who are far more conservative in their politics than the man under attack. They bring with them the backing of professional associations that can apply considerable pressure on universities by blacklisting, refusing to carry ads for positions in their newsletters, and releasing embarrassing publicity. And they are often successful in righting such academic wrongs. Only rarely does a university administration or board of trustees make an action such as dismissal stick when there is reason to believe that it was taken in retaliation for political activity.

But when an ordinary, traditional, nonactivist male academic defends his more radical fellow academic he is, in a way, aggrandizing his own self-image. He is assuring himself that the academic profession that has given him security, salary, and ego sustenance is an open and liberal profession that does not penalize people who pursue truth in their own idiosyncratic way. Indeed, it protects them. He is convincing himself that the only thing that really matters in achieving success in academe is merit and that political opinions and free-time radical activities are irrelevant. He is reinforcing the notion that academe is a true meritocracy and that he, by virtue of his success, is truly meritorious.

Why, then, does this same academic often find it impossible to defend a woman whose only "political" activity is to complain of sex discrimination? The answer is so obvious that most academics fail to see it: male radicalism is most often aimed at institutions outside the academy, but a charge of sex discrimination is aimed at the very institution that has given the male academic sustenance. It is a complaint that the meritocracy plays favorites and that those who make it may not necessarily be as qualified as those who do not. It is an attack against *their* establishment.

The direction of the attack is all important, as one male tenure reject from UCLA recently pointed out: "You could have radical politics, but if you never expressed them here—*never applied them to how the University works*—you'd have a better chance than if you expressed your politics in the University. If you express a vocal, dissenting view in the Academic Senate or the *Daily Bruin,* no way will you get tenure here" [emphasis added] (Peterson, 1974). When the challenge is directed against the internal status quo it calls for a no-holds-barred counterattack. It calls for both passive and active resistance, for injecting delay and confusion into the development of affirmative action plans, for court action on reverse discrimination complaints, for the publication of inflammatory articles that appeal to the emotions of male academics and raise the specter of impending mediocrity for those who might suspect themselves to be mediocre.

I would not suggest that all white male faculty members have thought enough about the issues to see discrimination complaints as clear threats to their personal prestige and their private economy. Many men in the academic world are undoubtedly sufficiently unthreatened to examine the problem rather than attack the individuals or agencies calling attention to the problem. And, no doubt, most men in the academic world do not think about the issue at all—at least not until it touches their sphere of interest. But a surprisingly large number of presumably intelligent men unthinkingly grasp at the liberal rhetoric of merit, since it allows them to maintain their own self-image while dismissing those who press discrimination charges as advocates of discriminatory quotas and as enemies of excellence.

There is a tactic so common that it might well be labeled the first natural law of discrimination complaints: when charges of discrimination are made, many men automatically locate the problem with the woman who has made the charges, not with the system nor with any of the circumstances in which they themselves might have played some role. This particular tactic focuses attention on the person claiming discrimination rather than on the issue itself. Whether through court cases or publications outside the university or through delay or direct attack inside the university, the effect is to hurt those who are most vulnerable: the effect is to cause further mistreatment of women who are already claiming mistreatment.

For a woman, deciding to file a charge of discrimination may mean that she has determined for herself that she has had enough of second-class citizenship, enough of being shunted into useful secondary roles, enough of doing the work and watching a male boss or colleague take home most of the salary. For many men confronted by a woman who has filed such a charge, the meaning is different: the woman has a problem. She has become a pushy broad, she is dissatisfied and maybe even bitchy. The cure is a good screw.

This common analysis always seems to provide a few laughs. And regardless of the level of subtlety or crudity, the analysis has one powerful and paralyzing effect: it shifts the problem from institutions to individuals. It thereby eliminates the need to reexamine institutions.

One woman, or a few, claiming discrimination, need not bring about an investigation. The claim can be written off when one writes off the claimant as peculiar, pushy, unpopular, inept, or even physically undesirable. These qualities (real or imagined) become sufficient explanation for so strange and disruptive an act as filing a discrimination charge. There is, then, no further need to deal with the charge itself.

A second law follows quite naturally from the first and applies to those same men who prefer to demean the woman rather than to deal with the issue: the closer a man is to the particular charge of sex discrimination, the more vociferous will be his insistence that the problem is with the woman and not the system.

No woman should undertake to file such a charge lightly. Once she decides to make that deceptively simple demand for equity it is no exaggeration to say that almost every man in a position of authority in relation to her own position and almost every man inadvertently touched by the repercussions of her complaint will react with anger and evasion. Even in a setting where dedication to truth is supposed to be the hallmark of professional activity, such a challenge inevitably will serve to provoke a plethora of

evasions rather than a spirit of exploration. Even men who appear
to be sympathetic and many men one may have thought were
friends will find no room for sympathy when their own territory is in
some way challenged or threatened.

My husband's coresearcher provides an example. For years
he lent a sympathetic ear to my complaint. But in the summer of
1973, HEW refused to give the university clearance for $2.4 million
of continued federal funding for a research project this man directs
with my husband; the contract was delayed pending an attempt to
negotiate a settlement of my complaint. It is true that my husband
had a personal interest in the outcome of my case and had pointed
out to university officials that a failure to bring the university into
compliance might eventually lead to a drying up of federal contract
money. But my husband's coresearcher seemed to believe that my
husband and I were using his contract to gain my job. No one,
including that formerly sympathetic researcher, seemed concerned
that the issue was discrimination or that the cure was an end to
discrimination.

It might be appropriate to point out here that the husbands of
discrimination complainants on university campuses quite commonly
become corecipients of the anger generated by the male academic
establishment. Such anger might result in petty efforts to annoy,
such as attempting to remove a man from desirable office space and
establishing him in some dusty and remote corner of a campus or
delaying such normal faculty prerogatives as sabbaticals. Or it might
result in more serious harrassment, perhaps seeing that salary checks
are delayed on some pretext or even attempting to achieve permanent removal of the offending male from the campus. The anger
that is generated in this manner is seldom directed toward the
administration that has ignored compliance with government regulations. It is directed, instead, at the woman who charges discrimination and at those who are close to her.

The first law is a matter of kind: reactions to charges of sex
discrimination tend to be diversionary and serve to refocus the
problem on the women rather than the issue. The second law is a
matter of degree: the more personally threatened the individual
may feel, the more he will exert himself in the effort to refocus.

Given these laws, there is room for a great deal of individual variation on the theme. One response, often the first one encountered on filing a charge, is anger. Anger is probably the easiest response to understand, for it is the most direct. It is, moreover, a response that is clearly leveled at the challenger rather than at attempting to discover the truth of the challenge. Anger can display itself rather directly: the Equal Employment Opportunity Commission, after investigating my complaints, found that well-controlled anger on the part of a number of faculty members figured prominently in their refusal to reconsider tenure in my case. The EEOC letter of determination quotes one professor, in response to my charge that the refusal was a form of retaliation, as saying, "She is half right. No one is retaliating, but neither is anyone pleased with the label she put on the group."

A second typical response, possibly inspired by anger, is the attempt to malign or defame the individual claiming discrimination. This reaction was amply displayed in my case by the New College review committee that managed in a preliminary report to impugn my academic credentials by stating that the director designate of New College had been selected without care or concern and had no qualifications for that or any other academic job and by demanding that the college pick a new director as a condition of survival.

A third response (one that might be labeled almost a non-response) is to ignore the complainant. Doing nothing seems to be a favorite technique of middle-level bureaucrats in dealing with sex discrimination complaints. While it may seem to arise more from indifference than any felt need to challenge the challenger of the Weltanschauung, inaction does serve a purpose. Most complainants, if ignored for long enough, will be forced by time and the need for employment to go away. If a complainant cannot go away, she may become discouraged—something that can easily happen when one's complaint seems to be so trivial that administrators do not even respond to it. Even if she does not begin viewing her own complaint as trivial, she will discover that administrative silence has the effect of eroding whatever limited support she may once have had. Silence, when practiced for long enough, has the effect of discrediting one's claims.

The classic series of events (or nonevents) in which this technique was employed in my case surrounded my attempt to gain on-campus investigation of my charge of discrimination. That attempt began shortly after the president, Harlan Cleveland, released an "affirmative action policy" in February 1971 calling for immediate establishment of "procedures for the expeditious processing of complaints which may arise concerning equal employment opportunities." But a year later, in spite of my repeated attempts to gain some "expeditious processing," nothing had been done, and the chancellor waved aside my complaint by stating: "It should be noted, however, that my review did not take into account the question of sex discrimination since the issue was not reviewed by the P and T Committee." The rationale for his inaction was the previous inaction of a faculty committee!

A fourth form of response is labeling and name-calling. The complainant, if she should manage to ride out the anger and survive the inaction that faces her, will inevitably find herself labeled an extremist. This form of response is perhaps the most ironic. When push comes to shove in the academic world, an uncomfortable male colleague still will not examine the issues. Instead he will resort to name-calling. This can occur in settings in which one can maintain a sense of detachment: my last meeting as chairwoman of the Faculty Senate Executive Committee provides an example. The male full professor who was to serve as "interim" chairman in my absence seemed embarrassingly eager to take over and two of his male, full professor colleagues on the Executive Committee were almost audibly sighing with relief at the thought that the heat was off—the chancellor had removed me by informing the Executive Committee that he would not deal with me. (It did not at all bother these three men that the integrity of the Faculty Senate in selecting its own leader might be involved.) All three of these gentlemen became suddenly very expansive and willing to share opinions they had previously kept to themselves.

"Well, we need someone who is more collegial in approach," harrumphed the first professor.

"Yes," echoed the second, "and, Joan, you are certainly too confrontational."

"Your approach is adversary," whined the third.

I suppose that nothing I could say would have changed their mutual opinion. But I felt obliged to point out, before I left, that going "through the system" for three years, obtaining five favorable faculty committee rulings, and still being ignored by the administration was hardly my idea of being confrontational in type or adversary in approach.

The state assistant attorney general assigned to handle the university's defense in my case has stated that university administrators have been forced to put in "100,000 man hours" in fighting me. That is twenty-five people working full time for two years! While I find this figure incredible and perversely flattering, I find it saddening as well. Isn't it a shame that they could not have devoted some few hours to an honest investigation of my charges? The rhetoric of the male academic establishment would have us believe that the establishment is as appalled by discrimination and as anxious to overcome it as are its victims. But charges of discrimination are countered by obfuscation aimed at "proving" that the makers of such charges are at best sloppy researchers and at worst hysterical extremists.

If one is to accept both the general rhetoric and the specific denials, one would have to conclude that the male academic establishment is, indeed, opposed to discrimination but that such discrimination just does not exist! A very unlikely pair of circumstances. What is far more likely is that the male establishment has no intention of voluntarily recognizing or ending discriminatory practices that are advantageous to the members of that establishment. On the theory that the louder and longer one denies, the more truth there will be to the denial, the male establishment in higher education continues to attempt to discredit complainants with talk of illegal quotas, impending mediocrity, and reverse discrimination without ever openly stating that the real fear is equal opportunity for women.

7

Academic Women

> *"I quite agree with you," said the Duchess, "and the moral of that is—'Be what you would seem to be'—or, if you'd like it put more simply—'Never imagine yourself not to be otherwise than what it might appear to others that what you were or might have been was not otherwise than what you had been would have appeared to them to be otherwise.'"*
>
> Lewis Carroll, *Alice in Wonderland*

It may be a shock to discover that instant support from other women does not follow from the filing of a discrimination charge, even from women who may be suffering the same kind of oppression one has come to recognize in one's own life. Women sometimes react to such a charge, or to the individual who has filed it, with resentment, suspicion, or outright hostility. The charge, especially

111

in the case of women who have or think they have "made it" in the higher education system, seems to represent a threat to their own hard-won status or perhaps a challenge to some carelessly thought through notions they may have about themselves as exceptional women.

To understand this phenomenon it is necessary first to explore the hard facts of the working situation in which women find themselves in universities and next to examine the traditional excuses and explanations applied to that working situation.

According to a study released in 1973 by the American Council on Education, women made up only 20 percent of the faculty members on American college and university campuses during the 1972/73 academic year. The figure represents a gain of only nine tenths of one percent over a five-year period. Even among those women who do gain employment in higher education, the comparisons to male colleagues are revealing. Women make up 40 percent of instructional employees at junior colleges and less than 10 percent of the instructional employees in the top prestige universities. Of all college and university instructors 32 percent are women, but only 8 percent of all full professors are women (WEAL, 1970, p. 310. *U.S. News,* Dec. 13, 1971, p. 79).

Exactly what do these statistics mean when translated into the day to day reality of a single campus, for those few women who are lucky enough to be there? The University of Hawaii may be no worse than most universities. I certainly hope it is not better! A look at it may help in arriving at an understanding of what it is that academic women are up against. At this writing the Psychology Department, with twenty-six full-time faculty members, employs not one woman, though a quarter of recent Ph.D.'s in psychology are female. The Political Science Department, with twenty-eight men and no women, has announced with political astuteness that it will not hire anyone but women for the next three years, three years in which the rapidly shrinking budget of the university and the even more rapidly shrinking number of students attracted to political science studies indicate that *no* hiring will be done in that department. The History Department has never, in recent memory, promoted a woman on first, or second, application.

Meanwhile, and despite a severe budgetary cutback and a

freeze on instructional hiring, the upper-level administration has hired at least five new high-paid male administrators without bothering to observe the university's own rules and the federal law requiring a search for qualified women for all positions. One of these high-paid employees was put in charge of the university equal employment opportunity program. Overall, women on the faculty earn $2000 per year less than men of comparable background and experience—a conservative figure since salary data are not available on 8 percent of the men who are in special off-scale (higher) salary steps. Only 3 percent of the university's few women are in such steps.

The university, in its attempt to comply with HEW requirements, released figures recently on actual terminations over the past three years. To no one's surprise, those figures revealed that 33 percent of all terminations were for women. When compared with the total number of men and women on campus, the turnover rate for female faculty members is 21 percent per year. The rate for men is 14 percent.

The traditional excuse for this sorry state of affairs is that our campus is no worse than any comparable campus and is, therefore, not really guilty of gross discrimination. Widespread practice is taken as a moral palliative. A vice-chancellor, for example, once ran chi-square tests on a number of departments in our College of Arts and Sciences, where employment of women runs at 17 percent of total employment. He told me he could see no discrimination, since the departments tested were about the same as comparable departments at other universities! The fact there are few women at other universities is taken as proof of the scarcity of qualified women.

The reason there are so few qualified women, one explanation would have us believe, is that early socialization has forever damned women to a secondary and supportive role in society. Jo Freeman argues this eloquently: "Women have not needed such stringent social chains. Their bodies could be left free because their minds were chained long before they became functioning adults. Women have so thoroughly internalized the social definition that their only significant role is to serve men as wives and raise the next generation of men and their servants that no laws are necessary to enforce this. Where socialization failed, custom sufficed" (1970, pp. 279–280). Freeman goes on to label the socialization process as "the most insidious mechanism of social control yet devised." She discusses tests devised to study the end result of the process by asking men and women to list adjectives that apply to themselves. The results "showed that women strongly felt themselves to be such things as uncertain, anxious, nervous, hasty, careless, fearful, childish, helpless, sorry, timid, clumsy, stupid, silly, and domestic. On a more positive side women felt they were understanding, tender, sympathetic, pure, generous, affectionate, loving, moral, kind, grateful, and patient." Freeman concludes: "This is not a very favorable self-image but it does correspond fairly well with the social myths about what women are like. The image has some nice qualities, but they are not the ones normally required for that kind of achievement to which society gives its highest social rewards" (1970, p. 280).

One useful means of examining the socialization theory (a humbling one) is to recollect one's own past attitudes. During my undergraduate days at UCLA, I mentally dismissed a series of young men I had dated from my own list of potential "serious" candidates for a lasting relationship. One was not assertive enough in comparison to my own level of self-assertion. Another was not intelligent enough in comparison to my own assumptions concerning my intelligence. Still another had professional aspirations less lofty than my own. I had taken for granted, along with most young women, the notion that the man in my life had to be more assertive, more intelligent, and more prestigiously employed than I; otherwise I could not respect him. It seemed perfectly natural for me to wish to be put in my (secondary) place.

But I was not so totally captivated by the expectations of my society as to fall unquestioningly into a male-dominated relationship, for I also mentally dismissed one nice young man who insisted with great frequency that I refrain from opening car doors for myself and pulling up my own chair at restaurants. It is possible that this small suspicion about the system was the seed that blossomed into my present activism.

In spite of these small stabs at unconventionality, it never crossed my mind twenty years ago that it might be equally damaging to mutual respect in a mature relationship for a man to deliberately seek out a partner who was less assertive or less intelligent than he pictured himself to be.

Unfortunately, the socialization theory is not a completely satisfying explanation. No one stands still forever, and no woman is fixed forever by her childhood. As long as she continues to have experiences in the world and as long as some of those experiences are more stressful and less rewarding than others, she will be forced, even minimally, to reexamine her feelings about herself. This is especially true for women who have chosen careers, in the academic world or elsewhere. For already, by choosing to work, they have taken a major step toward behavior that deviates from the dictates of the socialization process described by Freeman.

Socialization, then, is not an adequate explanation for the lack of women employed in higher education. The theory, however, remains remarkably persistent. It provides a ready excuse to all concerned administrators for the fact that so few women—they think—want to be employed in higher education. These administrators would no doubt agree with psychologist Bruno Bettelheim, who seems to indicate that he has discovered what all these well-socialized women really want: "We must start with the realization that, as much as women want to be good scientists or engineers, they want first and foremost to be womanly companions of men and to be mothers" (1965).

More to the point here, the socialization theory provides a handy rationalization for those women who have "made it," when they must explain to themselves why there are so many other women who have not. Given this rationalization, the facts provided by the working situation can be put to use as proof in a self-fullfilling prophecy: there are few women in permanent career positions in the academic world; ergo, there are few women who *want* or are capable of gaining positions in the academic world; ergo, the socialization process has been effective in seeing to it that few women want or are capable of gaining positions in the academic world; ergo, there are few women in permanent career positions in the academic world.

This particular bit of circular reasoning neatly does away with discrimination, at least discrimination in higher education. It is all back there in early childhood. But it fails to explain a few things. What about those women who want positions in the academic world and cannot get them? And what about those women who have positions in the academic world and are not satisfied that they are being fairly treated in them? The socialization theory simply fails to explain all these deviants.

In view of the working situation and the persuasive explanations for it, it is not surprising that few women are willing to recognize the problem, and fewer still are willing to do anything about it. I do not know all the female faculty members at the University of Hawaii personally, though there are few enough of them. And I will certainly be the first to recognize that women, whether at the University of Hawaii or elsewhere, react to discussions and charges of sex discrimination in a highly individualistic manner. Nonetheless, I have found that there are certain recognizable categories of reaction. For anyone contemplating taking an active role in protesting sex discrimination it may prove useful, if oversimplified, to describe them.

For the most part, it is the individual experience of each woman that dictates her reactions. I have found, for example, that most women who have reached secure university positions are all too willing to adopt the attitude that, since they made it through the system, anyone who has not made it just does not have the ability to compete. To recognize that discrimination is a major factor in the system would be, for these women, to invalidate their own deeply felt conviction that they, at least, are meritorious and merit usually wins out. Women who fit this category have been labeled "Queen Bees":

> All social revolutions begin with a vanguard of militants and are soon followed by a vociferous band of countermilitants: people who organize and fight for the status quo. Their countermilitancy has its roots in their personal success within the system: both *professional* success (a high-status job with good pay) and *social* success (popularity with men, attractiveness, a good marriage). The true Queen Bee has made it in the "man's world" of work, while running a house and family with her left hand. "If I can do it without a whole movement

to help me," runs her attitude, "so can all those other women" [Staines, 1974, p. 55].

To recognize that women who are capable are not making it would be unacceptable to the Queen Bee. Such recognition would challenge her belief, a belief shared by men—that even those women who have completed all the requisite graduate work are not as qualified as men to fulfill academic duties. It is quite possible that some of these women have always shared with men the idea that women are less apt to be competent, productive scholars than are men. Indeed, one study revealed that women students underrate the work of women scholars: these women considered professional articles, when attributed to male authors, superior to the same articles when attributed to female authors. The researcher concludes, "Women *do* consider their own sex inferior, and even when the facts give no support to this belief, they will persist in downgrading the competence—in particular the intellectual and professional competence—of their fellow females" (Goldberg, 1968, p. 28).

A few women may even feel that their own inferior ability accounts for their slow rise in the academic establishment. But it is also possible that some women, finally having arrived, are all too eager to suppress resentment at the length of their journey and to adopt the dominant ideology. Certainly they have discovered that the system rewards this behavior. For once having reached a secure position, nothing is as likely to win the approval of male colleagues as the vocal insistence that the judgments of those colleagues are just and fair.

A glimpse of several women who espouse the dominant ideology might be instructive. Among the tenured women in my own former department, these vocal upholders of the system are particularly apparent. In order to place them in proper perspective, let me provide a closer look at the working situation in that department.

Over the past seven years, the English Department has had a faculty of between 40 and 50 percent women. About 62 percent of those women are on revolving-door appointments as instructors. Yet HEW and other agencies have failed to prevent the department from using these very statistics as "proof" that it is not discriminating. Following a visit by HEW, the English Department chairman put out a memorandum and once again emphasized the department's stubborn refusal to understand. "We believe," he stated cheerily, "that our staffing situation with respect to women is very good. Certainly it is much better than the situation in any English Department with which I have been associated, and any that I know about. Approximately half the teaching people in our department are women. . . . I think there is no question that our department is virtually unique in being quite literally an equal opportunity employer for women."

What the new chairman failed to mention, of course, is that most of the women so honored by the department's largesse would not be there in a few years, that they were never considered promotable or tenurable or quite the equal of the men who come to stay on as part of the permanent staff. He failed to mention that 40 percent of all the women terminated over the previous three years by the *entire* University of Hawaii at Manoa were women who had held teaching posts in the English Department. He failed to mention that only four women were even considered for permanent academic tenure by the English Department between 1969 and 1974 (while twenty men were considered). He failed to mention that none of these women gained tenure (but fifteen men did). And he could not mention (because it happened a few weeks after his cheery memo) that one of those four women, partly as a result of her own unwarranted faith in the "system" walked into the ocean two days after she was told of the department's decision to deny her tenure. She was listed by the police as a probable suicide.

The case of this woman cannot be glossed over lightly. On several occasions she had prematurely but vehemently upheld the system in arguments with active feminists. She insisted that she had "made it" and that activists should stop complaining about the system and start concentrating on behaving in such a way that their excellence, if any, would be rewarded. She was sufficiently convinced by her own arguments that she could not shift gears when she was denied tenure.

This young woman's unhappy situation should serve to emphasize one of the most striking differences in approach between the individual grimly set on making it in a man's academic world and the feminist who has learned that the problem is often systemic and not individual. For the woman committed to the individual solution, defeat can mean that she herself is at fault and victory can mean that she herself is superior to her sisters and the equal of her male colleagues.

An interesting variant to the individual solution of the problem was voiced recently by Marjorie W. Farnsworth in a strange book called *The Young Woman's Guide to the Academic Career* (1974). In her book, Farnsworth, who apparently has retained little respect for the males among whom she works, passes along survival tips to young women who wish to make it in the academic world. "Survival in such surroundings," says Farnsworth, "is not easy for anyone, but it is far more readily achieved by mediocre men than by brilliant women" (p. xiii). Her advice includes (for graduate students) methods of coping with the exploitative tendencies of publication-hungry professors and (for new professors) methods of glombing on to as many graduate students as possible for the purpose (of course) of exploitation to ensure publication and, thus, to ensure tenure and promotion. Farnsworth shows an exceptional degree of awareness of discrimination: "In short, a woman with a degree from the best institution in the country, with extensive postdoctoral training, and numerous high-quality publications may have to settle for a position that no man of equivalent training, experience, and potential would even consider. Indeed, a mediocre male candidate enjoys a significant and real advantage over a superlatively trained woman when both apply for the same job" (p. 55). But the unfortunate fact is that Farnsworth, for all her awareness of the situation in academe, can see no farther than the individual in seeking a solution. In all of her ascerbic little book one finds only advice on how to get a job and keep it in a system she clearly despises and feels is unfair.

In the University of Hawaii English Department, one of those who did make it left a note on my office door shortly after word had circulated that I was complaining of sex discrimination. It was written out of "my regard for you as a teacher and as a person." It informed me that its author could "no longer support" my plea for tenure reconsideration. I cornered this woman later and discovered that she had supported me for tenure and had intended to support my appeal for reconsideration. However, since I had charged discrimination she was withdrawing her support; my qualifications for tenure had evaporated in her view. It is said of the Queen Bee: "By insisting that the present system is open and fair to all and that success is a direct result of personal talent and striving, the Queen Bee allows herself the luxury of self-congratulation. She is not at the top because of favoritism or fortune, but because she deserves to be there" (Staines, 1974, p. 55).

Another system upholder is the former assistant chairwoman of the department. She has herself probably suffered from blatant salary discrimination. In this regard she is not unusual. Ann Harris took note of what may be a common condition among women administrators: "I suspect that these women are among the most financially exploited group of all and are also the women whose abilities and leadership potential are most completely ignored by their male employers" (1970, p. 255).

Following the investigation of my sex discrimination complaint by the university president's Commission on the Status of Women in 1972, this woman felt obliged to write to President Cleveland to insist that his commission was guilty of "specious arguments that are being put forth to support charges of discrimination, when in fact no discrimination exists." Among these "specious arguments" was the commission finding that, in the English Department, the role of the assistant chairwoman was "to take care of people when they collapse, to substitute teach, and to schedule." In her letter to the president she went on to describe the importance of her scheduling role, a role handled at some universities by computers. She went on: "As for 'taking care of people when they collapse,' well, yes, I help with that when the occasion arises. That can't be all bad. . . . Rather than denigrate the functions I perform I should think the commission would want to recognize the fact that a woman has been entrusted with what I believe is the key position in this department."

Her letter recalls Jo Freeman's point: *The image has some nice qualities, but they are not the ones normally required for that kind of achievement to which society gives its highest rewards* (1970, p. 279). I do not, by any means, wish to denigrate either this woman or her accomplishments. It is hardly appropriate to belittle anyone for reacting in an acceptable and unsurprising way, especially in view of the fact that such activity brings rewards. (This woman was recently promoted to a similar post in the chancellor's office where, presumably, she can help people at a higher level when *they* collapse!)

Indeed, in one case, a small breach of acceptable behavior caused one woman in a secure academic position to react in an even stranger manner. Before I charged discrimination, I often ran into this woman on campus. She confided in me on occasion, especially with regard to her family. Once she expressed some resentment toward her husband, who is a professor in a different department. They both did the same amount of work, she complained. Yet when they came home each day, he opened a can of beer and sat down to read the paper while she had to tend to the kids, cook dinner, and clean the house. "Sometimes I'd like to sit down and read the paper, too," she said.

During the year of my tenure consideration, this woman conveyed a small bit of information to me that ordinarily would have been kept from a tenure candidate. Her motives were above suspicion: she was simply angry at what she felt to be totally improper and irrelevant considerations that were influencing the decision in my case. And indeed such leaks are common from male professors to their male protégés. But a few months later, when I asked her to discuss her information with an HEW investigator, she told me that she had talked it over with her husband and she was wrong; it had all been a joke. Months later, she anxiously told another investigator how fair her department had always been to her, how they had allowed her credit toward advancement when she had gone on half time because of young children, and how she owed them so very much. And still later I encountered her at the local supermarket. I smiled and opened my mouth to say hello. She turned deathly white and fled from the store.

What a shame to live in such needless fear—fear, I suspect, not of me, but of some unspoken black mark on her record and possibly even of a challenge I may have come to represent to her own self-esteem. This woman illustrates, all too painfully, that neither becoming nor remaining a Queen Bee is easy, that the

rewards that come with such a position are hard-won and the punishments for even momentarily dropping the expected pro-system stance can be terrifying.

A second category of reaction is that of lukewarm activism. Among those who react in this way are some women who both know and admit that something is wrong, but who cannot or will not do whatever is necessary to correct the situation. These women often adopt the general rhetoric of the activists and are willing to deal in large numbers: the statistics, they will admit, are appalling and strong actions are needed. But when it comes to particular cases, they seem to demand an excess of proof that injustice has really prevailed. And like my onetime supporter who could no longer exchange a greeting in a supermarket, they are affected by the passage of time and become more and more suspicious of the merits of any particular case.

In spite of their reluctance to act, many of these lukewarm activists already have the security of tenure. They are, perhaps, Queen Bees who are somewhat more secure than their antifeminist sisters, for they can afford the luxury of antiestablishment rhetoric. Administrators instinctively seek them out for posts on committees on the status of women and for positions as equal employment opportunity officers. It is risky, since occasionally one such woman will take action that might embarrass an administration. But for the most part, they are content to limit themselves to militant statements without risking the actions needed to back them up. I suspect that the reasons for this behavior are much the same as the reasons for the behavior of those who uphold and swear by the system—the unspoken fear that later rewards may be withheld and the suspicion that any challenge to the system is a challenge to their own claim to merit. To avoid suspicions concerning one's own merit, one must adopt the belief that the system that has rewarded that merit really works. Therefore, women who have not made it through the system might not be meritorious. To support them is to support the notion that the system, and one's own merit, are in doubt.

The excuses offered by the lukewarm activist are always plausible. When I was fired the first time a number of faculty members circulated a petition demanding my immediate reinstatement. One faculty woman, active herself on the State Commission on the Status of Women, refused to sign the petition because "the movement needs martyrs." Another faculty woman, one who served for a time as campus EEO coordinator, was also a member of the State Commission on the Status of Women. When I was fired, this woman called to commiserate and to tell me that the state commission should take some public stand concerning what appeared to be blatant retaliation. But ten minutes later she called again to tell me that she hoped I had not misinterpreted her remarks and she hoped I did not expect a statement from the commission because, of course, they had to preserve their "credibility" and so they could not take stands on every little thing that came along. They had to save themselves for "the big issues."

The commission, saving itself for the big issues, has yet to speak up on anything.

Yet another faculty woman has gained a reputation as an apologist for the campus chancellor. She served this man for some time as both assistant chancellor and as campus EEO coordinator. My own discrimination complaint was handled by her in the most evasive style and ultimately she advised me to simply drop the matter. Other women have reported similar treatment of their discrimination complaints. Her reactions should not have been unexpected to me: during my aborted term as chairwoman of the University of Hawaii Faculty Senate, I attended a number of meetings in the chancellor's office, meetings also attended by various deans and the heads of a number of campus divisions. The assistant chancellor (and EEO coordinator) attended the meetings religiously. Unlike the rest of us, she was never called on to report on the latest problems and issues, and (at least while I attended the meetings) she never participated in the discussions. She just sat there, as I am sure she is sitting there still, with her steno pad, taking shorthand.

I should emphasize again that it is not surprising to find so many faint hearts and weak knees among educated women. Life has neither trained nor equipped most of us to face the kind of struggle that demands that we deliberately efface the images we have of ourselves and one another. And life has certainly not prepared most of us for a system that, while it only grudgingly rewards behavior that reinforces the ideology of the establishment, actually punishes behavior that challenges that ideology.

Immediately on entering the academic world women are placed in an intolerable situation. Acceptable behavior, and thus rewardable behavior, appears to be quite different for men and for women. Women may see that the real rewards are reserved for behavior that is considered unfeminine—initiative, control, dominance. But they are not so stupid, for the most part, as to interpret all this as a sign that they should become aggressive, controlling, or dominating. In fact, these characteristics may bring on instant punishment. Thus, if women compete with men, using the qualities that seem most often to be rewarded in men, they lose. If they remain "feminine," they immediately place themselves at the mercy of others. It is possible their passivity will be rewarded. But it is just as possible that they will lose. Losing, either by competing or by remaining passive, does not allow one room to complain. If one has been passive and lost, one can be accused of expecting special favors because of one's sex and chastized for not competing actively and fairly. If one has competed "fairly," and possibly jeopardized one's chances by behaving in a "masculine" manner, one cannot very well complain of losing. After all, if you are going to scrap with the big boys, you cannot ask them to dry your tears afterward.

In view of these intolerable binds, it is a wonder that any woman accepts the challenge, confronts the ideology of the majority, and thereby takes her place in category three as an antidiscrimination activist.

One may well ask what possible rewards there could be for such behavior! Dr. Bernice Sandler discusses retaliation against university women who file sex discrimination complaints and concludes: "Unless women band together and protest as a group it is virtual academic suicide to protest sex discrimination on practically all campuses" (1970, p. 302). Certainly my own experience bears out Sandler's conclusion. If anything, her conclusion is an understatement, for there have been instances where banding together has served only to increase the number of individuals who may be intimidated.

In view of the very real possibility of academic suicide, perhaps becoming an activist is an irrational act akin to tilting windmills. But I would venture here the notion that taking on the challenge offers more than bruised bones. It offers some small but valuable rewards. There is, for example, a sense of satisfaction when other women begin to look more critically at their own situations and begin to take part in efforts to improve them, even when they are aware of the drain such efforts will become on their time and possibly on their emotional well being. There are the rewards that come when students, like those at New College, decide that they prefer integrity to back-room bargaining. Other rewards are internal, and perhaps more significant. One gains a growing sense of awareness about one's own life situation and a growing sense of pride simply in no longer accepting the intolerable.

Had I been rewarded for my teaching ability and for my publications, I might have been as suspicious of activism as are so many other academic women. I might find myself among those Queen Bees who are suspicious of group efforts to change the system. Like them, I might insist that it is individual effort alone that can improve the status of any individual woman. My situation, however, forced me to think beyond so simple a reaction. But I would like to believe I would have thought, in any case. A growing number of women are joining the ranks of the activists, and they are learning to work together toward the equitable representation of women on campus. Administrators cannot escape this effect of university intransigence.

But for those women who have not yet considered their situation there is a theory concerning juvenile delinquents which would seem, in part, to apply. According to this theory, it is the parents rather than the children who are responsible for delinquent behavior and who must pay the price for it. While it might be very comforting for the juveniles (as for women) so involved to blame those significant others in their lives for their behavior, it would also seem that there comes a time when one must break free of the influence of others and take responsibility for one's own behavior.

If there is anything at all to resent in the all too understandable pattern of academic women who will not wholeheartedly support the struggle for equal employment opportunity, it is this: theories of socialization may provide a rationalization for such behavior, even a sympathetic one. But they cannot provide a reason.

There comes a time for women who do manage to break through in academic surroundings to throw off the easy suspicions that they are intelligent exceptions to the rules about women and begin seriously analyzing the validity of those rules. It may indeed be difficult and risky, but it is nothing short of an obligation to intellectual honesty.

8

The Faculty Committee

The voices didn't join in, this time, as she hadn't spoken, but, to her great surprise, they all thought in chorus (I hope you understand what thinking in chorus means—for I must confess that I don't).

Lewis Carroll, *Through the Looking Glass*

The nature and structure of most universities, unlike other large institutions, make for pluralistic decision-making. While I will grant that even General Motors would not for long get away with imposing policy from above that was anathema to a majority of its workers, the situation in universities should be even less conducive to the imposition of decision-making from the top.

First of all, university professors do not like to think of themselves as employees. A part of the self-image discussed in preceding chapters depends on the idea that a professor is a professional man (and occasionally a woman) and not a mere salaried worker—albeit he or she is, in fact, a salaried worker. He or she is, therefore, supposedly concerned with professional standards and with upholding the reputation of professional peers.

Second, professors have a kind of dual citizenship. They are members of a discipline—historians, electrical engineers, sociologists, physicists, or whatnot—that extends to other universities and other countries. And they are members of the academic profession at a single institution; they are Harvard professors or Southern Illinois professors or Yale professors.

Universities are conglomerates of academic fields, and professors, with this dual allegiance, believe they are in a better position to select incoming colleagues than are university administrators. They supposedly can judge excellence (or incompetence) in their own fields better than an administrator who may come from another field (or no field at all). They are in contact with members of the discipline from other institutions and can exchange information about bright young graduate students or older professional colleagues who are seeking a new institutional environment. Thus the professional hiring system at most universities is fragmented, as is the system of recommending promotion and permanent tenure. Each department and each program composes a primary hiring unit. And each of these units is responsible for the initial recommendation in all faculty personnel decisions.

In an effort to establish some uniformity, most universities have an internal review process for new employees and for tenure and promotion recommendations that originate in the departments. Review committees are responsible for redressing violations that occur out of prejudice or failure to observe due process at lower levels of decision-making and for assuring some semblance of uniformity on an institutional basis.

While the system may sound somewhat complicated, it has certain obvious advantages. Ideally, it offers sufficient checks and balances to minimize abuse. Top administrators and university governing boards should share a common interest with faculty members at both departmental and review levels in maintaining or upgrading the capabilities of their institution. Thus it would appear to be in the best interest of both faculty and administration to make the system of diffused decision-making work as smoothly as possible.

However, the system seldom works as well as one might be led to believe by reading the statements of faculty senate committees or such organizations as the AAUP. The problems inherent in the system are many. The largest is that administrators and faculty members are not always either enlightened or in agreement as to the interests of their institution. Faculty judgment may be based on irrelevant factors. And, unfortunately, administrative acceptance or rejection of faculty wisdom may be based on equal irrelevance.

Peer judgment may be colored by petty jealousy, favoritism, fear of competition, political leanings, and other unlofty considerations. Knowledge of these abuses lies behind the distrust many women feel toward the system set up to judge their merit. In view of the persistence of the myths about women, such a system is bound to work to the detriment of women. In truth, many women would feel better about peer judgments if there were some indication that universities in general or particular groups of scholars from each discipline knew how to articulate criteria of excellence. One hears that it would be unwise to pin down criteria too narrowly, since the very best people may not fit so stiff a mold. But no one hears exactly how those very best people are recognized. Sometimes very best may mean nothing more than adherence to a certain style or doctrine within a discipline. Marxist sociologists, for example, may be loath to hire sociologists of more conservative bent. Or very best may simply mean that an individual has come from the same school and been trained by the same professor as the department chairman doing the defining.

Another flaw in the system is that peer judgment, when placed within the context of ninety or a hundred departments in a major university, may become somewhat chaotic. The interests of one department might best be served by bringing in a prestigious and high-salaried scholar. These might be in direct conflict with the interests of another department that also wishes to bring in a prestigious and high-salaried scholar, especially during a tight budget year. And the interests of both groups might be in conflict with the interests of undergraduate students facing classroom crowding in required courses if funds that could pay for five or six class-room instructors are spent to bring in one or two prestigious scholars who shun contact with undergraduates and demand light teaching loads.

Still another flaw is that mediocrity in higher education tends to breed more mediocrity. If second- and third-rate academics are in noticeable profusion in an institution, they are unlikely to run their committees in such a way as to call attention to themselves or their mediocrity. They will tend to fear excellence when they recognize it, since excellence will reflect badly on them and on their brothers. And their committee decisions will tend to bolster, and rationalize, the mediocre status quo.

The review process, too, has shortcomings. What is good for the university may not always be what is good for a particular department, but review committees are made up of people from particular departments. Faculty members serving on committees set up to review departmental decisions may find it relatively easy to see where one department is "going wrong" in seeking to hire a specialized researcher instead of someone to cope with a flood of undergraduates (or, conversely, they may be able to see where a department is judging incorrectly by developing a tenured staff just to service basic student requirements when those requirements may be about to change). They will be less likely to maintain that objectivity in relation to their own department or to closely allied departments.

In a series of answers to interrogatories in my state court case, two University of Hawaii officials presented a picture of the kind of abuse that can occur in such a system. In one series, President Harlan Cleveland made it clear that recommendations from review committees would not necessarily influence him: "Peer evaluations at the department level are generally considered of prime importance," he wrote. Yet in another interrogatory, he was asked if he had ever overruled that decision of "prime importance." He admitted that he had. He was then asked to list the decisions he had made that conflicted with the peer group recommendation and to state the reasons and circumstances surrounding such decisions. His response: "Answer would require enormous research effort, for which legislature has not provided sufficient funds to undertake without suspending most current personnel operations." In another pair of questions. Cleveland was asked if he had ever made recommendations on tenure that differed from those of the major review body, the Faculty Personnel Committee. He admitted that he had. When asked for specifics, he replied: "Answer would require enormous research and disclosure of confidential personnel files of other faculty members."

In this series of answers Cleveland revealed one of the most basic abuses that can develop in a system where decisions are allegedly based on broad consultation: without open procedures and without clear criteria for decision-making, the treatment of individuals may be neither fair nor uniform. Administrators can manipulate the system at any time and for any reason and need never be held accountable for their manipulations. Neither peer judgment nor the judgment of review committees is sacrosanct, and a university president need offer no standards for the acceptance or rejection of recommendations at any level of review.

In a similar set of interrogatories, my former department chairman was asked if the department had ever reversed tenure recommendations following a review committee recommendation that drew a conclusion opposite to the departmental conclusion. He claimed that the department had never done so. However, he did say that the department had reversed negative recommendations *after they had been endorsed by review committees.* In other words, he arrogantly claimed a policy of department *uber alles:* the department could reverse its own negative recommendations, even though review committees agreed that they should be negative. But the department never had, and probably never would, reverse a negative recommendation if a review committee had questioned their judgment and recommended positively!

Behind the hundreds of class complaints and the thousands of individual complaints of discrimination filed with government agencies against universities is the claim that both the standards of judgment and the procedures used for judging are unclear, subjective, and applied unevenly.

In personnel matters the University of Hawaii provides a rather common and unhealthy picture. Even the system set up to redress injustice operates in a vacuum, with administrators depending on their own peculiar motives in choosing to accept, reject, or totally ignore the outcome of any single appeal. The Faculty Senate Privilege and Tenure Committee, for example, is the major appeal body for investigating and recommending action on faculty grievances. Most universities have a similar committee. At the University of Hawaii, over the past five years, that committee had an abysmal record. The administration either completely ignored their findings or disagreed with them without offering more than a few words of explanation. The cases where the administration agreed with the committee were most often those where the committee found in favor of the administration and dismissed the complaint.

In recognition of this state of affairs in her own university, Farnsworth has offered the following comment: "The formation of a committee serves two general purposes: the delegation of necessary or unpleasant tasks to a smaller group; and the postponing of decisions until long past the time when any recommendations for action are pertinent. The first purpose is more frequently observed within a department, whereas the second is more likely to be used by the administration" (1974, p. 84).

Where timorous faculty members and weak faculty governance are the rule, faculty committee work may serve no other function than to keep alive the illusion of participation. My own case produced several examples of this kind of committee work. In two pairs of complaints, two faculty committees demonstrated their ability to back down when confronted by a rerun of an unsolved problem—a rerun precipitated by the very timorousness of their initial actions. I have talked to a number of women around the country whose experience has confirmed my own: faculty committees do not like to take strong stands and are made especially uncomfortable if asked to follow up once they have written a report.

The first pair of complaints was made to the Faculty Senate Privilege and Tenure Committee. On the first occasion, I asked that committee to review the initial decision not to tenure me. I pointed out that a review body, the Faculty Personnel Committee, had recommended unanimously for tenure and that there appeared to be several procedural irregularities in the handling of my case. I also pointed out that the mishandling was probably discriminatory. The committee declined to rule on the question of sex discrimination, but it did find due process violations and did recommend unanimously for tenure. For a long time that recommendation was simply ignored and, finally, it was rejected. But at no point did the committee feel the need to involve itself further.

On the second occasion, one year later, I was forced to file another complaint, since nothing had been done to implement the Privilege and Tenure Committee's first recommendation and because of this I was still in a tenuous employment situation. This time I charged that the administration had arbitrarily assigned me a 91.667 percent of full-time job for the specific purpose of denying my full-time prerogatives.

The written documentation for my second complaint was far more convincing and clear than any documentation I had been able to provide for my first complaint. In fact, the only documentation supplied for my first complaint was one letter with my charges stated in it. Nonetheless, I had made a mistake. One should never ask a committee to look into a problem that would have been resolved if, the first time around, they had insisted that their recommendations be accepted. This is probably particularly true in cases where sex discrimination has become embarrassingly prominent as an issue, for committee members may regret that they did not dismiss the complainant at an earlier stage of the game.

The first report from this committee was nonargumentative in nature. But the second year, the same committee reacted with undisguised anger. The members concluded that *"no* administrator should arbitrarily designate *any* position as 91.667 FTE," but went on to say that they, certainly, could not conclude that the position had been assigned arbitrarily. The mere fact that the previous assistant director of New College had worked full time in the same job, that the director of New College stated that I was doing the same job, that my salary had been considerably raised over my previous full-time salary, and that the dean in sworn testimony had admitted that no noticeable difference existed between my job and the job of my predecessor did not prevent them from concluding that "the duties Ms. Abramson chooses to fulfill do not establish that in fact she was assigned the duties of Assistant Director of New College."

The second pair of complaints went to the Committee on Academic Freedom, another Faculty Senate committee. The first complaint to this committee was delivered in early October 1972, when I had been newly fired from my job at New College. I alleged that removing me from my job in midcontract was a violation of academic due process and of my academic freedom. The committee finding was clear, to the point, but not very forceful. Even though I had been returned to my job by the time the report came out, the committee concluded that "the administration's action of September 29, 1972, removing her from her duties at New College without prior notice and without a hearing, did deprive Mrs. Abramson of her academic freedom."

They took matters a little further by stating a general position that was later endorsed unanimously by the faculty senate: "When the administration has made the commitment of employment to an individual to the extent that it has allowed the individual to assume academic duties, and in fact those duties have been assumed, the individual is entitled to the rights of academic due process."

All very well. But just as in the case of the Privilege and Tenure Committee, neither the committee nor the Senate Executive Committee made any attempt to follow up. They demanded no explanation for my dismissal nor even a commitment by the administration to the basic principle of academic freedom they presumably were defending. The dean was given not so much as a mild reprimand for firing me during a valid contract period.

The result of their timidity was predictable. One year later I was once again fired in midcontract and once again brought the issue to the Committee on Academic Freedom. But by this time my discrimination complaint had become somewhat of an embarrassment, a situation that added to the reluctance of the committee to remain consistent with its own past ruling.

In most respects my second complaint was identical to my first one: I had been fired in midcontract without benefit of academic due process. But this second time around, I was in a far more prominent position and had far more documentation of my charge. The complaint was filed against the chancellor, not the dean, since it was the chancellor who had first told me my contract would be approved and then, two months after I began work, had informed the Faculty Senate Executive Committee that I was "not a member of the faculty."

This second time around, the Committee on Academic Freedom, after four months of delay and equivocation (that included an effort by one committee member to get me to "prove" that merely being fired from an academic position was a violation of my academic freedom) did not even choose to write a formal report. On January 12, 1974, just two days before my state court hearing was to be held, I received a registered letter from the chairman of the Committee on Academic Freedom. It was sent on his own departmental stationery and did not bear the signatures of any other members of the committee. And it bore no indication that copies had been sent to anyone else. The letter informed me that the Committee on Academic Freedom could not find much substance in my complaint and that "any activity in which you engaged after June 30, 1973 was at your own choice, and that you were not requested to act on behalf of the University by Dean Contois. It is the conclusion of the Committee on Academic Freedom that the university administration has followed due process and therefore your academic freedom was not in jeopardy."

My complaint was never against the dean, but the chancellor. The dean had nothing to do with approving my contract—the chancellor did. The dean had nothing to do with firing me—the chancellor did. And standard faculty senate procedure demands that committee reports (not private letters) be written by the senate committee and that those reports be sent to the Senate Executive Committee (not directly to the individual involved) for action. There was something very peculiar about both the form and content of that registered letter.

That something came to light two days later, in court, when the university's attorney waved a copy of that private registered letter in front of the judge in an attempt to prove that I was not considered to be a faculty member. Thankfully, the judge refused to accept the letter in evidence.

At my request, the Senate Executive Committee later looked into the propriety of a senate committee finding being released to the university administration's attorney during a lawsuit rather than to the Senate Executive Committee. As one might well imagine, it all turned out to be a regrettable but understandable and forgivable mistake.

The lesson is apparent: if a grievance is found to be accurate and if nothing is done to correct it, the grievant may reappear with a similar complaint. But that second time around spells trouble—not for administrators who have seen fit to ignore remedies, but for the grievant. Committee disapproval is not directed at the administration that has failed to listen and to act, it is directed at the grievant who has had the bad taste to come back when no action was taken on the first legitimate complaint.

The same pattern was repeated with my complaint of sex discrimination. On the first occasion, a committee found unanimously that the complaint was accurate. On the second occasion, a different committee, one recently formed for the specific purpose of handling such complaints, found that they could not even hear the complaint. Their reason, amazingly enough, was that the complaint was against the administration, and the committee procedure was not set up to handle complaints against the administration. One wonders, since the administration is normally the employer in a university, just who else such a complaint would be lodged against.

In a broader arena, the same pattern was repeated on the occasion of two of the university's dismissal actions against me. When I was first dismissed in September 1972, even some of the conservative professors on campus found it in their hearts to sign a petition demanding my immediate reinstatement pending the usual academic due process. And even the AAUP fired off a wire to the chancellor requesting that due process precede any such firing. And the press, of course, found room for headlines. But I was fired again in September 1973, in remarkably similar circumstances—except that I was in a more prominent position. And there was not a whimper on campus or off. Once again, the message seemed clear: if you are wronged twice, the fault is yours.

In universities where faculty governance is merely a game to keep the faculty feeling reasonably busy, content, and collegial, it is simply gauche to remind committees and senates that no one with any authority is listening. It may be easy to understand how these things could occur in places like the University of Hawaii where weak faculties and weak governance prevail. But it is unfortunately true that such systems predominate in American higher education. Fewer and fewer universities can claim strong faculty governance.

This may be partially due to the timidity of faculty members who prefer back-room machinations to democratic governance as a method of pushing their own self-interest. It also may be partially due to the rapidly increasing complexity of universities. Administrative bureaucracy has grown almost geometrically of late.

In his history of American institutions of higher education, Frederick Rudolph comments on the process:

> The structure of the colleges and universities in the end made room for an extremely professionalized faculty and for a governing board whose professional competence lay outside the main interests of the institution itself. This anomaly had historic roots. But it also reflected the process of organization going on in many other American institutions, including the press and the church, which were being caught up in all the efforts to deal with growth, numbers, expanded purposes, and enlarged responsibilities. It therefore did not seem an anomaly, especially to the governing boards, *to have the pre-eminent organizers, the model managers, in control at the colleges and universities* [Rudolph, 1965, p. 427, emphasis added].

It is simply not possible in most large universities for any single full-time faculty member to understand the complexities of the rapidly growing university bureaucracy. Those faculty members who have the inclination to understand the bureaucracy rather than to become engrossed in their own fields generally allow themselves to become absorbed into the administrative structure—they, too, become administrative bureaucrats.

The degeneration of faculty governance also may be partially due to the increasing role of collective bargaining on the campus. As traditional faculty governance loses its power, more university faculties are turning to the collective-bargaining model, which in turn tends to weaken faculty governance still further. In fact, the bargaining model takes away from the faculty senate some of the duties that had previously been assigned to it: grievance processing and budget consultation, for example.

But even those universities where faculty governance is

healthy and where administrators have learned the value of meaningful faculty consultation are not likely to give sex-based complaints an objective hearing. Whether a faculty governance structure is weak or strong, the motivation of the faculty remains the same. That motivation is simple self-interest. And the self-interest of predominantly male faculties often coincides exactly with the self-interest of predominantly male administrations—after all, most administrators rise (or sink) from the faculty ranks. Disputes over whether departmental interest should prevail over more general university interests pale when the self-interest of the entire system is challenged by complaints of discriminatory application of the procedures within that system. The system does not readily admit to wrongdoing or back up such admissions by corrective action.

Such reluctance cuts two ways. An acquaintance who is attending the newly opened University of Hawaii law school called me recently to ask what steps one takes to gain dismissal of a tenured professor. When the law school opened in the fall of 1973, the students were greeted by several professors who had been hired with automatic tenure. These professors came so highly recommended (and so highly paid) that it was considered inappropriate to subject them to the supposedly rigorous scrutiny of their peers in the tenuring process. The luster of one of these tenured professors had dulled after a few short months. But I had to inform my acquaintance that short of dynamite there was little hope of getting rid of the man.

The same committee system that can never afford to take a stand on behalf of outsiders who challenge the system in an effort to gain admittance can rarely afford to endorse efforts to oust those on the inside. Tolerance of incompetence is readily accepted and rationalized, when it is recognized—and that is not very often. And efforts to point out incompetence—to get rid of the deadwood, as legislators, taxpayers, and students tend to call it—are rarely accepted as legitimate. Both activities are the same in their implications; both threaten the security of the system. The self-interest of predominantly male faculty members and administrators simply does not allow for a fair hearing of complaints of discrimination from those on the outside nor for complaints of incompetence lodged against those on the inside.

But attempts to displace the entrenched can be handled gently. They require supportive language for the faculty member concerned and a large dose of rhetoric about the protection of academic freedom. Student complaints of incompetence can easily be written off as mere dissatisfaction at tough grading or as an effort to muzzle unpopular views and thus damage academic freedom.

In contrast, discrimination complaints require harsher treatment for they represent a threat to the entire system. Philosopher Herbert Marcuse is quoted in the March 1974 *Stanford Observer* as commenting that the feminist movement is "potentially the most radical movement we have." While most professors probably have not thought about the issue enough to articulate it in just this fashion, I believe that most acknowledge that radicalism by their gut reactions against women who embarrassingly point out the gap between the rhetoric and the reality of the university employment system.

Faculty members in first-rate universities may be more articulate in expressing their findings on sex-based complaints. But the rationalizations used in arriving at findings (discussed in chapters five, six and seven) will not lend themselves to the open admission on the part of university committees that the system is unfair to women. In universities where such self-interest has been clearly thought out and forcefully implemented through faculty governance, I would very much doubt that even first-time grievances based on sex bias would have much of a chance. Strange as it may seem, a woman may be better off filing a complaint of discrimination within a university where weak governance exists. For in many states one must pursue all available administrative remedies before entering a state court complaint. The findings reached in those administrative proceedings will often be given considerable weight by the court. A fair court hearing would be made far more difficult if a woman's charge were found invalid at every level of university review and appeal. Courts prefer to endorse individuals who bring with them the previous endorsement of their peers.

Only where faculty members have not explicitly thought about discrimination and its implications for their very own system will faculty committees be likely to find in favor of someone with a sex-based complaint, even though they will avoid dealing directly with the issue if possible. This kind of finding is likely to be inadvertent. But should a woman have sufficient time to educate her colleagues on the significance of a discrimination complaint, they will probably demonstrate their learning ability by being careful to find against her the second time around.

9

AAUP: The Status Quo Seekers

The Red Queen shook her head. "You may call it 'nonsense' if you like," she said, "but I've heard nonsense, compared with which that would be as sensible as a dictionary!"

Lewis Carroll, *Through the Looking Glass*

On a local radio talk show not long ago six professors, all male and all tenured, gathered to discuss the subject of academic tenure. All were defenders of that institution. The next three hours were spent explaining how tenure developed and why it was so important to the academic freedom of university professors. The six professors demonstrated their hearty agreement with tenure as it has

141

been endorsed most recently by the American Association of University Professors (AAUP Commission on Academic Tenure, 1973):

> Academic tenure, rightly understood and properly administered, provides the most reliable means of assuring faculty quality and educational excellence, as well as the best guarantee of academic freedom. So central is academic freedom to the integrity of our educational institutions—and to their effectiveness in the discovery of new knowledge, in conservation of the values and wisdom of the past, and in the promotion of critical inquiry essential to self-renewal—that academic tenure should be retained as our most tested and reliable instrument for incorporating academic freedom into the heart of our institutions.

But it was not until five minutes before the program ended that the six professors were required to field the most interesting question of all. Someone called in and inquired, "If tenure is necessary to protect academic freedom, what happens to the academic freedom of the untenured?"

"Oh," said one professor, "untenured people have just as much academic freedom as tenured people. They are protected by the same academic due process."

There was not enough time left to ask the next obvious question: If the untenured *do* have the same protections as the tenured, why have tenure?

All six of those professors are members of the American Association of University Professors, and all six are eager defenders of its principles. The basic concerns of the AAUP today are the concerns that caused it to be organized in 1915: freedom of expression and job security. In the world of the association, and in the academic world that depends on the AAUP for maintaining and expounding its professional concepts, these two concepts have been given special labels: academic freedom and tenure. While few would argue with the idea that freedom of speech and freedom from economic sanctions are basic to the encouragement of excellence in universities, there is considerable room to question whether the system worked out by the AAUP actually serves the purpose of preserving these freedoms.

Most professors give surprisingly unthinking and automatic answers to questions about academic freedom and tenure. Academic freedom, they will insist, is a sacred and special right of university professors. It may resemble the freedom of speech guaranteed to all by the constitution, but it is different in degree because it is more important to the teaching profession than to other professions and because teachers are more vulnerable to its abridgment. Thus one past AAUP president argued, "It has been said that academic freedom should not be conspicuously advertised, lest it be resented, and that it should be presented simply as an aspect of general freedom of speech. Those who propose that we had better be silent about 'academic freedom' and talk only about 'freedom of speech' apparently fear that the people at large, who have long since been suspicious of the 'intellectual'—and particularly of the professor— will resent granting special liberties to the teachers of their children. . . . Granted, of course, that academic freedom is part of the general category of freedom of thought and expression, it is useful to recall the significant differences in their history, their legal status, their social function, and their institutional safeguards" (Machlup, 1955).

By the same token, professors will often proclaim that tenure is not at all the same as job security. While academic freedom may differ from freedom of speech in degree, tenure differs from job security in kind.

Thus adherents of the tenure system point out that it contains built-in procedures for eliminating incompetence, even if incompetence develops only after tenure has been granted. There are, in the academic rule book, procedures for peer hearings and, ultimately, for dismissal of tenured faculty members. The procedures are elaborate and judicial in nature. They involve careful statements of charges, formal hearings, the right of the faculty member being charged to counsel, and the right of the faculty member (whether tenured or serving on a nontenure contract when charges are brought) to retain both job and salary until (and unless) the hearing procedure results in negative findings. When critics claim that tenure is lifetime security for the deadwood as well as for the lively intellects on campus, advocates point out the basic AAUP statement on tenure containing the assurance that the service of academic employees can be terminated in cases of financial exigency or "adequate cause." Adequate cause, one is to assume, covers all those instances of incompetence and immorality that may develop. However, the association itself has never clearly spelled out the meaning of "adequate cause." A footnote to a later printing of the "1940 Statement of Principles on Academic Freedom and Tenure" (the basic statement of the AAUP) provides one of the few clues: "A resolution adopted by the 1953 Annual Meeting states that, 'The test of the fitness of a college teacher should be his integrity and his professional competence, as demonstrated in instruction and research'" (Joughin, 1969, p. 56). How to conduct such a test is not spelled out.

Those who argue that tenure is not at all similar to job security fail to point out that the procedures for dismissal are activated only in extreme cases of moral turpitude and are rarely called into play for mere incompetence. And even moral turpitude may become a matter of local definition. Here and there a professor may get caught in some violent and illegal political act, bombing a building perhaps. As a consequence he may face dismissal. Of course, he would be subject to criminal prosecution under such circumstances anyway. But overall, the incidence of dismissal of tenured professors is so low that it is statistically insignificant. The tenure system of job security is about as exempt from standards of excellence in job performance as any system can be.

The process of evaluation, called a probationary period, that leads to tenure consideration is also used as an argument to demonstrate that tenure is not job security. Job security, according to the defenders of the tenure system, is available to any federal or state government employee after a short trial period where no one is really careful to analyze job performance. Most large corporations, they insist, have equally little control over the excellence of the work done by employees who have lifetime job security written into their contracts through the union negotiation process. In contrast, academics are highly selective in granting tenure, they insist. The tenure probationary period is long and arduous. Young hopefuls have to show that they are going to be useful and productive and excellent for a lifetime. Tenure, according to the tenured and according to the AAUP, is not granted casually.

Proponents, however, fail to point out that no system is an automatic guarantor of good decision-making. A prolonged probationary period and careful evaluation may tend to result in a lower percentage receiving tenure than the percentage receiving job security in other industries. But it does not necessarily follow that those who do receive tenure are excellent or even that they are the best of the group under consideration. Of late, academic administrators are becoming more outspoken about the system of granting academic tenure. One wrote the following appraisal: "In the academy itself, tenure is on the way to becoming a job rights system for the protection of mediocrity rather than the right of free inquiry" (Denny, 1974). Thus, the same system the AAUP extols and defends can be described by another observer in another fashion: "On the surface, it would seem that great care and painstaking effort go into this process to ensure that only truly creative and deserving persons receive tenure. On closer examination, it becomes apparent that the system is wide open to abuse and covert reprisals against individuals who are not 'right thinking' or 'sound' in any one of a number of ways" (Farnsworth, 1974, p. 97).

If the only guarantor of academic freedom is tenure, it should be obvious that the untenured, by definition, do not have any guarantee. In order to obtain it they must manage their probationary years with great care: they must not step out of line too far, must not become too controversial, must not voice ideas that will be considered too wild by tenured professors who are watching them —particularly when it comes to the politics of their own university. So one UCLA tenure reject claimed that even for those who can pass the test of publication tenure is not a sure thing: "The second [test] is political, in the broadest sense of the word. It's not just if you're a Communist or a Democrat, but your political style, the way you look at things and respond to the University hierarchy. . . . The final test is social. You have to fit into the cocktail circuit, be a presentable, acceptable person to the hierarchy. If you were socially unacceptable, even if everything else were all right, that would do it" (Peterson, 1974).

The probationary years can become a training period where self-constraint is substituted for tenure as the guarantor of the job. It is a kind of training that may be difficult to overcome. To gain tenure, and thus to gain academic freedom, one must often forfeit academic freedom. What may only begin as temporary self-constraint may easily become a permanent posture.

Tenure is, for now, the only game in town. If one is in university teaching there is no way at the present time to continue practicing one's profession without becoming tenured. With few exceptions, tenure is an all-or-nothing system. If one continues teaching beyond a fixed number of years at the same institution, one gains automatic tenure under AAUP regulations. Institutions are therefore careful to give tenure consideration and to make tenure decisions before automatic tenure sets in. And if one is turned down for tenure, one cannot continue full-time teaching for more than a single terminal year in the institution that turned one down.

But this system may soon have to undergo radical changes because some universities are becoming totally locked in, with no available positions and with completely tenured faculties. The academic job market, in fact, is rapidly closing down. Daniel P. Moynihan made a point of this in an address given at Andover Academy in 1973: "Find out what it's like to live in a society where, if you want to be a professor, you wait until the man who is professor dies. Then the fifteen of you who want the job compete in various ways. One of you gets it. The rest hope for the best for their sons" (quoted in Holmes, 1973, p. 1). Unthinkingly, perhaps, Moynihan also seemed to assume that even such limited possibilities were not available to their daughters.

An increasing freeze in the academic job market may eventually reduce the institution of tenure to a puzzling vestige of the past. Even the AAUP is beginning to concern itself with the problem of tenure in relation to the closing academic job market. In 1971, the organization (along with the Association of American Colleges) sponsored a Commission on Academic Tenure in Higher Education, which suggested some modifications in the current system. The most controversial had to do with setting limits on the number of tenured employees at any one institution. The commission suggested "that each institution develop policies relating to the proportion of tenured and nontenured faculty that will be compatible with the composition of its present staff, its resources and projected enrollment, and its future objectives. In the commission's nearly unanimous judgment, it will probably be dangerous for most institutions if tenured faculty constitute more than one half to two thirds of the total full-time faculty during the decade ahead" (Adams, 1973, p. 134). The major argument of those who opposed the quotas was the argument of "merit." Whatever modifications might be proposed had to be measured against the true belief that tenure ensures the primacy of merit. Thus, at their 1973 annual meeting, the professors of the AAUP rejected much of the criticism that was to be found in the tenure study. They preferred, once again, to blindly endorse the system that had helped them to achieve academic security. The rationale for rejection, like the rationale for tenure itself, was based on academic freedom and academic excellence: "The annual meeting itself, in its resolution on quotas, voted that the association should oppose their imposition, viewing them 'as an expedient dangerous to academic freedom and academic life.' The delegates reaffirmed the principle that 'decisions on tenure must represent, first and last, judgments on individual merit'" (Adams, 1973, p. 134).

Meanwhile, all over the country, individual university faculties gathered to vote resolutions in support of the old ways. At Stanford, a two-year faculty committee study rejected any basic changes and called tenure "indispensable . . . for the kind of high-risk, creative inquiry which universities alone can provide for society" (*Stanford Observer,* March 1974). Facing the same fear of decreased growth, the faculty of the University of Iowa in early 1974 came out with a report voicing similar views: ". . . tenure will continue as a cornerstone of the university's relationship with faculty members. Tenure is not only consistent with academic vitality but essential to it. . . . No system of tenure quotas is contemplated." And at the same time the University of Hawaii faculty released a report that rejected quotas or any other limitation to the current system of tenure and concluded, "The granting of tenure is more likely to raise standards, than to protect inefficiency."

The pro-tenure argument that the system weeds out incompetence and promotes excellence is at least partially challenged by statistics revealed in the AAUP study of tenure. The report disclosed that 42 percent of respondent institutions awarded tenure to *all* eligible faculty members, while two thirds of all respondent institutions awarded it to "70 percent or more of those under consideration."

But while the debate goes on in the universities, with the consensus apparently for the status quo, the implications of government affirmative action in relation to tenure are becoming clearer. Tenure has, in effect, worked to exclude women from permanent academic positions. As one team of observers speculates, "Compliance with affirmative action regulations may well end, or at least dramatically transform, academe's most established and distinctive personnel practice—tenure" (Chalt and Ford, 1973). They go on to point out that the burden will fall on colleges and universities to prove that their present practices and the criteria used in granting tenure are significantly related to job performance.

> [For example,] if only lip service is paid to teaching effectiveness and what really counts is the candidate's publication record, then the institution, as the employer, must be able to prove that the publications are 'demonstrably' related to the job, which is teaching. . . .
> To the extent that tenure practices discriminate against minorities and women, external authorities will undoubtedly order the system revised or even eliminated.
> Thus, while academicians discuss the merits of tenure and eminent commissions walk a tightrope to consensus, the courts may dramatically end the debate. It would not be the first time the courts, prodded by minority groups, interceded to overhaul educational practices. The most noteworthy casualty was segregation. Tenure may be next [Chalt and Ford, 1973].

But the momentum of the tenure arguments is not easily reversed either on individual campuses or within the professional organization of academics. Rather than seeking creative solutions to the problems of "tenuring in" and of access to academic jobs for women and minorities, the standard reaction of male academics and their committees and organizations is a proliferation of bigger and better tomes in defense of the institution of tenure.

In fairness it must be said that the AAUP *Bulletin,* the major journal of the association, has been willing to discuss the problem of discrimination. Alongside the articles in defense of tenure, the *Bulletin* pages have included a number of articles by women about academic discrimination and excellent reports on what needs to be done to end it. In the summer of 1973, for example, an AAUP committee that included the former head of the HEW Office for Civil Rights, Higher Education Division, reported on affirmative action in universities and began with what was, for the AAUP, strong language: "We begin with the premise that discrimination against women and minorities in higher education is both reprehensible and illegal, and reaffirm the emphatic condemnation of such practices by the AAUP" (AAUP *Bulletin*, Summer 1973, p. 178). Such reports and articles may, over the years, have a salutary educational effect on the vast majority of the AAUP members who would prefer the comfortable status quo.

In the interim, however, a woman faced with academic discrimination must decide if her professional organization will, indeed, attempt to seek an equitable solution or whether she would be better off channeling her appeal through such agencies as the Equal Employment Opportunity Commission or HEW. Certainly the signs of interest are there, in *Bulletin* articles for the most part. And if one wishes to take seriously the association proclamations on the necessity of excellence, one can conclude that abuse is restricted to the local campus and that the national organization would be more than willing to set things right. The AAUP has, after all, sponsored numerous studies on the nature of fair and equitable procedures for tenure and promotion. And it has developed its own system of investigating complaints of procedural abuse, a system complete with censure lists for universities that blatantly break the rules. The system puts the national AAUP into the same category as government agencies and the courts. Like the agencies and the courts, the national AAUP has a mechanism for the investigation of complaints of abuse on individual campuses and can bring to bear considerable pressure in resolving complaints that are found to be legitimate. And, on first glance, it may appear to many professional women to be preferable to have their grievances aired within the profession rather than going to government agencies that may not have the least notion of correct academic procedure.

With just such thoughts in mind, I sought assistance from the AAUP in the spring of 1972. Indeed, I had already registered a complaint with HEW, but nothing had come of it. The slow pace of the federal investigative effort seemed to reinforce the idea that it would be better to take the matter to an academic organization.

My first encounter with the organization was quite favorable. At that time the local chapter of the AAUP had thrown in with a group called the Alliance and was competing with two other groups to become the elected collective-bargaining agent for the faculty. Even though I belonged to a rival union, the AAUP was anxious to take on the grievance. Wins on grievances were important politically for all the competing groups, and as a result people who had grievances during this period found the potential bargaining agents scrambling to help. Besides, there was a large overlap in membership: many people, even though not supporting its bid to take over the collective-bargaining role, belonged to the AAUP and considered it their primary professional affiliation. I must confess that I did not belong to the AAUP at the time. I joined in 1972, though, out of a sense of obligation for the work that was done on my case. Moreover, I had the distinct feeling that though the organization claims to represent faculty rights in general, it would be more inclined to represent the faculty rights of dues-paying members than of nonmembers.

I asked the organization to investigate my grievance in March 1972 and the local chapter grievance chief, after an enormous amount of work, pulled together an academic amicus brief on my behalf. But a month after the brief was written, several members of the local chapter of the AAUP, who also happened to be professors in the Department of English, raised objections. The amicus brief was clearly an attempt to state my claims, state the remedial action sought, and outline the chronology of the case according to the available documents. Its purpose was to help facilitate an informal resolution to the problem rather than to affix blame. However, the grievance chief did not count on the aroused feelings of members of my department, which undercut the AAUP attempt at informal settlement.

The ill will raised by the amicus brief can be illustrated by the following excerpt from a letter sent by a professor from my department:

> You know that I am opposed to quotas of any
> kind (*de facto* or *de jure*) based on the crude manipula-
> tion of statistical ratios to "prove" that discrimination
> exists. However, if you and the AAUP accept such evidence
> and demand that hiring be conducted according to the
> proportional representation of any group in this depart-
> ment, I would like to suggest that we examine the ethnic
> origins of the members of the department to discover if
> any group is overrepresented. If it should turn out that
> Ms. Abramson does, in fact, fall into this classification,
> whatever it may be, then our obvious duty is to hire
> someone whose ethnic group is not adequately represented.
> It may turn out that our highest priority in redressing
> any imbalance may be in the hiring of a black, a
> Hawaiian, or a Samoan.

Shortly after this particular tirade was issued, AAUP officials outside of Hawaii soothed my feelings somewhat by pointing out that such faculty overreaction was typical and that was exactly why the organization tried to handle cases outside the local arena.

In June 1972, a formal complaint was sent to the national office of the AAUP on my behalf. After administration rejection of the three unanimous committee recommendations in favor of my tenure on the University of Hawaii campus, it was a relief to contemplate removing the issue from campus long enough to get an outside opinion. But beyond a post office return receipt, the AAUP did not acknowledge my complaint. I confess that I expected more.

By the time the summer of 1972 drew to a close the AAUP had still made no commitment either to investigate my complaint or to set a timetable for deciding whether to investigate. Richard Peairs, the western regional director of the organization, suggested that I meet with a woman from the national office of the AAUP since the case appeared to be a "women's issue." In late August 1972, I did just that. The woman claimed a great deal of interest in the case and in the subject of sex discrimination. She urged me

to stay clear of the courts and the agencies and let the AAUP handle
the matter. And she pointed out that the AAUP did not like to get
involved when things were going the legal route, though occasionally
they did submit amicus briefs on important court cases.

I told her that I preferred to have the whole issue resolved
in an academic setting anyway. But before I could promise to stay
clear of the courts, I would have to have some commitment from
the AAUP as to when they would handle the case.

In spite of repeated promises that some commitment would
be made within a week or two, it took a combination of an impending collective-bargaining election and the university's illegal dismissal
of me in September 1972 to get any sign of support from the AAUP.
With the election breathing down his neck, Peairs wrote our
chancellor a lengthy letter. When boiled down it simply noted that
significant issues had been left unresolved and that the AAUP would
advise a complete hearing of my case within the university.

The letter concluded by stating that "it appears that a new
structure should be promptly established by the senate, or its executive committee, which will offer the faculty its own internal,
professional means for the sound resolution of this aspect of a
nonreappointment dispute which the association is now encounter-
ing nationally with increasing frequency." After two years of
senate committee investigations and rulings on my campus, and
after telling me that it was often best to remove such issues from the
campus, all that the AAUP would suggest was yet another committee
on the campus!

Under pressure of the upcoming election, the AAUP did take
one other action. Since I had been fired on September 29, just a
few weeks before the election, I could hardly be ignored. On
September 30, I appealed to Peairs, pointing out that by firing me
with no prior notice and no hearing the university was violating my
academic freedom and ignoring the procedural steps the AAUP
considered essential before dismissal. With the union election ap-
proaching, Peairs sent a telegram to the chancellor urging that I be
reinstated "pending precise description of terms of her appointment
or determination in appropriate faculty proceedings to resolve the
issue." His request was couched in suitably noncommittal language
and was sprinkled with phrases such as "situation appears to be

summary dismissal" and "if our understanding is essentially correct."

It would give me great pleasure to be able to state that the AAUP was responsible for getting my job back after that first summary dismissal. But it was the Labor Department that negotiated my contract and saw to it that I was returned to my job. In my case the AAUP took two actions so timorous that they had no effect at all. The first was to suggest that I be returned to work pending negotiation of a new contract or a statement of charges against me (a suggestion that was ignored all around—I was allowed to return to work only after a contract had been negotiated). The second (which was also ignored, given the fact that five campus committees had already dealt with the issue) was the suggestion that another faculty committee be established and be charged with investigating my case.

The second suggestion was tinged with added irony: I was told that the AAUP national office could not conduct an investigation, since there had been as yet no "full hearing" on my campus. Several months later (and for the first time in years) the University of Hawaii administration drew up a set of charges and launched a faculty hearing for the purpose of dismissing a male faculty member who, naturally, retained his teaching post and salary during the proceedings. Should that rare hearing result in his dismissal, he will have the right to a national AAUP investigation. In contrast, because the administration dismissed me, more than once, without stating reasons and without requesting a hearing the AAUP claimed that I am not entitled to a national investigation since the local hearing has yet to be held!

Between October 1972 (shortly before the AAUP lost the collective-bargaining election in Hawaii) and August 1973, I received not one word of written communication from that organization. And what little oral communication there was proved frustrating and useless. Again and again I wrote to ask for a status report on my complaint. Again and again my letters went unanswered.

In July 1973, I found myself back in the national office, talking, once again, to the woman who had advised me to stick with the AAUP and forget about court or agency action. And, incredibly enough, I found her telling me that the AAUP could do *nothing* until the hearing so timidly suggested to the University of Hawaii

administration one year before had been completed. I asked if such
hearings were essential in all cases handled by the AAUP, since it
was obvious that not all universities had hearing procedures (or, like
the University of Hawaii, had procedures that could be initiated
only by the administration and thus could be left uninitiated at will)
and since the AAUP officials I had dealt with had themselves told me
that there were times when complaints should be investigated by
off-campus groups.

I was told that, indeed, such hearings were not always
needed. There were some cases in which the violations were so clear
that everyone could see them. And then I was treated to a recitation
of recent AAUP decisions that had been made with and without
campus hearings, but with a noticeable absence of women among
the complainants. Had the AAUP ever solved a case involving discrimination on the basis of sex, I asked. The reply was that several
such cases had been filed. There was no mention of solutions.

My own complaint was formally buried in mid-August 1973
when Peairs finally wrote to me again. His letter insisted that the
position of the AAUP had been made clear long ago—that a full
hearing on the campus was needed. The letter contained some mild
handslapping and complained of my going outside the profession
to attempt to resolve the complaint. I was informed that my complaint, generated over two years earlier on the University of Hawaii
campus, was being returned to that campus, where the local chapter
of the AAUP would see to it. In August 1973, I wrote to the local
chapter president to ask how he intended to see to that complaint.
As of February 1975, I have received no answer, though the AAUP
managed to bring about another collective-bargaining election and
is now the official faculty bargaining agent on our campus. I have,
though, received several printed reminders asking that I renew my
membership. Among the concerns these reminders claim need urgent
AAUP attention: the status of women in academe.

The mechanism used by the AAUP to resolve tenure disputes
had seemed reasonable to me. As a way of maintaining self-
discipline rather than allowing outsiders to set the rules of the game,
it resembles the model preferred by professional organizations such
as the American Bar Association and the American Medical Association. But none of these systems can be better than the people

who maintain them. Computer people say it very simply: garbage in, garbage out. If men in the academic world cannot deal directly with challenges that require them to reexamine that world, a woman cannot expect the professional association organized and controlled by those men to deal directly with her challenges. At the present time the AAUP is the last place a woman should go if she is asking for a reexamination of the system. The AAUP is set up to police and enforce that very system.

If I had realized this three years ago I would have saved myself a lot of effort.

10

The Department of Labor: Guardian of Equal Pay?

"You couldn't have it if you did want it," the Queen said. "The rule is, jam tomorrow and jam yesterday— but never jam today."

Lewis Carroll, *Through the Looking Glass*

It is a long time since the Lord lectured Moses on the market value of the Children of Israel: ". . . thy valuation shall be for the male child from twenty years old even unto sixty years old, even thy valuation shall be fifty shekels of silver after the shekel of the sanctuary. And if it be female, then thy valuation shall be thirty shekels" (Leviticus 27:3–4). Nothing much has changed since that early directive. Indeed, in 1973, that same biblical ratio could be reported: "By 1970 more than half of all women worked, in contrast with about

156

80 percent of men. Comparing full-time workers in the same occupations, *women earned only about three fifths of the wages of men,* a fact which is remarkably constant all over the Western world. The American ideology of equal opportunity holds that equal qualifications and hours worked should bring equal rewards. But it does not apply to women" [emphasis added] (Huber, 1973, p. 765).

In the United States, where the idea of equal opportunity has long been an accepted if not an accomplished goal of education, the idea of unequal compensation for equal work also has been accepted for quite some time. Indeed, the concept of low or no pay for women has been decorated with the rhetoric of dedication, purity, and selflessness. Volunteerism is still rampant in our society, and women are still made to feel greedy and mercenary for making such crass demands as higher salary for their work. Somehow a man's work is valued more highly when it is paid for highly; this is often the argument academic men put forth when they talk about consulting rates. Their research, they insist, would be considered insignificant if it did not come at a high price. The notion of the value of a male consultant can be carried to ridiculous lengths: the ideas of a $100-a-day consultant are simply not going to carry much weight, whereas the $1000-a-day man can expect to be listened to with deference. Value also increases with distance, and the consultant whose travel costs must be paid is therefore more desirable than the local one. Thus the East Coast expert sometimes finds himself flying to the Pacific on consulting jobs, perhaps crossing paths with the West Coast expert who is on his way to Europe to consult in the same field.

But for women the argument is different. John Kenneth Galbraith has provided an analysis of unpaid and poorly paid labor classifications, a phenomenon that has been encouraged in our society by the use of what he calls "the convenient social virtue." Through it, society is able to keep certain classes of people, usually women, engaged in menial tasks such as housework. At the same time, these people are kept by the same social pressures from competing for jobs in the more lucrative professions. Thus morality is put to work on behalf of the role of women as the menial glue of the family unit—and not at all incidentally as the primary consumer in a consumption-oriented society. "The ultimate success of the convenient social virtue," says Galbraith, "has been in converting women to menial personal service." Thus a woman receives moral remuneration for staying in the home: "If she discharges these duties well, she is accepted as a good homemaker, a good helpmate, a good manager, a good wife—in short, a virtuous woman." Nor may she take on financially remunerative employment without censure: "Convention forbids external roles unassociated with display of homely virtues that are in conflict with good household management. She may serve on a local library board or on a committee to consider delinquency among the young. She may not, without reproach, have full-time employment or a demanding avocation. To do so is to have it said that she is neglecting her home and family, i.e., her *real* work. She ceases to be a woman of acknowledged virtue" (all quotes, Galbraith, 1973, p. 32).

Thus laws that sanction unequal compensation for women often derived their rationale from the morality of convenient social virtue while helping to reinforce it. It was right for women to be paid less and protected from longer hours and from engaging in certain occupations if the primary occupation of women was the home. Laws making unequal compensation part of the American scene derived from English common law as codified in 1765 in Blackstone's *Commentaries on the Laws of England*. Under English common law, women were legally invisible, being identified as one and the same as their husbands. Given this basic premise, the growth of protective labor legislation was quite natural.

Protection, when it was applied to women, often seemed to mean protection from equality. On the theory that women, like children, are in need of special protection from exploitation, women have been prevented from working at night (when restaurant and bar customers pay their highest tips), restricted from earning overtime wages (when, for some higher paying jobs, the freedom to take on overtime work is a requirement), and kept from "hazardous" (that is, high-paying) occupations. Such legislation, which not only barred women from earning as much as men but also barred them from taking up some of the more prestigious and lucrative male occupations, has been upheld all the way to the Supreme Court.

A Supreme Court decision in *Bradwell* v. *State of Illinois* (1873) upheld a state law forbidding women to practice law. It read in part: "Man is, or should be, woman's protector and defender. The natural and proper timidity and delicacy which belongs to the female sex evidently unfits it for many of the occupations of civil life. The constitution of the family organization, which is founded in the divine ordinance, as well as in the nature of things, indicates the domestic sphere as that which properly belongs to the domain and functions of womanhood. . . . The paramount destiny and mission of woman are to fulfill the noble and benign offices of wife and mother. This is the law of the Creator. And the rules of civil society must be adapted to the general constitution of things, and cannot be based upon exceptional cases" (Cary, 1973, p. 31).

And another, in 1908, reads in part: "History discloses the fact that woman has always been dependent upon man. He established his control at the outset by superior physical strength, and this control in various forms, with diminishing intensity, has continued to the present. As minors, though not to the same extent, she has been looked upon in the courts as needing especial care that her rights may be preserved. . . . Though limitations upon personal and contractual rights may be removed by legislation, there is that in her disposition and habits of life which will operate against a full assertion of those rights. . . . Differentiated by these matters from the other sex, she is properly placed in a class by herself, and legislation designed for her protection may be sustained, even when like legislation is not necessary for men, and could not be sustained" (Hole and Levine, 1973, p. 33).

Difficult though it may be to believe, equal pay for equal work did not become part of the law of the land until 1963. And it was not until 1972 that the concept was extended to cover the professions. And though it may be even more difficult to believe, it was not until 1971 that the Fourteenth Amendment to the Constitution, which guarantees equal protection of the law to all citizens, was legally interpreted as being applicable to women. The Supreme Court, in *Reed* v. *Reed* (1971), reversed a long string of judicial interpretations insisting that the amendment did *not* bar protective legislation and thus apparently did not extend its coverage to women.

Although the original backers of protective legislation and the Supreme Court justices who upheld the laws may have been well-intentioned, there is some evidence that a parallel exists between the incursion, or attempted incursion, of women into certain areas of employment and the development of protective laws restricting the terms and conditions of employment in those areas. Thus, writes Jo Freeman,

> As women acquired education and professional skills in the wake of the Industrial Revolution, they increasingly sought employment in fields which put them in competition with men. In some instances men gave way totally and the field became dominated by women, losing prestige, opportunities for advancement, and pay in the process. The occupation of secretary is the most notable. In most cases men fought back and were quick to make use of economic, ideological, and legal weapons to reduce or eliminate their competition. . . . The most onerous of all are the so-called "protective" labor legislation. Most of this was passed at the turn of the century as part of a general reform effort to improve sweatshop conditions. It has since been used to deny overtime pay, promotions, and employment opportunities to women [Freeman, 1969a, pp. 276–277].

One may well wonder just whom such legislation was intended to protect.

The academic world still provides an example of exclusionary philosophy and practice. And among the major discrepancies, salary remains painfully obvious. Of the number of studies on the relative salaries of male and female academics, all agree that discrepancies exist and are related to the sex of academic employees. One of the most conservative and careful of these studies concluded: "But nevertheless, women generally hold lower ranks and make lower salaries, however comparable their backgrounds, work activities, achievements, and institutional work settings to those of their male colleagues. Considering the many variables in these analyses, one can only conclude that sex discrimination is rampant in academe" (Astin and Bayer, 1972, p. 108). The study attributes a considerable salary differential to discrimination between men and women of the same rank—about $1000 per year on the average. But the authors caution that the figure is exceptionally conservative and point out that discrimination in rank between men and women of the same background increases the average figure substantially. And Astin reports that follow-up work shows the situation to be even worse in 1974 than the initial study indicated.

Such results are hardly surprising, for one of the most persistent ideas in the academic world is that women do not need as much money as do men. The men who decide initial salary rates and salary increments often see nothing odd in taking into consideration what they assume to be the needs of female faculty members, or of any female employees. Single women are often presumed to be supporting no one but themselves. And the level of support they will need is often underrated: if the man deciding the salary decides that a woman is even reasonably attractive, he is likely to imagine that other men will probably provide her with a certain amount of food and entertainment, or he may assume that, being single, her job is temporary and she will need no savings when she finds the right man and leaves her job for marriage. And married women are presumed to be supporting nobody, not even themselves. They may be reminded that their husbands are earning enough, that they live in nice houses, and that they do not need to work for a living. Some married women have even reported that male faculty members do not bother to hide their resentment at the comfortable life style an academic woman and her husband may be able to provide for themselves. Yet in spite of this persistent notion that academic women do not require salaries as large as those of academic men, no one has suggested that financial need should govern salary decisions for men. From each according to his ability, to each according to his need, is not yet the rule among male academics.

Given existing wage discrepancies, the equal pay laws certainly seemed promising. The heart of the equal pay concept is found in the 1963 addition of subsection (d) to section 6 of the Fair Labor Standards Act of 1938: "No employer having employees subject to any provisions of this section shall discriminate, within any establishment in which such employees are employed, between employees on the basis of sex by paying wages to employees in such establishment at a rate less than the rate at which he pays wages to employees of the opposite sex in such establishment for equal work." The law basically requires that equal pay be provided to men and women holding jobs that require equal skill, equal effort, and equal responsibility. A broad interpretation has been placed on these three terms—equal does not mean identical.

The extension of the law under the Education Amendments of 1972 for the first time gave women in the professions a direct legal means of seeking equal pay for equal work. What is more, access was far more immediate than through either Title VII as administered by the Equal Employment Opportunity Commission or amended Executive Order 11246, which is enforced by HEW. By 1972, both EEOC and HEW had developed enormous case backlogs. Once having filed a complaint, a woman could expect to wait months or possibly years before her case was investigated by either of these agencies. In contrast, the Wage and Hour Division of the Department of Labor, which has the responsibility of investigating and enforcing the Equal Pay Act, seemed not only willing but eager to take on new complaints. Wage and Hour Division offices often had little or no backlog. Cases could be investigated as soon as they were filed. Furthermore, the law itself confines and limits the issues that can be investigated, making it reasonable to assume that investigation, once it began, could proceed with dispatch.

I have been told that my equal pay for equal work complaint was the first complaint by an academic woman to reach resolution under the extended law. My complaint was filed on September 18 and "resolved" on November 3, 1972. The resolution was given a modest amount of publicity. ("Annual Pay Upped $4330," read one headline.)

But although the resolution of my complaint may have looked remarkably efficient and advantageous to those unfamiliar with my case and the Labor Department investigation of it, it looked remarkably shaky and inauspicious from my point of view. Indeed, my encounter with the Wage and Hour Division (and the subsequent encounter a year later because of the agency's unsatisfactory handling of things the first time around) amply demonstrated some of the serious shortcomings in the way the Equal Pay Act can be handled for professional women.

It is possible that these shortcomings are built into the law itself. I am inclined to think not. The law allows for latitude in interpretation and could be, in the hands of a serious enforcer, a powerful weapon in ending wage discrimination in the professions and in the academic world. Unfortunately, the enforcers do not always seem inclined to utilize their weapon. In fact, the most serious problem that exists today in the struggle to achieve equal employment is the unwillingness of federal employees to do the job that they are paid to do, the unwillingness of these people to enforce the laws. On all too many occasions one gains the distinct impression that some of the enforcers do not believe in the laws they are paid to uphold and that they uphold them (if at all) at the lowest possible level consistent with not losing their own jobs. Let me illustrate by briefly outlining my own experience with the Wage and Hour Division.

During the 1971/72 academic year, I had worked on a split appointment with part of my time spent in the Department of English and part at New College. New College then offered me a job as assistant director for the 1972/73 academic year. For a number of reasons outlined in detail in earlier chapters, the college was not permitted to give me an ordinary instructional position. Instead, the dean merely maintained that he could not prevent an offer of a lectureship position. The result was that for more responsible work I was to receive a substantial cut in pay and transfer to a nontenure track position. My male predecessor had received a 22 percent pay increase and a tenure track position. Needless to say, I had replaced him because the New College administration felt he was not doing an adequate job.

On September 18, 1972—after over two months on the job (without pay)—I filed an equal pay for equal work complaint with the Department of Labor. On September 26 a Labor Department investigator interviewed the dean. On September 29 the dean fired me. It was at this point that the dean tossed out a number of interesting diversionary smokescreens in an attempt to confuse both the faculty—which did not, initially, like the idea of a faculty member being fired in mid-contract—and the Labor Department. As it turned out, the faculty was thoroughly confused by them, but the Labor Department was not.

The Labor Department investigator ascertained without any

great difficulty that my predecessor thought I was doing the same job he had left, that both the acting director and the director of New College thought I was doing the same job, and that the dean himself could not quite say how my job differed from that of my predecessor. Having determined that, regardless of the title, I had been assigned the same job as my predecessor, it took the local office of the Wage and Hour Division exactly five weeks to get me back to work with a new contract, retroactive to July 1, the day I had actually begun work on the new job.

But behind the headlines featuring my supposed 53 percent pay raise and behind all the congratulations, the fact was that the Labor Department had negotiated a most fainthearted settlement—one that left me vulnerable. The Labor Department official who negotiated with the university had worked out the settlement within a narrow framework: first, he had placed the narrowest possible construction on the meaning of equal pay for equal work, and second, he had preferred to look the other way rather than recognize an obvious case of retaliation, though retaliation is specifically forbidden by the law itself.

In interpreting the meaning of equal pay, the Labor Department negotiator decided not to consider the possibility that my pay may have been unequal to start with, when I first had entered the university as an instructor. Nor did he consider university regulations that should have made review for promotion mandatory for me that year. The regulation stating that academic employees in their sixth year are tenured was ignored also. Thus equal pay meant I would receive a salary of $11,900 in a job designated "not eligible for tenure" compared with the $16,000 received by my predecessor in a tenure track position.

Using the same narrow definition of the law, the negotiator also allowed the university to designate my job as less than full time. By skipping my salary three steps higher (steps that would normally have taken three years to achieve) and by giving me a contract that entitled me to 91.667 percent of the full-time salary at the new level, the "correct" salary was achieved. But the negotiator claimed that the designation of a full-time job as full time was beyond his control. Thus arose the anomaly that I was receiving "equal pay" for equal work, while the university was allowed to define the work as unequal. The settlement left a large question unanswered: if, indeed, the work was "unequal," what was the Labor Department doing participating in the negotiations to return me to work?

An even more serious failing on the part of the Labor Department negotiator was his preference for ignoring retaliation. The Equal Pay Act clearly forbids dismissal, harassment, or discrimination against individuals because they have made complaints. And the Labor Department had a witness who revealed that on the very afternoon of the day the department investigator had talked to the dean, the dean was considering firing me as one way to handle my Labor Department complaint. Three days later he did fire me.

The Labor Department negotiator's preference for ignoring the implications of the incident unquestionably served to signal administrators that it was all right for them to try again. And they did. In December I was informed that my employment would come to an end the following June. And the following September, in spite of the fact that I was offered a new contract in June and had worked under that contract all summer, I was fired once again. But the same Labor Department official refused to see the dismissal as retaliation, and therefore it could not be treated as part of my original equal pay for equal work complaint. Nor could it be treated as any form of sex discrimination. In fact he informed me that he only had authority to enforce the *minimum wage law!* He would, said he, look into my claim that I had worked all summer and had not even received the minimum wage of $1.60 per hour that was required by federal law.

However, this small investigation took somewhat longer than expected. A hearing had been set in state court on my charge of due process violation by the university administration in the handling of my case. The Labor Department ruling would have been very useful in court, even though it addressed only the minimum wage issue, to help me prove that I was working with the knowledge and consent of the university administration during a seventh consecutive year. I had no wish to pressure the Labor Department for an early ruling, nor would such pressure have been possible. However, I did expect that the ruling would be made and released within a reasonable period after the investigation was completed. My court hearing was scheduled for November 14, 1973. But later it was postponed until mid-January 1974. My last day in court was Friday, January 18. And the following Monday I finally received the Labor Department ruling in the mail. It was dated January 18, 1974—the day my court case closed. But, the date was typed on a strip of white paper that had been pasted over an older date: November 23, 1973—a safe number of days after I was supposed to have gone to court in the first place! The Wage and Hour chief explained that he was really very sorry, but the letter had been sitting on his desk all that time with the carbon copy on top of the original, which led him to believe that the original had already been mailed. He had just happened to discover that this was not the case on the closing day of my state court hearing.

The ruling: that I had been working with the knowledge and consent of the university administration for a total of nine summer weeks at sixty hours per week. This entitled me, said the Labor Department, to $1008 in unpaid back wages (figured at the minimum wage of $1.60 per hour plus time and a half for overtime!). The ruling also reminded me that I could take the claim to court; the Labor Department, of course, would not do that since the claim was too small for them to bother with.

The sum total of my equal pay for equal work victory did not amount to much, in spite of all the publicity that was given to it. I am inclined to believe that the first encounter university administrators had with the Labor Department emboldened them considerably. It demonstrated that retaliation was a perfectly safe and effective tool for coping with complaining women. Bernice Sandler, testifying from her experience as head of the WEAL Action Committee for Federal Contract Compliance in Education, told a House subcommittee that a number of female academics have asked WEAL to file discrimination complaints against their universities. All, she says, have pleaded for anonymity since they fear retaliation (Sandler, 1970, p. 302).

In fact there is room for debate on the advisability of retaining anonymity or of having others file for one in a discrimination complaint. It is clear in individual cases at least that an employer will generally discover who the complaint is about. The more specific and concrete a complaint is, the easier it will be to prove. But by the same token, the more specific and concrete a complaint is, the easier it is to identify the complainant. And it is possible in some instances that anonymity can encourage retaliation since, if one has not filed on one's own behalf and is then fired, one can hardly complain that dismissal is an act of retaliation for having filed a complaint. On the other hand, openness does not seem to offer much protection either. Despite the fact that every major piece of legislation prohibiting discrimination has in it a clause forbidding retaliatory practices, retaliation continues—as I learned from my own experience. University administrators, when it comes to women filing sex discrimination complaints, do not always suffer moral qualms about breaking the law. And agencies set up to monitor the law sometimes show little more enthusiasm for it than do university administrators.

The Equal Pay Act has the strongest prohibition against retaliation of all the antidiscrimination legislation at the present time—the provision includes the possibility of six-month jail sentences for willful violation of the act. One can imagine that it would take but two or three deans sitting in jail for a few months to convince a number of other deans across the country that retaliation is unwise. However, the penalty is apparently considered too severe to impose. One is forced to conclude that federal officials consider the penalty paid by women in low pay, harassment, and even dismissal the lesser of two evils.

One may well ask why any woman would sign an agreement which fails to acknowledge past retaliation and clearly permits future retaliation. Again, my situation was hardly unique. After negotiating for five weeks (certainly not full time, however), a process that took him through three contract proposals, the chief of the Wage and Hour Division told me that he had done all he could and advised me to sign. The implication was clear, though politely worded: If I did not accept the contract, the Labor Department would pull out of the picture, and I would be left without any job at all.

No law, however well it may be designed, can solve the problem of discrimination. The Equal Pay Act amply demonstrates that fact. Some may say that it is too early to judge Labor Department performance in enforcing the newly extended act, but it is certainly not too early to judge enforcement of the 1963 provision, which covered the largest percentage of salaried workers. Despite the fact that the law has been in effect for more than a decade, women are still bringing home that same biblical three fifths of the salary of men in comparable positions.

About a month after the extended Equal Pay Act went into effect, I talked with the head of one of the Justice Department civil rights divisions about the prevalence of sex discrimination on university campuses. The white male lawyer brought in one of his subordinates (another white male lawyer) to take notes. I had the feeling that he was making sure that his superiors knew he was a busy man. Toward the end of our discussion he told me I was the first person who had ever come in to talk about sex discrimination in the academic world—"so it couldn't really be a very big problem, could it?" He went on to tell me about the really big problems. And he made it clear to me that women in the academic world did not have it so bad, most could depend on high-salaried husbands to keep them in clothing. After I left his office, I wandered through a warren of other offices, all inhabited by white males, and stopped to read the names at the reception room door, all male. It was not difficult to understand why sex discrimination was not an important problem. But it is still hard for me to accommodate to the fact that, as a taxpayer, I am helping to support the many, many bureaucrats whose job it is to enforce the law but who spend more time in obstructing than enforcing.

Good laws are not enough. The past has taught us that men do not always rush to obey the law voluntarily. What is needed is people who pay attention to the jobs that they are paid to do: people who enforce rather than obstruct the law. Such people are not readily available in government agencies.

Women who impatiently point to the failure of the newer agencies—the Equal Employment Opportunity Commission and the Higher Education Division of the HEW Office for Civil Rights—are sometimes told to have patience since it takes several years to work out the kinks in an agency and to begin the smooth enforcement of the law. But the decade that has gone by since the Equal Pay Act first came into being does not lend much support to the preachers of patience. One can walk into the Honolulu office of the Wage and Hour Division on almost any day of the week and find at least one person, one male employee, sitting there with nothing to do. Yet equal pay for equal work has still not become a reality.

11

HEW: The Reluctant Dragon

"I don't think they play at all fairly," Alice began, in a rather complaining tone, *"And they all quarrel so dreadfully one ca'n't hear oneself speak—and they don't seem to have any rules in particular: at least, if there are, nobody attends to them."*

Lewis Carroll, *Alice in Wonderland*

On March 1, 1974, HEW Secretary Caspar Weinberger and Labor Secretary Peter J. Brennan announced that a conciliation agreement had been reached between government civil rights officials and the University of California at Berkeley, thereby releasing previously withheld federal government contract funds. The story went almost unnoticed by most newspapers in the United States. Yet the

169

Berkeley settlement was probably one of the most significant events in the effort to eradicate discrimination in higher education. It marked a turning point in government action, if not in prevailing government attitudes.

Berkeley had been under government pressure to produce an acceptable affirmative action plan for needed improvements in the employment situation for minorities and women. The conciliation agreement announced by Weinberger and Brennan allowed Berkeley an additional six months to do employment studies and gather more data and once again to come up with a plan. Berkeley officials described the agreement to the press as a "plan to have a plan" and claimed there was "no basic disagreement between the campus and OCR" (HEW's Office for Civil Rights). Waite Madison, Jr., chief of the higher education branch of the San Francisco office of OCR, agreed. Berkeley officials, he said, had "a basic commitment to do what needs to be done" (Trombley, 1974c). But NAACP Western Regional Director Leonard Carter called the settlement a "travesty and an insult to the minority community." And Ann Scott, legislative director of the National Organization for Women, claimed it was a violation of federal regulations "so serious it threatens the viability of contract compliance" (Levy, 1974). Added one West Coast commentator, "The message they [other universities] have received from recent events at the University of California at Berkeley is that compliance is not necessary, that the government does not mean what it says" (Trombley, 1974a).

As if to prove the pessimistic observers right, only a few days after word of the Berkeley settlement traveled through university administrative circles, one university president is said to have phoned HEW officials in Washington and asked, only half facetiously, to have his own university brought into compliance with the law in the same way as Berkeley.

The Berkeley agreement came after a long and complicated struggle by several women's groups to apply presidential orders forbidding discrimination on the part of federal contractors to the situation in higher education. Executive Order 11246 was signed by President Lyndon B. Johnson in 1965. It prohibits discrimination by federal contractors on the basis of race, color, religion, or national origin. Two years later, after heavy lobbying by women's groups,

Executive Order 11246 was amended by another executive order that prohibits discrimination by federal contractors on the basic of sex.

Under the executive orders, the Secretary of Labor is responsible for administering the prohibitions against discrimination. Each federal contractor, simply by accepting federal contract funds, agrees to refrain from certain discriminatory practices and promises, in the language of the orders, to "take affirmative action to ensure that applicants are employed, without regard to their race, color, religion, sex, or national origin." The penalty for noncompliance is severe: "In the event of the contractor's noncompliance with the nondiscrimination clauses of this contract or with any such rules, regulations, or orders, this contract may be cancelled, terminated, or suspended in whole or in part and the contractor may be declared ineligible for further government contracts." It would be hard to imagine a more effective penalty for institutions that depend on federal contract funds for much of their work.

However, the executive order is not without a loophole: the Secretary of Labor can exempt a contractor from the provisions that demand nondiscrimination if "he deems that special circumstances in the national interest so require." The loophole was not overlooked in the Berkeley settlement.

The executive order recognized the necessity of setting up some kind of investigative mechanism to determine compliance. The primary authority for the establishment of that mechanism is assigned to the Department of Labor, Office of Federal Contract Compliance, which in turn has delegated much of the task to various federal agencies. As part of that delegation of authority, HEW's Office for Civil Rights was assigned investigative and compliance chores for university contractors.

Federal contracting agencies such as the Department of Defense and NASA are obliged under the executive order to ascertain the compliance posture of potential contractors before assigning contract funds. They can do so by notifying the Office for Civil Rights and obtaining the necessary clearance. Presumably that office either will have cleared the potential contractor in a normal check of institutions that receive large numbers of federal grants, or it will be equipped to check the institution and then issue a letter to the government agency seeking to give contract funds.

In the early 1970s several national organizations concerned with civil rights for women began filing class complaints against universities. Three hundred class complaints were filed by 1972 and probably over five hundred by 1974. (HEW does not seem to have records of the numbers of such complaints it has accepted.)

The Contract Compliance Division, one of three divisions in the Office for Civil Rights at that time, was not equipped to handle the complex university-based complaints, and by June 1972, when the backlog had grown to embarrassing proportions, a new Higher Education Division was formed to take on the task of university compliance.

But compliance is proving difficult. The rationalizations offered by university officials, especially in regard to the employment of faculty members and professional personnel, are complex and sophisticated, and the availability of women and members of minority groups in the general labor pool cannot be translated automatically into jobs in institutions that require highly trained professionals.

The flood of charges that engulfed the Office for Civil Rights in the early 1970s left it bewildered and unable to cope. Although there were undoubtedly some skilled and intelligent investigators, the history of higher education complaints is marked by a number of botched investigations. Unskilled investigators were (and are) easily befuddled by the sensible-sounding rationalizations offered by university officials with years of experience at befuddling university professors. And university officials, trained in the art of the intellectual put-on, are adept at making investigative heads nod in profound, if bewildered, agreement. And if nothing else is convincing, their anger at complaints is certainly genuine and convincing enough: there is nothing that so unifies academics as a complaint to an outside agency, something that nowadays could be referred to as the Serpico effect.

A further complicating factor is the obvious reluctance on the part of many government bureaucrats to undertake the same kind of effort on behalf of women that was earlier undertaken on behalf of blacks. While commitment to end discrimination against women was never a high priority item under the Kennedy or Johnson administrations, the commitment to end racial discrimination led to high morale and a fair level of affirmative action accomplishment. If there was reluctance to extend the fight to discrimination on the basis of sex, it was not obvious in the general atmosphere of antidiscrimination activity. The real push to end sex discrimination, unfortunately, did not gain momentum until the Nixon administration was firmly entrenched. And by that time the drive on the part of individual women and women's groups was met head on by growing bureaucratic indifference to civil rights in general and to women's rights in particular.

In July 1970, then Secretary of Labor James Hodgson even went so far as to state publicly that he had "no intention of applying literally exactly the same approach to women" in regard to enforcement of the executive order as had been applied to blacks, though the executive order had neither been rescinded nor softened (Hole and Levine, 1971, p. 46). Although he later modified his statement, it remains an accurate assessment of government willingness to act on behalf of women.

The Higher Education Division of the Office for Civil Rights works under a number of disadvantages. According to HEW officials a major one is that the regulations for implementing the executive orders were drafted by the Department of Labor with an eye to industrial situations. But a reading of the current regulations on affirmative action makes one suspicious of HEW or university officials who complain that industrial guidelines on discrimination cannot be made to apply in an educational institution. The regulations seem clear. Claims of confusion, while they may be valid on occasion, also can be used as a device to avoid compliance. And any complex set of regulations, including one that spells out what is needed for antidiscrimination compliance by federal contractors, allows sufficient latitude for deliberate confusion. Even unclear regulations could be made to work with a high level of commitment on the part of either the agency or the universities or both.

Another problem that has plagued efforts at enforcement is the lack of leadership within the Higher Education Division itself. From its formation in June 1972 until June 1973, the division had no permanent director. Yet in January 1973 the division had to take on a new task in addition to its other uncompleted ones. As of that month, all institutions of higher education that received federal funding were required to have affirmative action plans on file. Before that time, only private institutions that had federal contracts were under this obligation; public institutions needed only to produce "corrective action" plans, if they had been found out of compliance with the law. The new requirement obviously demanded an enormous amount of agency time and attention, but during that first year the Higher Education Division did not manage to attract or keep a permanent director. Two interim directors filled in at various times but did little to organize the division or formulate plans of action. And in early 1973, when for a few weeks the division did have a permanent director, her time was spent in political infighting. Just before the new director took over, Columbia had been found out of compliance, several pending contracts had been withheld from the university, and a letter had been sent asking Columbia to correct the alleged violations or to show proof that they had not occurred. The new director began her job just in time to take the brunt of the political pressure to let Columbia off the hook. She fought that pressure, and then, rather than cave in, she resigned. By mid-March 1973 HEW was once again looking for someone to head its Higher Education Division.

In June 1973, a year after the division was formed, the fourth director was selected. She was a former political science professor from the University of California at Fullerton, Dr. Mary Lepper. While Lepper made headway in internal administration of the division (in such matters as the efficient tracking of cases, keeping records, and answering correspondence—all areas that had been neglected before), she was left with a legacy of problems that were allowed to compound over the years through bungled investigations, political pressure, and lack of concern. She fought to make the Higher Education Division effective but lost almost all her battles.

One of Lepper's problems arose from the Nixon philosophy of governmental decentralization that gradually allowed regional directors of dubious competence and dedication to take over much of the authority for civil rights enforcement. For the most part these regional directors take a dim view of the effort to achieve equal employment opportunities for women. And Lepper was also forced to fight higher level officials in her agency for the right to do the job she was hired to do. Enforcement of civil rights legislation is not a big item with the current administration. Because of these political factors staff morale within the division is low, at least among those who care about enforcement of the law. "Better than half the staff doesn't give a damn," claims an HEW insider.

Under the circumstances it was not surprising that the Berkeley situation became a cause for battle, not just between Berkeley and HEW but within HEW itself. The Berkeley struggle began in April 1971, when the League of Academic Women, along with the National Organization for Women, filed a class complaint with HEW against the Berkeley administration. The complaint alleged sex discrimination in both academic and nonacademic employment. But HEW was not prepared to handle the complaint. No investigation was launched, and the university went right on receiving clearances for federal funds. The Berkeley women waited ten months for HEW to take some action and then in mid-February 1972 filed suit in federal court. The suit asked for an injunction that would have affected hiring and termination rates until an acceptable affirmative action plan to remedy past discrimination was worked out.

A hearing on the suit was held at the end of March 1972. But by that time HEW had belatedly begun its investigation. The judge ordered the agency to finish its investigation as rapidly as possible and continued proceedings on the plaintiff's motion for preliminary injunction for forty days. But it was November 1972 before HEW was able to release a determination. It found Berkeley out of compliance with the law and demanded that the university submit plans for ending discriminatory employment patterns on the campus. Since mandatory affirmative action plans were not yet required of public institutions, the HEW letter gave Berkeley thirty days in which to come up with either a corrective action plan or an affirmative action plan. Under government regulations Berkeley should have been well on its way toward losing federal funds if a suitable plan could not be drawn up within that time. Thirty days, however, is not a fixed amount of time in HEW parlance, and by July 1973 Berkeley had submitted only inadequate bits and pieces of material. But the agency still had not imposed contract holds on the university. Berkeley was not only long overdue in relation to the HEW letter of findings but three months overdue in having on file the by then required affirmative action plan.

In July HEW finally felt a sufficient sense of urgency to send a letter asking Berkeley administrators to devise an adequate affirmative action plan within thirty days. Part of this new enthusiasm for enforcing the law undoubtedly was generated by the fact that Lepper had taken over as director of the Higher Education Division in June. The letter was followed up by a meeting between HEW officials and Berkeley Chancellor Albert Bowker. HEW officials came away from Berkeley with a promise that the university would submit an acceptable affirmative action plan by the end of August. But the "plan" submitted at the end of August was, according to one official, "no better than anything else they had submitted."

However, HEW officials did not respond by withholding federal contracts. It took weeks of heated discussion within the agency before Lepper and Office for Civil Rights director Peter Holmes, Lepper's immediate superior, went to Berkeley in mid-November and delivered a letter giving Berkeley notice that if something were not done a thirty-day show-cause letter would be issued. (A show-cause letter informs an institution that federal funding will be stopped unless the institution is able to demonstrate that it has ended its discriminatory practices. But the Higher Education Division has only twice issued such letters—to the University of Washington and to Berkeley. In the case of Washington, the agency backed down, and, in September 1974, the university produced an affirmative action plan described as "worse than Berkeley's." The Berkeley affirmative action plan is discussed below.) In effect, the document finally sent to Berkeley in November 1973 was a sixty-day show-cause letter and indicated to Berkeley officials that if no better affirmative action plan was forthcoming within that sixty-day period, contracts might be stopped.

The new Berkeley affirmative action plan arrived in Washington in December 1973, thirteen months after HEW had first demanded that such a plan be submitted within thirty days. But once again it was inadequate. Higher Education Director Lepper again decided to fight. But the fight, unfortunately, was not merely with Berkeley. Once again it was with officials inside the Office for Civil Rights as well. According to one HEW insider, "it had just become obvious that they were willing to find any nit-picking reason they could not to send a show cause letter. I believe they were second guessing [HEW Secretary Caspar] Weinberger all along. I believe they felt that Weinberger would be very upset if Berkeley got a show cause letter."

In mid-November, Lepper had been able to impose several temporary contract holds on Berkeley. One involved a $2.4 million contract from the army for computer research on the campus. But, in violation of government regulations, the army released contract funds without the required letter of clearance—a letter that is supposed to be written before any federal contract funds can be released and that assures the contracting agency that the recipient of funds does not engage in discriminatory practices.

On another contract involving NASA-sponsored research for 1975 Soviet-American joint space flight, Lepper received cooperation from the contracting agency. NASA had its collective fingers burned in October 1973 when its internal administrator for equal opportunity, Ruth Bates Harris, was sacked, precipitating an uproar among women's groups across the country (Holden, 1973, p. 804). NASA was not about to follow up that disturbance by releasing funds to Berkeley without the proper clearance. In fact, according to HEW insiders, NASA officials were so cooperative that they were willing to assign the research project to another institution.

In January 1974, Lepper went to Berkeley again, this time accompanied by Martin Gerry, the acting deputy director of the Office for Civil Rights. But by January, it was clear to Berkeley administrators that there was pressure within HEW to avoid implementing the agency's own regulations. Government officials were all too willing to participate in the game of negotiations and delay rather than to enforce regulations that required them to withhold or withdraw federal contracts. Even worse, when a serious effort to implement the regulations was finally made by Lepper, both regional HEW officials and supervising officials in the Office for Civil Rights fought that effort. Enforcement of the law was being prevented both by Berkeley's delaying tactics and by active collusion on the part of HEW officials.

The January session ended with a conciliatory statement by Gerry, who told reporters that "things are moving in the right direction" and predicted "a lessening of restraints" on Berkeley (Trombley, 1974b). By this he could only mean that the NASA contract, which NASA itself was not pushing to release, would in fact be released.

But in February, *Los Angeles Times* reporter Bill Trombley questioned Lepper, who had remained silent after the January session with Berkeley administrators. By that time, Lepper was ready to give the press an honest assessment of Berkeley's efforts. The new plan, Lepper said, "contained no policies or programs that would lead to a satisfactory solution." She went on to list a series of flaws in the plan, including its failure to deal with revolving-door appointments (the low-ranked, impermanent appointments that beef up university statistics on the number of women and minorities who are employed but never allowed to move into the ranks of permanent members of the university community) and including the noticeable omission of hiring plans by most of Berkeley's academic units. Berkeley had submitted such plans for only four units out of a total of eighty academic departments and seventeen colleges and professional schools. Lepper told the *Times* that she was "disheartened" by the Berkeley situation. "I really don't understand why Berkeley couldn't come up with an acceptable plan," she said. "After all, they've been working at this since November of 1972" (Trombley, 1974b).

Peter Holmes, director of the Office for Civil Rights, immediately removed Lepper from the case and placed Martin Gerry in charge of negotiating a settlement with Berkeley. With Gerry in charge, a "settlement" did not take long to achieve. In late February 1974 a settlement was announced, and NASA was informed that it could release funds to the campus. But NASA officials, still wary after their internal squabbles over affirmative action, were not ready to release the funds. Instead, they went to the Office of Federal Contract Compliance (OFCC) in the Department of Labor, the agency that is authorized to supervise compliance with the executive order and that technically has supervisory authority over the HEW Office for Civil Rights. NASA inquired whether or not it was permissible to release contract funds. And the OFCC, instead of going along with the Berkeley-HEW agreement, insisted that Berkeley's affirmative action efforts were inadequate and advised NASA to continue withholding funds.

It was the OFCC refusal to go along with the Berkeley agreement that brought Weinberger and Brennan into the picture. The two cabinet officers agreed to call off the Office of Federal Contract Compliance. That agency, having advised NASA that Berkeley was out of compliance, announced in late February that the contract funds would be released after all, because it was "in the national interest" that the NASA project go forward (Levy, 1974). A few days later, Brennan and Weinberger held their press conference and publicly announced that the Berkeley-HEW conciliation agreement was acceptable to both HEW and the Department of Labor.

Berkeley had tested HEW and found it vulnerable. The gamble paid off and funds were released. Berkeley could take another six months to once again attempt to come up with an acceptable affirmative action plan.

But the story does not end there. Back at HEW in Washington, a memo was removed from circulation. Intended for higher officials including Weinberger, it had been drafted by an HEW attorney to inform them that HEW was, and would continue to be, in violation of its own regulations if it did not take immediate action to declare Berkeley out of compliance and to withhold all federal funds from the campus. The memo was never sent.

And on March 15, 1974, Holmes sent a congratulatory letter to Berkeley Chancellor Albert H. Bowker assuring him "that UCB has demonstrated that it will be able to comply with the equal opportunity requirements of the Executive Order." It concluded: "Before closing let me offer my apology for the statements allegedly made by members of my staff (as reported by the *Los Angeles Times* of February 8, 1974) regarding both the efforts and intentions of the Berkeley campus toward the development of an acceptable Affirmative Action Program. These 'quotations' are particularly regrettable because they appeared at a time when OCR on a day-to-day basis was fully aware of the substantial efforts of Berkeley officials, on a close cooperative basis, to move quickly to finalize the development of an acceptable Affirmative Action Program. The spirit of positive cooperation which has characterized the relationship between you and your staff and representatives of this office during our negotiations is appreciated." In one letter Holmes had congratulated Berkeley for its "spirit of positive cooperation," a spirit that had apparently marked the previous two years of delay

and resistance, and chastised his own Higher Education director for
pointing out that Berkeley was not exactly cooperative!

Reaction among those who understood the law was not as
sanguine as the Holmes letter. In Berkeley, court action was
activated again by local women trying to get the courts to enforce
the laws, since the agency set up for this specific purpose was apparently unwilling to do so. And Berkeley member of the House of
Representatives, Ron Dellums, asked the Government Accounting
Office to investigate the Office for Civil Rights. Contract compliance enforcement, one of his aids pointed out, is following a
"pattern of governmental lawlessness" (Levy, 1974).

Predictably, the new plan submitted by Berkeley over the
summer and fall of 1974 was found totally inadequate by officials
in the Higher Education Division in Washington, who gave it what
they called "the most comprehensive analysis." The plan was also
given an extensive legal review and was passed on to the Office of
Federal Contract Compliance of the Department of Labor for
still further review.

Shortly before year's end, the Higher Education Division
sent its recommendation to Director Holmes: a show cause letter
should be sent to Berkeley. According to HEW insiders, politics once
again took over at this point. First an effort was made by Holmes's
office to intercede with the HEW General Council by claiming that
the Higher Education Division made an erroneous and inadequate
analysis of the Berkeley plan and by insisting that the Berkeley
problem was not serious enough to call for the sending of a show-
cause letter. The internal politics become a little vague at this point,
but Holmes's recommendation that no show-cause letter be sent was
somehow reversed and a show-cause letter was drafted by Gerry
for delivery to Berkeley at the end of January 1975. The month-long
delay before issuing the letter apparently was due to the desire of
Higher Education Division officials, chary of past accusations that
they had not done their analysis in thorough enough fashion, to add
further substantiation to the show-cause letter.

On January 17, 1975, officials in the Higher Education
Division were convinced that the internal battle was over and the
decision firm: HEW would release a show-cause letter on January
27. But on January 20, two Berkeley vice-chancellors "just hap-

pened" to be in Washington, and Holmes, after meeting with them, decided once again to delay sending the show-cause letter. On January 22, the two vice-chancellors were able to announce to the press that Berkeley would get additional time to gather data and analyze its situation. If Berkeley did not come up with the needed data, they added, HEW might then send a show-cause letter.

In what appeared to be a prearranged scenario, Holmes delivered the long delayed show-cause letter to Berkeley officials on February 18, 1975, and was handed Berkeley's new affirmative action plan on the same day. Holmes accepted the plan the same day, making the show-cause letter moot while making onlookers somewhat skeptical about the care with which the two-volume, 1000-page plan was analyzed.

A suit brought by several women's groups in November 1974 against HEW and the Department of Labor for failure to enforce the antidiscrimination laws probably caused some pressure on the agencies, according to insiders. It may even have been behind the seemingly firm commitment that developed inside the agencies in late December 1974 to send Berkeley a show-cause letter. And the suit caused a flurry of talk about enforcement. But the flurry was short-lived, and furthermore, in February 1975, insiders claimed that Lepper, the first full-time director of the Higher Education Division to remain for more than a few weeks, was on her way out, to be replaced by a white male. While Lepper did not please women activists who expected more from the agency and who point to instances where she might have managed better and gained better enforcement, at least part of her problem in many instances was in trying too hard to gain enforcement. Berkeley was one such instance, and there undoubtedly were others.

In its entire history of control over the higher education enforcement of the executive order, HEW has only rarely delayed contracts, has only twice sent a show-cause letter, has never held an administrative hearing (a step that occurs after an institution has been declared out of compliance), and has neither disallowed nor cancelled a single federal contract.

In October 1974, the sixth full year of the executive order came to an end. In that six years there is little one can point to in the way of advancing the cause of equal employment on American college campuses. But at least, until Berkeley, HEW was viewed by campus administrators as a *potential* threat. Even that threat has now faded.

For people who have filed individual complaints of discrimination with HEW, the situation seems even worse than for those who have filed class complaints. Before 1972, the executive order offered the only protection against discrimination available to most women academics. Title VII of the Civil Rights Act of 1964 exempted both private universities and state agencies until it was amended in 1972. Since academics were not covered by Title VII, HEW continued to accept individual executive order complaints from them until 1972. When authority to accept complaints from state employees and employees of higher education institutions was given to the Equal Employment Opportunity Commission in 1972, HEW stepped out of the business of investigating individual complaints. But in the spring of 1974, the agency reversed its position and stopped automatically forwarding individual complaints to the Equal Employment Opportunity Commission. Officials reasoned that most individual complaints had class implications and should therefore be investigated. (EEOC has maintained this reasoning all along.) But HEW investigation of an individual complaint of sex discrimination is not necessarily a favor to an individual woman. The individual complaints filed before the spring 1972 cutoff decision were retained by HEW: Given the HEW distaste for record-keeping, one might well wonder if the reason for the agency's reluctance to give up its old and unresolved complaints in 1972 might have been that the agency could not have produced a list of those complaints. All are now over two years old, most have remained unresolved, and some have been so badly botched that the women who filed them have no recourse but the courts.

A number of women have reported that even though the agency has found in their favor, no effort was made to secure their jobs. Other women have been fired or let go after filing complaints. One woman reports being forced to accept a small financial settlement, even though HEW found in her favor and even though she claims to be blacklisted by every university that offers courses in her esoteric field. Still other women have reported that HEW refused to investigate their cases and sent them, instead, to the Wage and Hour Division of the Department of Labor, though the issues involved went far beyond the jurisdiction of the division. Others have reported that their complaints have gone uninvestigated for years or that investigation (or multiple investigations) did not result in any findings. Others report completed investigations that did not even include an interview with the complainant. And even where investigations have been completed in a satisfactory manner, women report that agency attorneys are reluctant to act on them.

One incident from HEW's overlong involvement with my own complaint may serve as an illustration of the treatment women have had at the hands of the agency. That complaint was filed in June 1971 and was investigated twice over the following two years. In the summer of 1973, Lepper and Madison came to Hawaii to negotiate a settlement of my discrimination complaint. A few weeks before, contract funds had been delayed on a $2.4 million NASA grant to the university. The contract covered the largest single research project at the University of Hawaii, a computer-satellite project that happened to be codirected by my husband. Lepper and Madison were confronted by nine university administrators (the vice-president for business affairs, the vice-president for academic affairs, the chancellor, vice-chancellor, assistant vice-chancellor, university secretary, dean, personnel director, and assistant personnel director), all men. The campus EEO coordinator, a woman, was not present. Those nine men had the upper hand. Not only did they outnumber the HEW contingent, but more importantly they had no fear of losing the $2.4 million contract. The chancellor had made this quite clear in a meeting a few days earlier. He assured the two directors of the research project that, if necessary, the university president would use his good contacts in Washington to guarantee that the contract would not be taken away. My husband tried to explain, to no avail and perhaps naively, that the proper solution was to comply with the law, not pull strings in Washington.

Lepper and Madison left the islands with a "compromise." They would release the funds, and the university would allow me to continue my job as an untenured instructor. That was in July. However, in September, when funds for the contract had been released, the administration had no qualms about breaking what was, at best, a bad bargain for me. The chancellor declared that I was not a faculty member, retroactive to June 30—a date well before the bargain had been struck with HEW. The university had not needed to pull strings in Washington. The contract that had been withheld specifically because of my discrimination complaint was released, I was fired, and HEW did nothing.

With enforcement of the executive orders a shambles, it is no surprise to discover that the Office for Civil Rights has a poor record on the other antidiscrimination provisions placed in its charge. In addition to the executive order, HEW's Office for Civil Rights has been entrusted with supervision and enforcement of Title IX of the 1972 Education Amendments and Titles VII and VIII of the Public Health Service Act. Title IX includes the provision that "No person in the United States shall, on the basis of sex, be excluded from participation in, be denied the benefits of, or be subjected to discrimination under any education program or activity receiving Federal financial assistance." Title VII prohibits the granting of funds "for the benefit of any school of medicine, osteopathy, dentistry, veterinary medicine, optometry, pharmacy, podiatry, or public health or any training center for allied health personnel unless the application for the grant, loan guarantee, or interest subsidy payment contains assurances satisfactory to the Secretary that the school or training center will not discriminate on the basis of sex in the admission of individuals to its training programs." Title VIII invokes the same prohibition with regard to nursing schools.

Yet enforcement of these federal laws has been as lax as enforcement of the executive orders. Although Title IX was enacted into law in early 1972, final regulations enabling enforcement had not been released by HEW as of January 1975. Titles VII and VIII became law in November 1971, yet (as of January 1975) final regulations for the enforcement of these two titles were not promulgated.

In the fall of 1974, the failure of HEW to enforce these laws caused a number of organizations and individuals to file suit against the agency in Washington federal district court. The organizational plaintiffs are the Women's Equity Action League, the National Organization for Women, the National Education Association, the Federation of Organizations for Professional Women, and the Association of Women in Science. Among the charges against the agency are failure to enforce the executive orders, failure to review contractor records, failure to conduct precontract award reviews or continuing compliance reviews, failure to require contractors to provide affirmative action plans, failure to review and evaluate plans when they have been sent in, and failure to initiate sanctions when plans prove inadequate. Of importance to individuals who have filed complaints, the court complaint charges failure to investigate in a timely manner, failure to protect individual complainants against intimidation and retaliation, failure to investigate properly and adequately, and failure to act on agency findings once discrimination has been established.

The court action will, of course, take some time. But the fact that it was filed should put both university administrators and agency officials on notice. Women will not give up when they discover that government officials neglect or subvert enforcement of the law, nor will they graciously accede to university administrators who believe neither in the law nor in the government's willingness to enforce it. Inside HEW, sympathetic officials do not expect much from the lawsuits. They feel that without the will to enforce the regulations no amount of pressure from the courts is going to have any real effect. Such pressure might speed up investigations, they point out, and the issuance of letters of finding. But it cannot guarantee that findings will be adequately researched nor that they will be sympathetic.

Women involved in such lawsuits do not agree. After experiencing disillusionment with the enforcement of existing laws, they see court-ordered enforcement as one of the few remaining avenues for ending sex discrimination. But until the test cases go through the courts, Berkeley remains the model of HEW enforcement. As matters now stand, the Higher Education Division of the Office for Civil Rights is totally ineffective, in spite of the efforts of a few of its top officials. Those few officials have faced massive indifference. They have also been hamstrung by active efforts to subvert the intent of the executive order and the civil rights laws on the part of both regional officers and their own superior officers. For the present at least, HEW's Office for Civil Rights is following the Watergate model. The government is in the business of breaking the laws it was set up to enforce.

12

EEOC: The Paper Tiger

◆◇◆◇◆◇◆◇◆◇◆◇◆◇◆◇◆◇◆◇◆◇◆◇◆◇◆◇◆◇◆

"If there's no meaning in it," said the King, "that saves a world of trouble, you know, as we needn't try to find any."

Lewis Carroll, *Alice in Wonderland*

In spite of the fact that HEW has once again entered the field to investigate individual complaints of discrimination, the Equal Employment Opportunity Commission (EEOC) probably will remain the major investigative agency in this area. At the very least, the agency offers the possibility of court action as a final step against intransigent employers. And both potential complainants and respondents might well be curious about the agency, for it has made large headlines of late in cases that affect whole industries—the steel industry, for example, and the telephone communications industry.

186

The EEOC functions under Title VII of the Civil Rights Act of 1964, which prohibits discrimination by employers, employment agencies, and unions on the basis of race, religion, color, national origin, or sex. The basic provision of Title VII is found in Section 703(a), which states the unlawful practices to be monitored and corrected by the agency. The prohibited practices are

> (1) to fail or refuse to hire or to discharge any individual or otherwise to discriminate against any individual with respect to his compensation, terms, conditions or privileges of employment, because of such individual's race, color, religion, sex, or national origin; or (2) to limit, segregate, or classify his employees or applicants for employment in any way which would deprive or tend to deprive any individuals of employment opportunities or otherwise adversely affect his status as an employee, because of such individual's race, color, religion, sex, or national origin.

Another important section of the law, Section 704(a), addresses the problem of retaliation. Like all the major laws and regulations dealing with discrimination, Title VII prohibits retaliation against an individual for either filing charges or helping others to file.

Although the 1964 version of Title VII held out promise in some areas of employment, it had two severe limitations: it did not cover employment in several important areas, and it contained no means whereby the EEOC could enforce the law. The Equal Employment Opportunity Act of 1972 was aimed at correcting these shortcomings. Under the 1964 version of the law, coverage was basically limited to employees in private industry. Government employees at the state, local, and national level were not covered. Nor were instructional employees of educational institutions. These exemptions quite obviously excluded major areas of employment for women—public school teaching and civil service. Moreover, it was apparent that in both of these areas, while women composed a large percentage of the workers, they composed a disproportionately small percentage of the managers and executives. The 1972 law added coverage for state and local government employees and for teaching employees of educational institutions. In doing so, the 1972 version of Title VII extended the jurisdiction of the EEOC to millions of government workers and to over 120,000 educational institutions with close to three million teachers and professional staff members. The 1972 amendments also added an encouraging timetable for agency action: the commission has ten days from the date a charge is filed to notify the respondent (employer). It is then expected to investigate as soon as possible, preferably within a 120-day period. If the investigation reveals probable cause to believe that the charge was accurate, the commission attempts to conciliate the case. If possible, the entire process of investigation, finding, and conciliation is supposed to take no more than the suggested 120 days. If no satisfactory conciliation is achieved after that period, the commission or the attorney general may take the matter to court. In states where there is an applicable state law forbidding discrimination in employment, the EEOC defers to the state for a fixed period of time. If the state agency does not achieve a satisfactory solution, the case then goes back to the EEOC.

If the commission fails to complete its administrative procedures on a charge within a 180-day period or if it has been unable to issue a letter of determination or enter into an acceptable conciliation agreement, an individual complainant may file suit in federal court. But the amendments approved by Congress in 1972 were specifically designed in the hope that this particular remedy would be "the exception rather than the rule, and that the vast majority of complaints will be handled through the offices of the EEOC or the Attorney General" (Manpower Information Service, 1972).

The whole procedure seems speedy enough. And since employers are notified of charges made to the EEOC, speed would seem to be essential to the peace of mind of the individual who has filed a complaint. However, the ideal timetable is seldom achieved. Even the requirement that employers receive notification of a charge filed against them within ten days after the filing of that charge by the EEOC is rarely fulfilled. And investigation within the recommended time period (let alone findings and conciliation) is almost unheard of.

The EEOC has been plagued by low budgets and a lack of sufficient trained personnel to fill even those positions it is authorized to staff. These problems, plus a certain amount of bureaucratic ineptitude and an unexpected deluge of complaints, have produced an enormous case backlog. During its first year of operation, according to the agency's annual reports, the commission received 8854 charges of discrimination. During its seond year it received 12,927, an increase of 46 percent over the first year. The load of incoming cases in year three grew to 15,058, and in year four to 17,272. By 1970, the incoming cases exceeded 20,000. In spite of the fact that the agency judged a number of cases to be out of its jurisdiction and sent still others to state or local agencies for handling, the backlog continued to grow.

In January 1970, in an effort to reduce the backlog, the Commission instituted "predecision settlement" procedures. The new procedures are intended to allow negotiated settlements before tightly worded, conclusive determinations are written up. When it believes prima facie evidence of discrimination exists, the EEOC may suggest to employers that a certain course of action would remedy the situation and avert further investigation or a formal and potentially embarrassing finding. The technique is used in cases where it appears that it might produce more rapid results.

An attempt at predecision settlement may be warranted in instances where there has not been excessive resentment generated by a complaint. In some cases the employer makes it quite clear that any such informal efforts would be fruitless. But even in cases where the EEOC has felt such an effort would be worth making, the results have been disappointing. In fiscal 1972, for example, only 14 percent of such efforts at predetermination settlement resulted in satisfactory agreements. By the time the 1972 amendments became a part of the law, little had been done that actually worked to reduce the backlog or increase the rate of satisfactory case settlement.

The threat of EEOC court action and the firming up of the investigative timetable that were added to the law in 1972 were intended to expedite the EEOC process. But the new amendments also extended coverage of the law to millions of additional employees. And the backlog has continued to grow. In fiscal 1972 (the last year for which complete statistics are available at this writing), the EEOC received 51,969 new charges. Of these, 28,337 were considered ready for immediate investigation; these were added to the 20,585 complaints from previous years still awaiting action. Yet only 726 cases reached successful settlement during the year—a mere 19 percent of the cases in which discrimination was actually found and 1.5 percent of the cases considered worthy of investigation during that year. Under the new, amended law, "unsuccessful" settlements (3000 in 1972) need not mark the end of EEOC involvement in cases. The agency can pursue cases in court and is doing so in some instances, but there is a pattern of diminishing returns within the agency.

John H. Powell, Jr., who was chairman of the EEOC until March 1975, took office in December 1973. During his tenure, Powell made the reduction of the agency backlog his first priority. But many agency workers do not view this goal as an indication that Powell was appointed for his determination to enforce the law with vigor. Quite the contrary, they claim that former Chairman William Brown III had exhibited too much determination, a quality that did not endear him to the Nixon administration. He was replaced, they claim, by a man whose convictions were more comfortably in line with the anticivil rights philosophy of the administration.

Many EEOC employees involved in the investigation and conciliation process were not happy about some of the initial steps that were taken by Powell in order to reduce the backlog. Among these moves are a rapid acceleration in "production" of case findings and conciliations and the wholesale deferral of cases for investigation by state and local agencies, many of them already known by EEOC to be inept at such investigation or even corrupt.

The acceleration of case findings will not necessarily add up to enforcement of the law. Under the best of circumstances, an employer is at an advantage in an investigation, since he controls access to all records. An investigator can obtain a subpoena to gain access to records, but an employer can launder records before a subpoena is issued. Or an employer may confront an investigator with so many records that it can take months and a high level of expertise to sort through them. And the very fact that most complaints have been waiting in the wings for months or years to be investigated often adds to their complexity—retaliation can and often does occur between the filing of a complaint and the arrival of an investigator.

The new policy may indeed reduce the backlog. But it is also likely to reduce the rate of successful settlements. Investigators point out that the chances of finding discrimination increase with the amount of time spent in an investigation. By the same token, the less investigative time spent on a case, the less likely the investigator will be to turn up the necessary proof that discrimination has occurred. The new policy is therefore likely to benefit those very employers who can cause delays rather than the many complainants waiting to have their cases investigated.

My own case, one investigator has pointed out, could never have been investigated thoroughly had a speedup in production been in force. A number of instances of retaliation complicated my case, and no single week of investigative time would have produced coherent, complete, or fair findings. Indeed, a week of intensive day-and-night effort on the part of the EEOC investigator and the HEW investigator working together was required simply to produce an adequate EEOC letter of determination. But the hours required just to write that letter were undoubtedly small compared with the hours required to gather the documentation on which the letter was based.

In my own case, sufficient time to conduct conciliation efforts would not have helped: EEOC did not even have the chance to send a conciliator to Hawaii. The agency's conciliation office wrote to the Board of Regents and proposed what they considered a minimum settlement: reinstatement with tenure at the rank of assistant professor, back pay for part of the time during which I had received inadequate pay and for the time during which I was illegally kept from employment; the reestablishment of New College with me as its director; and $20,000 in exemplary damages. But all the time and effort that went into the investigation of my complaint were stymied by the simple and arrogant refusal of the university administration and Board of Regents to sit down with EEOC conciliators and negotiate.

Their refusal illustrates another major weakness in the Title VII law: once EEOC has found that discrimination did take place, the agency is helpless to do anything to end it. No matter how well investigations are conducted and how well equipped EEOC officials may be to conduct conciliation meetings, those officials still do not

bring any real power to the negotiating table. Employers can, as
the University of Hawaii Board of Regents did, stymie the process
by refusing even to sit down and talk about the issues.

The 1972 amendments to Title VII included provisions intended to improve such situations. Under the 1964 law, once having
found that discrimination was present, the authority of the EEOC
was limited to "informal methods of conference, conciliation, and
persuasion." Unless the Department of Justice subsequently was
asked to look into a case and concluded that a "pattern or practice"
of resistance to the law was involved, a case could end with the
refusal of an employer to take any action. If the Department of
Justice did not feel a case was important enough to warrant legal
action, the individual complainant was left with no recourse short of
privately initiating court action.

The Senate Labor Committee viewed this oversight as a
serious one. In reviewing the original law, the committee stated:
"This failure to grant the EEOC meaningful enforcement powers has
proven to be a major flaw in the operation of Title VII." The
victim of discrimination, the committee added, has no recourse but
the courts, a recourse that at best "is time consuming, burdensome,
and all too often financially prohibitive" (Manpower Information
Service, 1972).

Under the amended version, the commission itself can go to
court in order to enforce the provisions of the law against private
employers. The Justice Department must still take cases against
public employers, and it is entirely at the discretion of that department whether such cases will be taken. Even in private employer
situations where the agency now has the right to take court action
the conciliation picture is not bright. To be sure, part of the blame
might lie with inept conciliation. But part rests simply in the fact
that employers often would prefer taking their chances in court to
settling out of court. Moral suasion is not a great weapon, and most
employers do not mind in the least if court action might bring them
into the public eye and label them as discriminatory.

Not every complaint in which discrimination has been found
will end in court action. Before EEOC had the right to bring such
action, the agency did not always ask the Justice Department to
pursue court action. It preferred to tackle only precedent-setting
cases where the law could be clarified or, as with American Tele-

phone and Telegraph, cases where an industrywide settlement might gain enough publicity to bring other industries into line with the law. Now that the agency has the right to bring its own cases against employers in the private sector, the attitude remains much the same. As the commission chairman has announced in EEOC's newsletter, *Mission,* "The Litigation Centers will probably recommend only about 20 percent of the cases they review for litigation. The rest of the cases may be small or dated, or duplicate the types of cases we have already brought. They are still important but can be better handled by private counsel. We will only recommend cases for government action which involve significant issues and/or large groups of people" (Jan. 1974, p. 3).

This policy is a far cry from the extended power to bring suit envisaged by the Senate Labor Committee in 1972. The intent of the Congress in granting EEOC new power was to do away with the necessity to sue privately. The EEOC's seventh annual report, released shortly after the newly amended law went into effect and while William H. Brown was still chairman, reflected the same intent: "For those who ask what can be expected of the commission over the next several years, it is fair to say that, having labored under the handicap of lack of enforcement authority for so long, the commission now intends to use that authority to its fullest and most effective extent in its efforts to achieve Congress' goal of equal employment opportunity for all people." But it would seem that former President Nixon's appointee shared neither the view of his predecessor nor the view of Congress as to the intent of the new authority granted to the EEOC.

Viewed against the thousands of instances in which the agency has found in favor of a complainant and has been unable to achieve an out-of-court settlement, the court action taken by the agency is unimpressive: between March 1972 and September 1973, EEOC had filed only 145 suits. But it is apparent that the agency is just beginning to pick up momentum—125 of those suits were filed in the first nine months of 1973. And the cases themselves often have been massive undertakings.

Perhaps the most publicized court achievement on Title VII by either the EEOC or the Justice Department resulted from EEOC taking on American Telephone and Telegraph. The suit was settled in early 1973, with AT & T agreeing to pay $35 million in back pay and raises and pledging more aggressive recruitment and promotion programs for women and minority groups. However there is some evidence that the settlement has done more to open previously "female" jobs for men than it has to open "male" careers for women. But the agency *has* consistently maintained a policy of bringing to court cases that may provide valuable precedents or may help to clarify the law, and it has been conscientious in listing the rulings that come out of such cases, whether brought by the agency or private parties. (Indeed, the tidiness of EEOC records is in marked contrast to the seeming inability to keep records that has pervaded HEW's Office for Civil Rights.)

Recently, the EEOC has tested such vague areas in the law as the burden of going forward in discrimination cases. For instance, once a plaintiff has demonstrated that he possessed the needed qualifications but was denied a job, the burden shifts to the employer, who must establish (if he wishes to win his case) that the denial of employment was related to job requirements rather than discrimination (*Green* v. *McDonnell Douglas,* 8th Cir., 1972).

In two other cases, the right of the agency to look at employer records, including computerized payroll files and computer printouts of W-2 forms, was upheld by the courts (*Rogers* v. *EEOC,* 5th Cir., 1971, and *Adams* v. *Dan River Mills,* W.D. va 1972). The legality of access to records has been extended more recently to personnel files of faculty members in universities (*EEOC* v. *University of New Mexico,* D.C., N.M., 1973).

One of the most important cases involving Title VII was heard by the Supreme Court during its 1970 term. In *Griggs* v. *Duke Power Company* (401 U.S. 424, 1971) plaintiffs, who were black employees of the company, challenged the company's right to require a high school education or the passing of standardized general intelligence tests as a condition for employment, transfer, or promotion. The challenge was based on the fact that neither standard was shown to be related to job performance, and both requirements disqualified blacks at a substantially higher rate than whites. The Supreme Court found the requirements to be unlawful. "The Civil Rights Act proscribes not only overt discrimination but also practices that are fair in form but discriminatory in operation. The touchstone is business necessity. If an employment practice which operates to exclude Negroes cannot be shown to be related to job performance, the practice is prohibited."

This particular decision may have future implications for the question of job qualifications and the question of the procedures by which those qualifications are measured. Within the EEOC there are some officials who see *Griggs* v. *Duke* as leading the way for future decisions that may force universities to pin down their now subjective and slippery notions of qualifications for academic careers and to explain the procedures by which academic men seem to attain rewards with so much greater frequency than do academic women.

Each new case opens the way for further clarification of the law. But the legal program of the agency is not without its problems. The first is obvious: the agency has failed to pursue a sufficient number of cases to cause any great change in employer practices. So far, at least, there has not been enough legal activity to prevent some employers from engaging in the same kind of practices that have been held to be illegal for other employers. This particular problem could be solved by time, if the agency is consistent in its demands on employers. Eventually there will be a body of administrative decisions and legal rulings that will serve as a healthy deterrent to certain employment practices.

But whether because of a belief that some solution is better than none, or because of simple lack of commitment to civil rights, the current commission leadership has not acted consistently. It has shown a willingness to rush into settlements that are less than satisfactory for the persons involved rather than to postpone settlement and clarify the issues in court. One industrywide agreement was arrived at in mid-April 1974 after EEOC, the Labor Department, and the Justice Department had jointly filed a complaint against nine major steel manufacturers and the United Steelworkers Union. All five groups were parties to the consent agreement. The affected classes of people—minority and women workers—were not.

Under terms of the voluntary agreement, the steel companies have consented to pay back wages estimated from $16 million to $31 million to some forty to fifty thousand black, Spanish surnamed, and women employees, who were relegated to the less desirable and generally lower paying jobs with the least opportunity for advancement. (The variation in the amount of money and number of affected employees comes from differences in the AP and UPI versions of the story.) The steel companies also agreed to hire more women.

Secretary of Labor Peter J. Brennan entered the picture here as he did in the HEW-Berkeley affair to make a laudatory statement about the settlement, which he called "historic." "It will ensure equal employment opportunity in hiring and promotion in one of our nation's basic industries," said Brennan, (*Honolulu Star Bulletin,* April 15, 1974). But the terms of the agreement do not support Brennan's contention. Workers will be required to sign waivers relinquishing their right to sue for further damages in order to get a few hundred dollars of back pay. And as part of the settlement, the Department of Justice and EEOC agreed to intervene *on behalf of the employer and the union* in case a worker refuses to sign a waiver and becomes a plaintiff in a lawsuit against the steel companies. And the government agencies agreed to exempt the steel companies from any equal employment suits for five years (Maslow, 1974, p. 36).

Herbert Hill, national labor director of the NAACP, was one of the first to publicly criticize the settlement. "The major steel corporations and the steel workers union are attempting to buy immunity from further litigation," Hill charged. He also charged the government with supporting the effort to bypass the law. Hill pointed out that the settlement had been arrived at without any participation from the classes of people affected and charged that the government's cheerful waiver of the rights of individuals to sue and its agreement to fight them if they do "is unconscionable and should be declared illegal" (*Honolulu Star Bulletin,* April 15, 1974). Not only did the agreement fail to redress past discrimination but it also failed to provide for the elimination of future discrimination. Discriminatory seniority lines were not ended by the settlement. Instead, blacks will be permitted to bid for jobs in white seniority lines when those jobs become available.

The provisions included in the settlement to redress sex discrimination are equally ineffective: the steel companies agreed to make "good faith" efforts to hire one woman for every four men added to the payroll in production and maintenance (management was not mentioned). At best, if these good faith efforts succeed perfectly, it would take a generation to achieve 20 percent women on the payroll.

Newspaper reports at the time the consent agreement was reached indicated that the district court had no objection to the voluntary settlement between these particular parties. This means, of course, that the affected parties—the only ones left out of the negotiations—will have to carry the burden of attempting to convince appeal courts that the entire settlement is invalid. In this they will be opposed by the joint forces of the steel industry, the steelworkers union, and the federal government—including the very agency set up to implement the law this agreement so clearly violates.

Until recently it was possible to temper impatience with EEOC's slow pace with the knowledge that at least the agency was, more often than not, pursuing important issues in the courts in order to clarify the law and set precedents that might gain liberal settlements for affected individuals in the future. And clearly the agency leadership under Chairman Brown was dedicated to implementing the law. But the steel settlement implies a change in direction for the agency that brings it more in line with the Office for Civil Rights of HEW. Even before Powell took over as EEOC chairman in December 1973, there was considerable debate within the agency over whether large class complaints should take precedence over individual complaints. Logic and the rapidly increasing backlog seemed to argue for handling complaints that affected the largest number of people first and leaving individual complaints for a later date. But thoughtful investigators pointed out the unfortunate flaw: such a system would expose countless individuals—more vulnerable than anonymous classes—to the possibility of retaliation and harassment when they had done nothing more than to ask the federal government to investigate illegal activity that disadvantaged them and when the law itself forces them to file complaints within a fixed time or lose all possibility of redress.

Under Powell, the answer to this dilemma did not seem to be more investigators and more attorneys, more investigations and more lawsuits. The answer seemed to be to make the current investigators and attorneys work faster (but not necessarily better) and clear up the backlog within a one- or two-year period. Apparently it did not matter that such a procedure might demoralize workers within the agency and leave thousands of complainants with inadequate investigations and unjust findings. And the answer—following the steel industry case—seemed to be to gain headline-making, industry-wide settlements that spread a thin layer of money over an area of endemic illegality in the hope that the dollar bills would serve as proper bandages.

13

The Courts: The Coward's Way Out?

◆◇◆◇◆◇◆◇◆◇◆◇◆◇◆◇◆◇◆◇◆◇◆◇◆◇◆◇◆◆◆

"No, no!" said the Queen. "Sentence first—verdict afterwards."

Lewis Carroll, *Alice in Wonderland*

University officials who take adamant stands against women with discrimination complaints may like to think that court was always the goal of these women, that they are litigious and uncompromising, that their very nature is adversary, and that their primary intent is to confront and embarrass the establishment. But without exception, the women I have talked with who have brought discrimination-based complaints to courts of law have shared my surprise that they have had to go so far to obtain a fair and open hearing.

There are a number of reasons for this. First, there is the

notion built into law that courts are a last resort and that administrative remedies are desirable, if not mandatory, first steps. Then there is the expense: most women would not even consider taking on the expense of attorney's fees when they first lodge complaints. Emotional expense is certainly another factor; no one wants to rush into a court of law. But most important, it is difficult to entertain the possibility that reason will not prevail at some earlier stage than a court hearing.

Of course, it is possible and even desirable to settle discrimination disputes at any stage of the game. The discouraging statistics of agency settlements do not reflect those cases that never reached the stage of outside investigation and were settled amicably within an institutional grievance system. However, the statistics should serve as a warning to those who experience discrimination: when one files a complaint of discrimination against a university, even if that complaint is first filed internally, one has a fairly high probability of ending up in a court of law. The reasons for this are implicit in the discussion of the previous chapters. But it might be advisable to spell them out more explicitly in this chapter and then go on to examine some of the risks that must be faced when a discrimination case heads for a court of law.

Attorneys like to tell their clients that most disputes are settled out of court and that the pressure of bringing court action— if one is clearly right in relation to the law—is likely to result in speeding an out-of-court settlement. It is possible that this is true in most civil litigation, where both parties agree to the basic fairness of the law and simply disagree as to whether or not the law has been violated. But civil rights litigation is apt to be quite different, for it is often a means of testing fairness and possibly even of expanding the interpretation of the law. Furthermore, civil rights litigation is quite often aimed at what a plaintiff feels is systemic discrimination. It therefore falls into that unsavory category discussed in chapter five—it is an attack against a specific system by an aspiring member of that system. It can be viewed by insiders as a thankless attempt to bite the hand that feeds.

Therefore, few of the normal patterns associated with civil litigation seem to hold true. Defendants, be they steel companies or universities, will rarely come to terms unless forced to do so by the courts. The track record of the Equal Employment Opportunity Commission (fewer than eight hundred settlements in fiscal 1972, for example) is ample evidence. Even in those rare cases where settlement is achieved before court action is taken, there is a telling bit of game-playing that accompanies settlement: defendants, when they give in and agree to compensate plaintiffs for past discriminatory practices, *do not admit* that they have, in fact, been practicing discrimination. The first item in almost every such settlement is a standard written denial on the part of the defendant stating that the actions being taken (whether reinstatement, back pay, salary increase, or whatever) are not an admission that any past practices were discriminatory.

Attempting to push civil rights cases in the universities is even more difficult, since university faculty members and administrators have great reluctance to admit that there is built-in discrimination in their procedures for hiring, firing, tenuring, and promoting. Administrators and male faculty members seem to feel they can ill afford the bad press of early settlement. Caving in, even with the standard denial of guilt, would be damaging to their liberal self-image. Women discover this when, because of the unresponsiveness of the internal system of appeal, they go to an outside agency: the wrath of the university establishment comes down full force at such a time. It is a fine lesson in the limits of what is permitted within the university system. Rather than encouraging early settlement, going outside provides administrators and male faculty members with the excuse that they cannot possibly settle the grievance in a gentlemanly fashion, since the aggrieved party has broken the unwritten rules and brought in outsiders. They fail to add what every woman knows by that point: there is little chance that they would settle in a gentlemanly fashion inside the system.

In a series of articles published in the spring of 1973, former University of Hawaii President Harlan Cleveland complained of the numbers of people who were turning outside academe for settlement of their grievances. His comments throw some light on the question of why discrimination cases so often end in court: "A growing proportion of all academic people who don't get what they want go to court about it. As this is written, I am defendant in a dozen lawsuits, either as university president or as an individual, usually both. The plaintiffs include a student who received a *C* and is suing for a *B* in a business administration course, faculty members who charge that adverse judgments on their new or continued employment were based on their sex or race, a professor who does not wish to retire at the mandatory retirement age" (Cleveland, 1973, pp. 23–24). While Cleveland bemoaned this inappropriate kind of activity on the part of so many, what he failed to mention—or perhaps even to notice—is that the grievants are members of power-less groups: students, ethnic or racial minorities, women, and the aged. He did not mention white males in their prime because they are unlikely candidates for outside action against a university: the system works for them. The system was invented by them and for them.

The heart of the problem of snowballing litigation on the part of faculty members, Cleveland seems to think, is a sudden clamor for clarity. The unhappy result will be "a pattern of written regulations in domains where a benign ambiguity previously seemed better to serve the interest of the faculty" (Cleveland, 1973, p. 23). But I believe it is far more likely that litigation has snowballed of late because of a rising level of expectations among persons largely excluded from the world of university employment. For the disen-franchised, the benign ambiguity Cleveland speaks of is not benign at all. It is a dual system of rules: it is a formal system of written due process rules and regulations that can be cited as needed to turn away outsiders as well as a system of informal, unwritten rules that keep insiders knowledgeable (and outsiders ignorant) as to when and for whom the written rules may be broken, bent, or bypassed. What is benign ambiguity to the establishment can be clearly singled out as abuse of due process to those outside the system.

The benignly ambiguous system of hiring, firing, and doling out rewards produces startlingly different perceptions. To Cleveland it is "a hardy chunk of conventional wisdom, the product of several hundred years of academic development. It is a trio of notions: that in a company of intellectuals, precise rules of behavior are nonsense; that valid judgments about rights and responsibilities within the academy can be made only by peers; and that within parameters set by peers, individual members of the academic club are free to inquire, to think, to teach, and to speak out in a socially protected sanctuary—and to do it for life" (1973, pp. 25–26). In contrast, to a female academic it "is wide open to abuse and covert reprisals against individuals who are not 'right thinking' or 'sound' in any of a number of ways." It is a system, she claims, where "survival . . . is far more readily achieved by mediocre men than brilliant women." And she adds, as for those who praise the system, "the self-laudatory claims of university administrators and professors as upholders of justice and humanitarianism are hollow indeed when their actions are so clearly self-serving" (Farnsworth, 1974, p. 97). Such polar views of the academic employment and promotion system indicate that the system may not function in the same manner for all groups of people.

In January 1973 I found myself in state court as a plaintiff against the University of Hawaii. My complaint was limited to procedural matters, since the issue of sex discrimination (while it could clearly be considered the motive for procedural irregularities) was still under investigation by several federal agencies. The state complaint provides a striking example of how the system functions differently for different groups of people and can, where there is a will, be manipulated to suit the powerful.

At the University of Hawaii, the written regulations governing the procedure for the granting or denying of tenure seem clear enough:

> The recommendation for or against tenure shall be initiated in the faculty member's academic department or academic division and passes via the chairman of the department or division to the appropriate dean or director for transmission to the Faculty Personnel Committee (FPC), who will review the case. The FPC will report to the president, who will forward the recommendations with his own to the Board of Regents for action.

President Cleveland admitted on the witness stand that this was indeed the current policy. Practice, however, differed: he, as executive officer of the regents, acted on all negative tenure recommendations. Thus he made all negative *decisions*. Only positive recommendations were passed on to the regents for their decision.

While this procedure is an interesting interpretation of

written policy, in my case it proved particularly important since the Faculty Personnel Committee had made a unanimous positive recommendation, yet the president had decided to make a negative *decision,* and thus the case did not go to the regents. (The next year, he took the nearly unanimous negative recommendations of all the committees and administrators below him on one man and turned the case into a positive *recommendation;* naturally the recommendation went to the regents, where it was endorsed.) The choice of what would be called a "negative decision" and withheld from the regents and what would be called a "positive recommendation" and forwarded to the regents was solely in the hands of one man—a man who, according to the written rules, was supposed to make recommendations only, not final decisions.

Further, the president stated, on the witness stand, that "any fool" would know that the university practice was for him to make all negative decisions and the regents to make the positive ones on tenure. The fact that the language in the handbook did not exactly spell out that procedure did not seem to matter. After all, he said, it was clear by reading the newspapers that only positive tenures were listed every year, so it should be obvious that these were the only ones acted on by the regents.

Cleveland complained that "if the practices are all to be committed to paper, codified in laws and executive orders and Board decisions and collective bargaining agreements and student contracts, none of which can be changed without cumbersome processes or bypassed without lawsuits, the resulting hardening of the arteries can only be devastating for the academy's role as the incubator of social invention" (1973, pp. 29–30). He failed to see that self-serving abuse of flexibility on the part of the establishment may perhaps drive the disenfranchised into court to secure due process. The present system already has "practices committed to paper, codified in laws and executive orders and board decisions." If the real fear is not of such regulations, it must be located in the second part of his statement—in being unable to change or circumvent those rules without being held accountable.

In talking about the large number of lawsuits in which he was a defendant, former President Cleveland bemoaned the fact that people who do not "get what they want" seem to end up suing the university. He does not speculate on what it is that they might want. He does not speculate that what people want when they go to court is not to rigidify the system but merely to ensure that, whatever system exists, it is applied in an evenhanded rather than an arbitrary fashion. Perhaps what academic women want—what they demand—is a system where the right to bypass the rules is not arbitrarily abused without reason to the detriment of everyone but the white male.

Those who have benefited from the current system are for the most part unresponsive to this kind of demand. If the demand is successful, it might reduce the power of those beneficiaries—or eliminate it altogether. It is not surprising then that so few of the victims of the system can gain a hearing within it and that so many of those victims end up so frequently in courts of law. All too often such action is taken only after interminable appeals and investigations both within the university system and with outside agencies. It is more often than not the unresponsiveness of the system rather than the destructive nature of the system's victims that leads to the courtroom.

In their seeming bewilderment at finding that the disadvantaged are taking them to court, many university officials may overlook the fact that this course of action is very risky for a woman complaining of sex discrimination. It is, of course, financially and emotionally expensive. The cost of such action must generally be borne by the individual (although here and there a union or a professional society or, more often, a feminist organization is beginning to help). The emotional cost cannot be shared: it is her reputation that is being discussed, her career, her claim to professional excellence. For defendants, the financial cost is borne by the institution and, if there are emotional costs, they are generally shared by deans, chancellors, and regents, so that all are able to bear up nicely. It should be clear that no individual woman (or no group of women for that matter) takes on such an expensive proposition frivolously.

The process of taking a discrimination complaint to court involves more pitfalls for the plaintiff than for the defendant institution. First, a woman must select an attorney who is not only competent but who also cares about the law and about her case— not an easy task. If she has limited resources, which is almost always true since she has probably been fired, her choice of attorney may be limited. If she is lucky, she will have a union or faculty professional organization that is willing to back her and that has retained a competent and sympathetic attorney. (This is not something that comes automatically with union or professional organization membership—the same academic establishment that has caused much of her problem is generally in charge of that union or professional organization.) And if she has done much looking she will have discovered that the two types of attorneys she may naturally assume to be sympathetic, civil libertarians and women, may not necessarily be so. She may discover that the first type, attorneys who have made reputations as defenders of liberal causes, are not necessarily defenders, liberal, or even reputable.

She may also discover that being a woman does not automatically qualify an attorney to take charges of sex discrimination nor, for that matter, to defend against them. The University of Hawaii took an unsurprising action in my case: administrators picked one of the few women in the state attorney general's office to defend them. The presumption, apparently, is that a judge would see that they were not discriminating just by her presence in the courtroom. Such cleverness rarely helps either side. Indeed, it can backfire, as one major corporation discovered: Celanese Corporation assigned their defense against an employee sex discrimination suit to a woman on their legal staff. The woman read the plaintiff's brief and then decided that she, too, had a case. She immediately filed a complaint of sex discrimination against Celanese with the Equal Employment Opportunity Commission (Bralove, 1974, p. 1). The process of entrance into law school, passing the bar, gaining a position with a reputable firm and sufficient clients to make a living, however, may serve to warp a number of women attorneys just as it does a number of women academics. By the time they achieve security in their profession, they may also have achieved a sense of their own special excellence: they can make it in a man's world, whereas the woman who complains of sex discrimination is merely whining because she is not good enough. There are few women attorneys, and even fewer among them who sympathize with a complaint of sex discrimination.

An important part of this potential pitfall is finding an

attorney with whom one can develop a satisfactory working relationship. An individual woman, while she may know far more about university matters than her attorney, must often fight to keep any control over her own complaint. Most private attorneys, when they come across a case of some interest, assume automatically that the case is theirs. The human being behind the case rapidly fades into inconsequence. Attorneys talk about *their* wins and losses, as if clients existed merely to supply them with the means to ply their trade. Even when one has forewarned an attorney that one intends to take part in strategy-making, there can be moments of relapse when one must either battle or give way to the more typical client-attorney relationship.

There are two very good reasons for maintaining some control. First, attorneys rarely know as much about universities and the way they function as do persons who have been employed in them. Second, attorneys seem to tend, as a class, toward procrastination. If a client does not push, a case may die of neglect.

The institutional defendant does not have to struggle to achieve a good working relationship with its attorney—it is clearly in control. It may be the employer of its attorney or may be able to pick and choose—and rechoose—from among several dozen attorneys from a state attorney general's office. It should be clear, then, that institutional defendants have a decided advantage over individual complainants in the business of retaining, paying for, and dictating the working relationship with attorneys. An institution is one of those rare clients that is really in control in an attorney-client relationship.

Institutions also have advantages when it comes to courtroom presentation of the evidence. An individual plaintiff generally will be forced to use self-restraint: self-aggrandizement can only backfire. But a defendant is bound by no such limits, and unfortunately, in most cases where discrimination is at issue (even if only in the background), universities are quick to present "evidence" that might serve to disparage plaintiffs. Difficult though it may be, a plaintiff will have to continually remind herself that not every insult and injury can be hauled into the courtroom to be countered and refuted. Perhaps one of the most frustrating aspects of the law

is that it does not always take up those questions one would like to
have taken up.

English common law, and thus American law, is largely based
on the protection of property rights. Personal rights do not amount
to much in the courtroom. Thus a woman may find that her complaint of injustice, when boiled down into terms a judge can cope
with, might sound more like a business transaction. Discrimination
may be translated into the illegal denial of a right to earn one's
living—a property right. Unfair treatment at the hands of university
officials may become the violation of contract terms—another
property right. The nature of the law dictates what can and cannot
be brought before a judge. And the personal insults one has had to
put up with, the telling statements of department chairmen, the
backroom votes that are revealed only by way of rumor, may all
have to be discarded as nonlegal trivia. But by the same token,
events or statistics that may seem inconsequential in terms of abstract
justice may prove to be of enormous importance to a legal case.
Certainly it is better to spread out the entire case before one's
attorney, debate the import of any single event or statistic, and only
then decide which can be included. Many times what may seem to
be a minor point—perhaps a written admission that this or that is
or is not a policy—can prove to be of considerable importance in
establishing some legal point. A good attorney undoubtedly would
prefer to be inundated with information and to sort out what is
useful. And a good client quickly recognizes that she knows infinitely
more about her case than does her attorney.

The evidence that enters into discrimination cases at the university level seems to fall into four major categories. The first kind
that appears in almost all cases of academic discrimination is statistical. Here again it should be obvious that an individual woman
may have a difficult time gaining access to university statistics.
Institutional defendants, on the other hand, not only have ready
access to such statistics but also control them and have, on occasion,
been known to manipulate them. Poor record-keeping, or the ap-
pearance of poor record-keeping, can aid universities in continuing
discrimination. Whether the statistics are in good order in university
files makes little difference when the university comes forth with
confused, noncomparable data and insists to judges and to govern-

ment agencies that it can do no better. Nonetheless, gross statistics covering the employment situation at a university are needed to establish a prima facie case of discrimination, either with an agency or in a court of law. And as difficult as statistics may be to come by and as important as they are, once a prima facie case is established, a plaintiff is still left with the necessity of proving that discrimination exists in her own case.

Departmental statistics may be useful in this. If a department has, over a ten-year period, consistently turned away female applicants for tenure and consistently found that male applicants are excellent, the statistics may provide additional—and more compelling—prima facie evidence of discrimination. But such evidence may still not be enough to gain a legal decision that one woman, turned away in one year, was in fact the victim of discrimination.

The burden of proving that a single individual suffered discriminatory treatment rather than being the victim of her own inferior qualifications still rests on the individual plaintiff. While there is legal precedent for the notion that the burden of going forward (that is, the burden of proving that discrimination did *not* take place) falls on the defendant once a prima facie case of discrimination has been established (*Green* v. *McDonnell Douglas Corp.*, 8th Cir., 1972), especially on a lower court level it is far more likely that the plaintiff will encounter just the opposite demand. A judge will look at the gross statistical evidence and then expect the plaintiff to prove that in her particular instance discrimination did in fact take place. And, even when the burden of going forward is clearly assigned to the employer, a plaintiff must be prepared to demonstrate discrimination, for a university will most often attempt to discredit the academic credentials of the plaintiff.

Statistical evidence, then, is a necessary but insufficient condition for establishing a case of discrimination. This leads to the second and infinitely more dangerous kind: evidence of individual qualifications.

Because it is so dangerous, most attorneys (and most clients) prefer to stay away from it. A major difficulty is that if the plaintiff sets out to establish merit before merit is challenged, the effect may be nothing more than to convince a judge that one is adept at self-congratulation. Defendants, on the other hand, generally do not attempt to stay away from this type of evidence. Any woman who decides to bring a discrimination charge against a university should be forewarned: the university will more than likely counter with an effort to denigrate her qualifications and to malign her character. Such efforts should not be surprising for, in the tradition of countering complaints of discrimination, universities seem far more inclined to attack the individual complainant than to examine the complaint—a phenomenon explored in some detail in earlier chapters.

Once a hearing bogs down in subjective issues of this sort, there is no telling which way a judge will rule. The two sides may even engage in the business of bringing in "experts" who, like opposing psychiatrists testifying to the sanity or lack of sanity of an alleged criminal, will build up or malign the plaintiff or each other—ad nauseam. As much as she may wish to be vindicated in the courtroom, a woman is better off when she avoids such issues.

So far, then, there is statistical evidence, which is not enough to prove a specific case, and evidence on personal merit, which is almost always extralegal in nature and tends to bog down in innuendo and counterinnuendo.

The third type of evidence, violation of due process, is perhaps the most useful to a plaintiff (if the least satisfying to her sense of outraged justice). This type lends itself less frequently to the kinds of innuendo that can shadow claims of merit. If a university administration has violated its own procedures, administrators are going to have a hard time defending themselves in court. But there is a serious shortcoming. It may be easy enough to prove that a university administration violates its own established procedures for the handling of faculty personnel matters. It may be equally easy to prove that administrators are capricious in the practice or violation of the rules. But the remedy might not be the automatic granting by the court of the reward that was denied through procedural violation. The remedy might be to send the whole matter back to the university, where correct procedures can be invoked—perhaps even to achieve the same result that brought one into court in the first place! The admonition to go back and do things correctly does not necessarily mean that the end result will be different. Administrators do not much like being told that they have done things improperly, and they may be sufficiently miffed by such a court directive that they will be doubly careful to proceed, quite properly, to accomplish the same adverse result.

The fourth type of evidence is the findings of committees or administrative agencies that previously have reviewed the issues before the court. Such findings are useful for they help to counter any attempts to discredit a plaintiff by making it clear that she is not alone in thinking that she has been injured. But in the case of university committees, positive rulings are not easy to come by, since it is generally the male academic establishment that provides committee members. And in the case of slow, inefficient, or even corrupt outside agencies, waiting for rulings in order to get evidence for court may be interminable. Here again, the difficulties for the plaintiff are far greater than the difficulties for the defendant. In the case of negative university committee decisions, the very same prejudicial treatment that has paved the way to the courtroom may be used by a defendant university as evidence that a case has no merit.

The admissibility of agency findings, such as those of the EEOC, has been an issue in court. In one case a federal circuit court found a lower court in error for failing to admit commission findings into evidence (*Smith* v. *Universal Services, Inc.,* 5th Cir., 1972). Nonetheless, the admissibility of this kind of evidence may be a matter for the judge to decide. Appeal from such decisions is, of course, possible. But appeal is a time-consuming and costly process. Clearly, the initial hearing is vital. And clearly, the character of a judge will have a great deal to do with the way that initial hearing is conducted and with its outcome.

Thus we come to what is undoubtedly the greatest risk a woman must face on going to court: the risk of drawing an unsympathetic or careless judge. But the risk here is one that is totally out of the control of most plaintiffs, for it is the court calendar that will generally dictate assignment of a case to one judge or another. Here again, the plaintiff's risk is greater than the defendant's, for a loss in court may mean her job or her entire career. A "loss" for a university may mean only that it is forced to employ a competent teacher and scholar. In the long run (and with sufficient numbers of "losses"), it may even mean a radical change in the employment patterns at American universities that could vastly improve the quality of American education.

Perhaps the single most important ingredient in a court settlement is the judge. I was given a graphic example of that fact during my own state court hearing in January 1974. On the last day of that hearing, the judge interrupted the assistant attorney general in midsentence and began contemplating aloud: How was it possible for the president of the University of Hawaii to make a recommendation on tenure and also to make the tenure decision? Didn't that put far too much power into the hands of one man? If he were working there, he would want the fullest possible review, said the judge. After all, it was an important decision, whether or not a person could continue to work at a university.

At that point, the assistant attorney general, who had argued that the right of the president to make negative decisions on tenure was a perfectly acceptable if not exactly literal interpretation of the faculty handbook, changed her tactics. In somewhat Orwellian fashion, she urged that if the university administration had done things wrong they should be allowed, albeit three years later, to go back and do things right! She urged the judge to order that the tenure decision be sent back for action by the Board of Regents. Otherwise "hundreds of thousands" of people would have claims against the university, said she: floods of people would come back to claim tenure, money, promotions, since the president had been the one who acted on all of them.

The argument verged on the absurd. And apparently the judge also felt the argument was faulty, for once more he interrupted the defendant's attorney to voice his view on sending the matter to the regents: "That would be the coward's way out," said he.

We broke for lunch a few minutes later. And just after the noon recess the judge ruled: the case would go back to the regents. I can only speculate unhappily on that particular noon recess.

The history of judicial pronouncement on sex discrimination is not encouraging. For centuries patriarchs and legislators enacted and judges upheld protective laws that limited women's sphere of operation and influence. And, as late as 1973, a federal appeals court, in an opinion written by none other than former President Nixon's would-be Supreme Court justice, Clement T. Haynesworth, upheld the right of a school district to force a pregnant woman to take unpaid maternity leave:

> Only women become pregnant; only women become mothers. But [the] leap from those physical facts to the conclusion that any regulation of pregnancy and maternity is an invidious classification by sex is simplistic. The fact that only women experience pregnancy and motherhood removes all possibility of competition between the sexes in this area. No manmade law or regulation excludes males from those experiences, and no such laws or regulations can relieve females from all the burdens which naturally accompany the joys and blessings of motherhood [Cary, 1973, p. 32].

Indeed, judges do not necessarily consider sex discrimination to be an important or even a real issue. On the first day of my state court hearing, for example, my attorney had all he could do to make clear to the judge that discrimination was an issue that was being investigated by government agencies and was *not* at issue in his courtroom. The judge was eager to decide that issue without either testimony or debate. He let us all know that sex discrimination was neither a real nor a serious charge and that, therefore, he would gladly and immediately rule that there was none so that we could all get on to serious business.

Can a woman expect to gain equitable treatment in a court of law? I have been in court twice during the past two years: once in connection with a suit brought by the faculty union in an effort to keep the regents' axe from cutting off innovative university programs and once as a plaintiff in my own case. Those two experiences were sufficient to permit me to form some impressions of the way two very different judges behave—and the relative chance of a sympathetic hearing on discrimination that may exist before such judges.

The two judges were almost opposite in their approaches to legal decision-making. In the innovative program case, the federal judge concerned himself with the law, to the detriment of human feelings of outraged justice. And the law does not protect students who see injustice in the closing of their program. The judge pointed out that they still had a university to attend and that the university was not under any obligation to provide one program over another. At best, this approach might have led the judge to decide that the university had a financial commitment to faculty members who had been promised jobs and to rule that they were entitled to monetary compensation. However, he decided that in all but a few cases faculty members had been notified in a timely manner that their contracts would end. But in his careful written decision he pointed out that several faculty members (I was one of them) did have valid claims to new contracts since notice of termination did not appear to have been given in a timely fashion. However, that was a state and not a federal issue, and he advised that it be taken up in state court.

The state court judge, on the other hand, concerned himself more with feelings than with the law. It was apparent, when we walked into his courtroom, that he had read about that "women's libber" and did not much sympathize. It took several days of exuding quiet dignity and decorum (including dressing like the stereotypic 1950s schoolmarm) to convince him that I was not a raging radical and that perhaps I had a point to make. Indeed, one of the most annoying aspects of the courtroom is that so much depends on the ambience a plaintiff (or a defendant) is able to create. I had the strong impression that this judge was going to decide which side he favored on extralegal grounds and then pick a law on which to hang his decision. His disregard for the law seemed to extend to judges who had regard for the law: one of our most trying moments during that hearing came when my attorney pointed out that the federal judge in the innovative program case had indicated that I was entitled to another year's contract. The state judge interrupted to ask my attorney whose courtroom he thought he was in and just why he thought that he, a state judge, need pay any attention to that other fellow.

During the week, the judge left the courtroom several times, occasionally interrupting testimony in midsentence, to conduct weddings in his chambers. He called in his secretary at one point to draw her a picture of a tire jack, explaining to all present that he was sending her out to buy one since his neighborhood gas station would not sell him more than $2 worth of gas at one time and he was, therefore, not going to give them his business should he get a flat tire. And he dismissed court early on one occasion because he heard of one service station that *was* filling tanks. (My hearing took place during the January 1974 gasoline shortage.)

I suppose one could call his performance colorful. And it was clear that issues of justice could on occasion receive a hearing in his courtroom, whereas issues of law were often pushed to one side. His attitude might provide a fine sense of satisfaction on those occasions when he allowed a plaintiff to expose all the injustices suffered, but it also opened the door for other, less satisfying kinds of irrelevancy.

One always hopes for a judge who is concerned with law and who will temper his interpretation of law with a sense of justice. I would suspect that the first judge comes closer to this model than the second. While it is clear that the first kind of judge can make legal decisions that may offend justice, the second can make decisions that offend both justice and law. Such a judge may allow more latitude for appeal. But it is far better to win a sound judgment in the first place than to put up with an involved appeal process. And although both kinds of judge may retain narrow views of a woman's role, the judge who concerns himself with law may still rule in favor of a woman on a discrimination complaint, though he may not like the law. The judge who concerns himself solely with his own sense of justice, on the other hand, may self-righteously ignore the law and uphold the age-old "moral right" of keeping woman in her place.

Unfortunately, it is all too often the case that a judge is not an unbiased party who merely weighs the evidence and applies the law. A judge's own preconceptions and the courtroom presence of a plaintiff may have more to do with the nature of a final decision than any amount of evidence mustered on the plaintiff's behalf or any amount of expertise on the part of an attorney in presenting that evidence. A presentation of evidence, whether well or poorly done, may serve only to make it more difficult or easier for a judge to follow his own initial inclinations. Judges, who are not exempt from human nature, will often lean first and seek persuasive and judicial-sounding reasons afterward.

Both the law and the evidence are on the side of those many women who currently are claiming that the system in American universities has a discriminatory effect on women. The ultimate achievement of equal employment opportunity in higher education will depend on judges who measure the evidence against the law rather than measuring—and stretching—the law to fit their own notions of what is important or right or even morally correct.

14

Toward Equity

"At any rate I'll never go there again!" said Alice, as she picked her way through the wood. "It's the stupidest tea-party I ever was at in all my life!"

Lewis Carroll, *Alice in Wonderland*

For women who have been involved in the effort to achieve equal employment opportunity on the campus, the 1970s have not yet offered much in the way of encouragement. What began as an optimistic, if naive, attempt to point out inequity and injustice turned into a protracted political struggle. The denials of university administrators and male faculty members to charges of discrimination evolved on some campuses into efforts to evade or delay enforcement and in some cases to malign the women who brought them into public view. Faced with an issue they do not understand, an issue which challenges their fundamental academic (and perhaps personal) beliefs, many academics prefer the comfort of myth to serious examination of the fact of inequity and the reasons for it.

Pressure from male groups has visibly influenced agency policies: an HEW ombudsman to protect the rights of white male academics was rapidly appointed because of pressure from such groups and the post was wiped out just as rapidly because of pressure from the very same groups since, in their collective opinion, the ombudsman was not pursuing the job vigorously enough. The same kind of political pressure from the same sources resulted in a series of House hearings in mid-1974 on the supposed dangers of reverse discrimination under current laws.

Within the professional organization of university professors, the AAUP, the challenge to rethink the whole system of tenure was met weakly and then was completely dismissed: the white male establishment prefers the protective system that guarantees their jobs and the jobs of their sons. And the AAUP has played a strange game, rhetorically insisting on the importance of resolving problems of discrimination within the profession while sometimes stymieing efforts to investigate complaints that come to it.

Those few women who have made it on American campuses are for the most part content to shun their less fortunate sisters. With disappointingly few exceptions they prefer to indulge in the gratifying notion that they made it on merit, therefore anyone can. And traditional faculty committees, whose charge it is to examine alleged due process violations, have not amassed a creditable record in this area. The committees, after all, are no better than the individual faculty members on them or around them.

The many wage and hour enforcers of the Labor Department have stacked up an unremarkable record over the years: women still earn three fifths the salary of men. The HEW Higher Education Division is in the throes of an internal struggle. A few of its myriad bureaucrats believe it is their job to enforce the antidiscrimination provisions of the law. But they must contend with regional officers who appear embarrassed by positive action and with superiors who have had no qualms about going even higher up to squash abortive attempts at enforcement. The Equal Employment Opportunity Commission, in many respects the most promising of the antidiscrimination agencies, has little clout when it comes to enforcement and is almost hopelessly mired in a backlog of uninvestigated complaints. And, worse, the Nixon administration carefully stifled any intent the agency had to pursue the law with vigor by removing a chairman who advocated court action and replacing him with a man who made it clear that, under him, the agency would not push very hard.

The courts present another series of obstacles for the individual woman. Attorneys are costly. Court calendars are full, and justice delayed is the rule rather than the exception. The choice of judge is often a game of Russian roulette, and plaintiffs can easily draw a chivalrous gentleman who has no intention of violating what he supposes to be the laws of nature in favor of the laws of the land. This leaves the way open for appeal—for more legal fees and more interminable waits for courtroom time.

Given the record of the past few years, those who are a part of the male academic establishment might well ask why women persist: can it be worth it to continue the struggle? My answer and the answer of a growing number of women will continue to be *yes*. First it will be *yes* because all the hassle, all the emotional and physical drain are balanced out by self-respect. To live with injustice is often more damaging to the individual than to fight it— even to fight it and lose. Second it will be *yes* because I believe there is still hope. That hope may not lie in the realm of individual complaints. There is little to be gained now by waiting in line for EEOC to investigate or to act, and there is much to be lost—one's job, for example, or the hope of gaining a new job. And few women can stand the monetary expense of lengthy legal proceedings. But there is still hope in group action. The cause of equal employment opportunity has allies, and together women can have an impact. Group action has a number of strengths. It certainly does not produce the sense of isolation and futility than can often accompany the individual woman in her individual struggle. It is far more tolerable financially. And it undoubtedly has far more political clout.

Looking backward, I would not change what I did, nor would I stop the process now. At the time my case began, only the most cynical thought that the academic world would not want to correct the situation once it was explained, and only the most suspicious thought the federal agencies were not in business to enforce federal law. But in the intervening years women have learned the ways of the academy and the agencies. Practically, the collective route is the most promising for academic women both because it seems most fruitful in the courts and because it may cause the message to get through rapidly to those in the academic establishment.

There are several intriguing avenues for collective action. The first is political. Possibly women are not yet perceived as a political force, particularly in Washington, where some agencies continue to bend to the will of male academics and where representatives still hold hearings and propose legislation that would result in weakening or killing civil rights laws. Women may be perceived as Republicans or Democrats, farm people or city people, blue-collar workers or professionals rather than as a voting block on women's issues. But women are beginning to elect and defeat political candidates on the basis of their stands on issues important to women. And feminists are running for office. A start has been made, and perhaps anger at the inaction of the agencies will stimulate a larger effort.

The second avenue is legal. A suit has been filed against HEW for failure to enforce the executive order and several of the civil rights laws that affect universities. Other suits have been filed against individual universities, and the plaintiffs point out, as part of their complaints, that court action is necessary because of the failure of HEW to act. It may prove necessary to file suit against the Labor Department for its unwillingness (or inability) to pull together adequate campuswide equal-pay studies and to enforce the provisions of the Equal Pay Act. And even EEOC, which seems to have tried harder but has made few gains, might need the push of court action. Continued pressure of this sort will be necessary for some time in order to convince universities and agencies to obey and enforce the law.

The civil rights that seem to belong to women from a simple reading of the constitution and of the laws of the land are not in evidence. But a look at the history of various civil rights movements in the United States should make it clear that rights are never passively conferred merely by their presence in the law—they are actively taken, even if only with the deliberate speed of civil rights enforcement. And usually they have not been taken without a fight and without a concerted effort by a politically powerful group. Women have not yet gained the reputation, or perhaps the organization, to be taken seriously as a political force. But the achievement of this goal is an important next step, a step that requires action in both the legislative and the judicial realms. And women are ready to take that next step.

The message to the male academic establishment should be clear: It is no longer possible to condemn the Watergate morality on the national scene while practicing it on the campus. There is a difference only of degree between the contempt for law displayed by Nixon and his aides on the Watergate tapes and the contempt for law that manifests itself in discrimination against women on American campuses. It is no longer possible to view illegal sex discrimination as just another issue on which opinion can differ and over which some women have acquired a distorted sense of mission.

Here and there, one can recognize signs that the message is being heard. University administrators who for years denied the existence of sex discrimination on their campuses are beginning to admit that there has been discrimination. Once in a while male academics have paused for breath long enough to wonder whether all the smoke might indeed mean there is a fire. And on occasion an administrator has even taken the step of writing down and publishing what was, and in the main still is, the unpopular belief that all is not well on our campuses. One such administrator pointed out that advocacy of merit is hollow if merit does not mean the selection of the best individuals from the widest possible pool; that tenure is rapidly becoming a system to protect the mediocre rather than a system that guarantees academic freedom; and that "merit, equal employment opportunity, and affirmative action are all soldiers in the same cause—a just, whole, fair, productive, and representative society" (Denny, 1974, p. 875). At least a few administrators are thus beginning to recognize both the justice and the necessity of change. They are beginning to believe, along with women, that if universities are to avoid protracted legal battles the time has come to take positive steps to correct the situation on our campuses.

How can this be done? Understanding a problem is an obvious and essential first step toward achieving an adequate solution. Yet understanding is not possible without communication, and communication between administrators and feminists is, thus far, rare. During one of the many HEW visits to the University of Hawaii campus, a woman government enforcement official set up a series of seminars intended to enlighten university officials on antidiscrimination measures. The first seminar, for all department chairmen, was followed by a seminar for chairmen of departments felt to be particularly recalcitrant. One of the men who attended the first seminar but was not required to attend the second went anyway. He took with him the assistant chairman of his department because he felt it was a perfect opportunity to see a "real bitch" in operation. Unfortunately, this attitude still seems to predominate in the academic world. Opportunities to learn about the law and to analyze the meaning of discrimination may be ignored or viewed as a perverse form of entertainment. Thus communication about the issues is blocked.

Indeed, the difficulty some administrators have in communicating with women about sex discrimination is a striking feature of the academic scene. Even in my limited experience I have encountered this problem again and again. With few exceptions, when I have attempted to explain my own situation to university administrators, I have been put off or put down. My files contain long series of memos requesting the time simply to discuss issues raised in my discrimination complaint. For months at a time those memos went unanswered. And when ignoring my memos was no longer possible, many administrators simply informed me that there was no need to talk. Those who did decide to talk often seemed to disengage their minds for the course of the conversation.

The tendency of those who stand to gain by rationalizing and justifying has been pointed out by Galbraith in discussing the economic system: "In considering the sources of the instrumental role of economics, nothing should be attributed to conspiracy and not much to design" (1973, p. 7). The same can be said of the male academic establishment in its efforts to rationalize and justify the academic status quo. It would be wrong to attribute natural self-justification to an organized and conscious conspiracy to keep women out. But the status quo does, in fact, serve the self-interest of the male academic, and it does keep women out. Only when the rationalizations are stripped off and and the mechanics of the status quo are exposed does support for it become unconscionable. To consciously support the status quo then would be to insist that maleness is a primary qualification for the rewards of the academic life. It would be to insist that the role of the male administrator and male faculty member is to screen out qualified people because they happen to be women, to protect other administrators and male faculty members who engage in such screening, and to intimidate and retaliate against those women who attempt to question the system. Few male administrators or male faculty members would be comfortable with such a definition of their activities.

To achieve this kind of explicit understanding of the status quo requires meaningful communication with just those women who have experienced discrimination. Thus my first piece of advice may not be particularly palatable: it is to invite in and to listen to the women one has been inclined to dismiss previously with bad jokes— the most outspoken women antidiscrimination advocates on campus.

The result of such discussion might well be an understanding, for example, that sex discrimination simply means that qualified women are being bypassed for jobs while men with lesser qualifications gain employment. It does not mean, as so many men have been eager to believe, that underqualified women are seeking employment at the expense of qualified men. Once this is understood, it should become clear to administrators that they have not been hiring, tenuring, and promoting the most qualified people; they have only been hiring, tenuring, and promoting the most qualified (or those they believe to be the most qualified) men. When administrators understand that increasing the pool from which they seriously select candidates can only increase the quality of the faculty, the first major hurdle will have been overcome.

The second hurdle is no easier. Having understood that ending discrimination means ending preference based on factors other than merit, administrators must next make a policy decision. Do they want to base judgments on merit? Or do they wish to maintain the current, sex-based preference system?

Unfortunately, it is all too easy, even after one has admitted that there might be a problem to continue to discriminate by inaction or by actions that are only diversionary. By such simple devices as requiring that new equal-employment questionnaires be completed for each personnel action an administrator can easily claim to be (or even believe he is) doing his job without in the least way affecting the employment picture. Many universities have initiated systems that merely require departmental officials to fill in an extra form justifying their sex-based preferences as the "most qualified" candidates. Such devices, even when they are sincerely intended to eliminate discriminatory hiring, often have the effect of generating support for the opponents of affirmative action. Filling out forms, as most department chairmen and faculty members already know, is but a paper game, and one they resent.

If administrators have made a policy decision to eliminate sex discrimination, adverse departmental reaction can be avoided, but not easily. Administrators must guard against implicit double-standard systems where women are turned away because they do not meet qualifications interpreted with the utmost rigidity while men are judged with the utmost flexibility. Administrators like to point out that rules should be applied intelligently and thus flexibly and that they should on occasion be broken intelligently. And they are correct. But the rules that are so often broken to accommodate male academics often become surprisingly inflexible when applied to women.

Even more important, administrators must move on to understand the meaning of affirmative action. Several years ago a dean at the University of Hawaii waved that term aside casually: "Oh yes," he said, "affirmative action; that means we have to discriminate to end discrimination." Not at all. Affirmative action simply means taking action to remove existing discriminatory preference systems, to substitute systems that are based on qualifications and merit rather than sex, and to bring to the employment scene those many women (and minority group members) who have been by-passed in the past.

Only those intent on obfuscation will assert that quotas and goals are the same. Quotas are quantitative and imply the hiring of women regardless of the possibility of hiring better qualified males. (It might be said that male quotas describe the current situation, that is, the hiring of men when qualified women are available.)

Goals, however, acknowledge qualifications (which should be clearly but intelligently articulated so they cannot be manipulated) and are a means of monitoring success in ending discrimination: if a university cannot meet even modest goals for hiring women, if year after year the statistics remain the same, the disparity between goals and achievement speaks to the insincerity of the goals and the continuation of discriminatory sex-based preference systems. To believe anything else is to believe that there is no discrimination now and that there simply are not enough qualified women.

Once a serious commitment to affirmative action has been made in the upper levels of a university administration, it is essential that the message get across to all levels, including those lower levels where hiring, tenuring, and promoting are initiated. For the pattern has been that lip service covers an oppressive atmosphere in which retaliation against women who seek to point out inequities is the everyday reality. Given the way things work in most universities, even the most sincere orders to implement affirmative action from the top administrator will not necessarily produce implementation. Such orders are sometimes interpreted by lower-level administrators as mere propaganda intended to make the university look good to the government. What may be read between the lines is that the lower-level administrators are supposed to do the dirty work needed to preserve the status quo, thus keeping top-level hands clean for making conciliatory gestures. Once when I pointed out to the dean of arts and sciences at the University of Hawaii that continued acts of harassment and retaliation could only put him uncomfortably in opposition to government antidiscrimination enforcement efforts, he replied, "That's what deans are for." His understanding seemed to be that presidential statements about equal employment opportunity and affirmative action were just that—statements. His job was to see that the statements were never turned into reality.

One of the most effective ways to signal the message that affirmative action is to be taken seriously is to clearly and publicly overrule and reprimand or replace a lower-level administrator who continues to act as if the policy is not a serious one. It might be pointed out here that the U.S. Department of Defense used a similar technique when the policy decision to end racial discrimina-

tion in the services was made. Promotion of officers is directly tied to
efficiency reports which include an item on each officer's record on
race relations.

Another point that might be made to administrators is that
their attorneys should sometimes be ignored. Attorneys are not in the
best position to run universities and calling them in to handle discrimination complaints often has the effect of putting them in
charge. Too many universities have allowed themselves to be backed
into a corner this way. When faced with a discrimination complaint,
an administrator may be tempted to seek legal advice immediately.
But a complaint should serve to warn an administrator of problems that have escaped notice, problems that might require careful
attention rather than the immediate assumption of a protective
legal stance. A difficulty with asking legal advice is that attorneys
like to win. They therefore prefer giving advice that may foil the
individual complainant but not get to the root of discrimination
problems. Clearly, if discrimination exists there are times when
administrators will have to admit that they or their procedures have
been wrong. They must, in other words, lose a few points if the
university is to work its way toward a more equitable system.

Another necessary step is to examine the qualifications and
attitudes of the women who are currently serving in equal employment opportunity capacities. Some of these women were appointed
at a time when no real commitment to affirmative action existed in
the higher levels and when none was expected from them. Some
may even have been selected for their loyalty to a dean or a
chancellor or for their own hostility toward active feminists. Such
women can do no good in equal employment opportunity positions.
Indeed they can do positive harm to themselves as well as others,
for they become nothing more than apologists for the administrators
they serve and buffers for the hostility that can develop on either
side. These women should be reassigned.

What is really needed is female equal employment officers
who understand the issues, are outspoken about them, are secure in
their positions, and are not beholden to any administrators. In
short what is needed is women who are not afraid to challenge
decisions when they are discriminatory. It would be useful if such
women had the power to stop and carefully investigate appoint-

ments, tenure, and promotions when there is good reason to believe that they have been granted in a discriminatory manner. But at the least, such women should have job security so that they maintain the power to point out illegal acts with impunity. This power could be persuasive when backed at the highest levels by the clear intent to achieve equal employment opportunity.

Something else should be made clear to the predominantly male administrators in higher education. There is an assumption in the academic world (and elsewhere) that women do not make good administrators because other women will not work for them. In Hawaii the superintendent of public schools made this claim in explaining why there were so few female principals in the state. When such positions open up, he claimed, women teachers often call to ask that a man be appointed since they cannot get along with women principals. And when I first moved into an administrative job at New College, the program director warned me that I would have to woo the all-female office staff because, he claimed, they were leery of working for a woman. As a result, I was given a new IBM electric typewriter so that I could woo them by not giving them any work. My male predecessor had no such slick typewriter and did not feel obliged to type his own reports and memos.

The notion that women cannot work for other women is largely a figment of the male imagination, though some women have bought it sufficiently to be standoffish at first. The notion is probably nothing more than a projection of the fear some men retain of working for women. Whether it is phrased in terms of female or male inability to work for a female, the notion is certainly useful as an excuse for not promoting deserving women. Yet when was the last time a deserving or even an undeserving man was not promoted because women—or other men—did not like working for a man? The best way to do away with this notion is to ignore it, promote deserving women, and allow those men and women who feel they cannot work for a woman to find another job. The women who have been led to believe they cannot work for a woman generally adjust easily and find they can, often with great enthusiasm. Men, if faced with the prospect of having to find other employment, might also find that they can adjust rapidly.

My next piece of advice for administrators seeking to implement affirmative action would be to survey the institution's male faculty with a cold and realistic eye and to acknowledge that there is often a difference between institutional goals of quality and actual hiring, tenuring, and promoting patterns. Such a look might be shocking in most universities. There are a few top universities that do manage, in the main, to control quality in the employment and promotion of faculty members, though quality is most often limited to a male pool. And there are often a few departments in other universities that maintain the same quality control but with the same limitation that excludes women. But in a large percentage of our universities there is an enormous gap between the rhetoric of excellence and reality. Thus it is all too easy to turn away women who do not meet the often unarticulated quality standards. But what about men?

In these universities—that is, in most universities—the following kinds of questions might be appropriate: How many ordinary men have been hired at a relatively late date because an engineer or a psychologist or a linguist was needed to fill in on short notice? How often have positions been found when an old male friend at a distant university needs a favor for one of his old male friends who wants to get away from the scene of a bad marriage? (And how many of these men have stayed on permanently?) How many times have exceptions been made for a fellow with fine experience but poor academic credentials or for a young man with no publications but great potential? How often has an older, underqualified male faculty member who was hired years ago been promoted out of kindly consideration for his ego or to enable him to retire at a higher rank and pension? (And how many older women have been retired at assistant professor rank after serving at that rank for decades?) How many men have slipped by and gained promotion with no noticeable achievement simply because one does not embarrass one's colleagues by keeping them at a lower rank for more than a certain number of years? (And how many women have been turned down for promotion on the grounds that they have not achieved quite enough?) How many men have been allowed to fudge on achievement, listing future publications that never seem to materialize or that appear in obscure or foreign journals that no one has bothered to check out? And when was the last time a man was turned down for anything because of such "personality" problems as overweight, loudness, or just plain ugliness?

The patterns are familiar, but they are not often acknowledged. If they were consciously acknowledged—something administrators can do by asking these kinds of questions—it might be a little harder to turn down a woman because she has not yet gained an international reputation in her field. Quality cannot mean the best in the nation for women (while barring women from jobs in which they might work toward such a reputation) at the same time that it means almost any male who meets some, but not necessarily all, of the written requirements.

A big factor to reckon with is that academic males are willing to take risks when it comes to their fellow males. Sometimes gambles turn out well, but often they are ill-advised. Yet yesterday's bad risk is often today's tenured professor or assistant dean. Risk-taking is rare when it comes to the employment of women. Quite the contrary, with women the assumption is often that since they *are* women, there is no risk to be taken: women *will* turn out poorly. An assistant dean gave a demonstration of just this attitude at one university when a women's studies program was started. Several women were hired to teach half time in the new program and half time in other departments. Toward the end of their first semester of employment the dean advised them to consider second-year contracts at 95 percent of full time. If they continued on full-time contracts, he warned, they could only work for four years. If they decided to accept euphemistically labeled "part-time" contracts, said he, they could be employed indefinitely. The assumption behind the offer was that the women could not even be considered risks so they need not even be considered for tenure. The best they could do was to accept tenuous part-time status and hope their contracts would be renewed each year in these second-class positions. Risk, administrators claim, is necessary to academic vitality. Yet women seem required to bring with them an ironclad guarantee when they come seeking normal tenure track employment. And those few who sneak in without the guarantee are often told later that they were warned that their chances were slim. For men, on the other hand, risk, and unfulfilled promise, often slide inconspicuously into permanent employment. It is not uncommon when this happens for colleagues and deans to assert human values and human kindness as motives: after all, the poor fellow is a friend and he does have a family to support.

Administrators must begin taking risks with women. They must stop assuming that marriage, babies, homemaking, future disinterest in the field, unproven research ability, and so forth, will prevent success for a woman. Such considerations, after all, are not assumed to prevent success for a man. Yet men get married, become fathers, maintain homes, may lose interest in their fields, and may never demonstrate research ability. Risks must be taken. And if they are unsuccessful, administrators should be careful not to generalize from single instances of failure. The path of least resistance is often to do just that: to point to a single "failure" with a female employee and assume all women will prove equally inadequate. This attitude pervaded the remarks of one physics professor when he told of his department's attempts to be kind to women. One involved providing a graduate assistantship for a woman student. Regretfully, said the physics professor, this generosity was not appreciated for the graduate student "got tired of lifting lead bricks or something" and left the university. That, he seemed to imply, is what happens when you do something nice for a woman. He failed to point out that men are called "enterprising" when they seek more challenging work.

Men also leave their jobs, and often for personal reasons. But administrators are rarely tempted to dismiss such occurrences with remarks such as, "Well, what do you expect when you take chances on a man?" If it is possible to get over this hurdle and learn to willingly take the same chances for women that are taken for men, where can administrators find women on whom to gamble? Administrators may not feel comfortable looking in the right direction, but if they do they will find that the women are there—in some cases those same administrators have already fired them.

Active feminists who have been edged out or actually fired are one obvious source of qualified women. It should be pointed out that such women are often in touch with networks of other women academics in the country and often know where to locate qualified individual women and rosters of women who are in the job market. Another obvious source is faculty wives. For years these women, many of them highly trained professionals, have been barred from employment in their husband's universities by nepotism rules which have now been declared illegal. Many of these women have accumulated valuable experience in nonacademic employment or as informal (and unpaid) research associates for their husbands. Another source should be women employed in part-time academic jobs within the university itself or in part-time and full-time jobs in junior colleges, where there has been less resistance to the employment of women. Any administrator who is serious about affirmative action will find among these women many candidates for permanent career positions.

Another source of women for academic employment is the nonacademic professional employee pool within most large universities. As a rule, women make up a larger percentage of these employees than of faculty employees. They are engaged as research assistants, programmers, technical experts in any number of fields, laboratory assistants, and associates in research. They often do the lion's share of the actual research on university projects managed by professors who claim to be too busy with their academic chores to devote large chunks of time to the laboratory. The only professional difference between these women and the men they work for may well be that the men are paid more and enjoy more secure positions. Many of these women have positions that are funded by federal money, soft money that could disappear with the end of a particular research project. While they may sometimes go on to other, parallel jobs in new projects, they do not always carry accrued seniority or employment benefits with them.

As a sidelight here—an important one, to be sure—it should be pointed out that the pay of those professional women who are on federal research funds may one day come back to haunt universities if it is inadequate. I know of a number of cases of women who work on federally supported projects and who are excellent candidates for equal pay adjustments and large back pay settlements when enforcement of the Equal Pay Act catches up with universities. If universities had voluntarily paid them fairly all along, their salaries would have come from federal funds. But when back pay and adjustment surveys are completed and settlement amounts are determined, those settlements will have to come from each university's own funds, be they state or private. The longer universities put off equal pay surveys and settlements, the larger these amounts will be. Administrators who prove recalcitrant in this area may well have to face their own accounting later with state legislators or private endowment trustees when back pay adjustments must be paid.

Another source of trained academic women is the larger professional community. An administrator need only look at the difference between the percentage of women graduates in a field and the percentage of women employed in the department of that field to recognize some problem areas. Psychology departments, for example, are notorious: while 24 percent of recent Ph.D.s in psychology were granted to women, many departments have remained steadfastly male. Those trained women are out there somewhere. Many have become practicing clinical psychologists or counselors, but they are not *all* there because they prefer the couch to the classroom. Some are there because they have met impossible employment resistance among the male academics from whom they received their training.

Professional organizations in the various fields can provide both good information about areas of female underemployment and good lists of potential female employees. The American Sociological Association, for example, has 15 percent female membership. The same organization has studied academic employment among female sociologists and found that only 12 percent of academic sociologists are women. The discrepancy is aggravated by the fact that most of these women are found at the lowest academic ranks. Serious administrators can get help from professional organizations, especially from the women's caucus groups of such organizations and from the separate women's professional associations that have been formed in recent years. Many of these groups maintain rosters of qualified women. The Project on the Status and Education of Women of the Association of American Colleges and Universities is a good source of information about such organizations.

Another rich source is the nonacademic professional world. There may be few female doctors and attorneys, for example, but those few are more readily overlooked than male doctors and attorneys when positions open up in schools of medicine and law. And in departments such as art, journalism, music, and drama, the search for qualified faculty members encompasses automatically men from the nonacademic world who do not have a doctorate. Yet the search rarely seems to reveal women with equivalent backgrounds. And women who are experienced in the nonacademic world are sometimes told that they do not meet academic requirements—an issue that is rarely raised with men from that world.

Graduate schools, which are turning out more and more female Ph.D.s, provide another source of qualified women. One of the most persistent complaints of men in the academic world is that they do not want to be forced to hire just any Ph.D. They want only the best. Aside from the offensive implication that women Ph.D.'s are "just any" rather than the best, the complaint overlooks, once again, the large gap between the ideal goal and the real situation that exists on all but a very few campuses. In reality, these same male academics who complain of being forced to hire just any woman will sometimes hire just any man, regardless of the quality of his graduate school or of his own standing within the profession. And it should go without saying that encouraging women to take on graduate work would result within a few years in a larger pool of women available for academic employment.

While most feminists support the idea of acceptance to graduate school on an equitable basis, it is interesting to note that at least one prominent male academic advocates going a step beyond this to a policy of affirmative discrimination in favor of women (Galbraith, 1973, p. 238). Such a policy, says Galbraith, is necessary to eliminate the effects of past discrimination. While there may be poetic justice in this, there are not many women who would advocate it since, in spite of discouragement at every step, the number of *qualified* women who are seeking admission to graduate schools has increased rapidly over the past few years. The problem is not to let in underqualified women who are knocking at the door. The problem is to assure admission to those many qualified women who already wish to enter. The flow could be increased by encouraging more qualified women to apply and by monitoring admissions operations to assure that they will gain places. At the same time it would hardly hurt to discourage those less qualified men who currently assume a place in graduate school as part of their birthright. The current situation, after all, is that such men are taking up places in graduate schools that could and should go to better qualified women.

But there is one area where Galbraith's system of affirmative discrimination can be justified: the evaluation and placement of older women. However, I would not use the term affirmative discrimination, for the intent of such a scheme would simply be to overcome past discrimination. The intent of the law is clear. It is not legal to discriminate against a woman for lacking certain qualifications when, in fact, the opportunity to gain those qualifications was denied her by past discrimination. Thus, a woman who was discouraged or prevented in the past from completing her doctorate should not now be called underqualified because she has failed to complete it. Nor should a woman who was, in the past, prevented from holding a job at anything but lecturer rank be called ineligible for higher rank. Employment outside the university or in nonacademic university jobs or even volunteer work must be seriously considered for what it might demonstrate about the skill and expertise a woman has gained. And those women who have learned their husband's field—in some cases better than their husband—by spending half their marriages at work on two-person careers should be encouraged to convert their skill and knowledge into paying positions. The current definition of qualifications will have to be largely discarded to make room for these women. It will have to give way to a broader definition that includes the most creative and imaginative look at the skills women may have gained through nontraditional channels. Such an intelligent approach to the question of qualifications may lead to a rapid achievement of the goal, which is, as Galbraith points out, to "bring a very great increase—potentially a doubling—of the supply of available intelligence" (1973, p. 238). No one is asking that unskilled or underqualified women be offered jobs that require skill and qualifications. What is required is that the skills and qualifications of women, whether acquired by traditional or nontraditional means, be properly valued.

The problem cannot be solved merely by encouraging more women to go into the academic profession in the future. Those women must have opportunities to gain employment in their fields once they are trained. And monitoring may be necessary for quite some time to assure that they have those opportunities. Nor can the problem be solved merely by hiring the women who are currently available under our broad definition of qualifications at only the lowest possible rank and salary, where they can be aced out later when the time comes for tenure decisions. Women must be encouraged to gain training and seek jobs in the academic world, and those who have gained their credentials already through nonacademic means must have those credentials properly valued by assignment to higher ranks.

A careful look at part-time employment for women and men may prove revealing as well. Administrators often claim that women prefer part-time jobs to the more demanding full-time tenure track jobs. But such a claim confuses two issues: the issue of part-time employment and the issue of professional status and remuneration. Few administrators would be willing to claim, for example, that women prefer low status and low pay. Yet this is exactly what they get in these part-time jobs. The assumption that women prefer low-paying part-time jobs is more often than not an excuse when, in fact, the real reason so many women are found in them is that they meet with less employment resistance in obtaining them. In contrast, the resistance to giving women full-time, high-status jobs is massive. They are, then, forced to take what they can get.

There is something else wrong with the part-time, low-status versus full-time, high-status university employment dichotomy. The unspoken assumption is that the work done by part-time employees, even on an hour-for-hour basis, is not as good or as valuable as the work done by full-time employees. Therefore it does not count toward tenure, promotion, salary increases, sabbaticals, or any of the other rewards of the academic world. Surely one of the things that can be done in any affirmative action effort is to make academic work relatively equal on a unit-for-unit basis. And surely there are few other institutions in the country where such a plan can so easily be achieved. If a person chooses to work half time, that person should be accumulating credit toward tenure, sabbaticals, promotions, at half the rate that the full-time employee accumulates such credit. And that person's rank should be assigned with regard to qualifications and merit, not with regard to the percentage of time worked. To automatically affix low rank to part-time jobs is to assume that the inability or unwillingness to work full time is a factor of qualification. This is a foolish notion at best and one that is belied by the fact that some men, having achieved permanent positions and high rank, voluntarily drop to half time or take frequent leaves of absence to reduce the amount of time put into their academic job. If an equitable system were set up, some women and some men would freely choose part-time employment, while others would choose to work full-time. But if a third option were open—part-time work that paid less and did not offer the possibility of permanent employment, higher status, salary increases, and so forth—no doubt there would be few takers.

There are a number of other things that should be done. For example, day care centers can relieve both women and men, students and employees, from the burden of providing one adult supervisor for each young child—an uneconomical arrangement at best and one that most often interferes with the education and professional employment of the female member of a marriage (or divorce) (Galbraith, 1973, p. 238). Student work rates, scholarships, and assistantships should be carefully reviewed to see that they are equitable in compensation for work performed, equitably distributed between male and female students, and are sufficient to cover the needs of students who depend on them.

The current lack of commitment to affirmative action among university administrators is signaled, among other things, by their reluctance to spend money on the effort. Equal employment opportunity duties are often assigned as extras to persons who already have full-time duties. (In one rather absurd effort to avoid cost while striking a sincere posture for government investigators, the University of Hawaii announced that EEO duties were handled by three administrators: the vice-chancellor had 5 percent of his time assigned to these duties, the assistant vice-chancellor 10 percent, and the assistant chancellor 20 percent. The assignment seemed calculated to ensure that no one would really oversee equal employment opportunity.) Yet it should be clear that the efforts suggested in this chapter will not be cheap. Not only will it be necessary to assign high quality administrators to supervise affirmative action, but it will be necessary to hire women at more than minimum rank and salary and to promote those women who are currently below rank.

Administrators should not be too quick to plead institutional poverty. Sooner or later the price must be paid. And the sooner it is paid the lower it will be. Delay will only add to the cost by increasing the back pay that will have to come from institutional rather than federal funds, adding to institutional legal bills (and to the cost of additional administrative time that must be spent on litigation), and increasing the likelihood that large punitive damage settlements will be assigned by the courts. The cost of employing women and paying them fairly is sure to be cheaper.

A beginning must be made toward real equity and toward overall improvement in academic quality. Perhaps this book can be a start: sometimes it is more comfortable to read than to confront directly. And perhaps this book will help to sensitize a few male academics enough so that they will admit that a problem exists and that their own perceptions of their self-interest might have to give way to other considerations. But eventually lines of meaningful communication will have to be opened.

The choice is to understand and cooperate in correcting the situation or to spend administrative time and effort and quantities of institutional resources in defense of an indefensible, illegal, and immoral position. Equal employment opportunity may be postponed because of intermittent government enforcement or unwillingness on the part of university faculty members and administrators to voluntarily comply with the law. But it cannot be prevented. Women mean business.

Bibliography

One of the most useful compilations of material on the subject of discrimination against women in higher education can be found in the two-volume transcript of House hearings conducted in 1970 by Congresswoman Edith Green and titled *Discrimination Against Women*. The volumes are available from the United States Government Printing Office. For convenience, the short title *Green Hearings* has been used in the bibliography. Where material is available both in the hearing transcript and elsewhere, page citations have been given for the *Green Hearings*.

Legal cases are cited in the text in order to facilitate location of legal opinions. Analyses of legal cases of importance to antidiscrimination enforcement are included each year in the annual reports of the Equal Employment Opportunity Commission.

Newspaper and magazine articles without listed authors have been included in the bibliography under the name of the newspaper or magazine.

Ad Hoc Senate Committee on Tenure. *Final Report*. Honolulu: University of Hawaii, 1974.

ADAMS, W. "A Letter from the President." *AAUP Bulletin,* 1973, 59(2).

ASTIN, H. S. *The Woman Doctorate in America.* New York: Russell Sage Foundation, 1969. Reprinted in part in *Green Hearings,* pp. 968–974.

ASTIN, H. S., AND BAYER, A. E. "Sex Discrimination in Academe." *Educational Record,* 1972, 53(2), 101–118.

BEM, S., AND BEM, D. "Training the Woman to Know Her Place: The Power of Nonconscious Ideology." In *Beliefs, Attitudes, and Human Affairs.* Monterey, Calif.: Brooks/Cole, 1970. *Green Hearings,* pp. 1042–1049.

BERNARD, J. *Academic Women.* University Park: Pennsylvania State University Press, 1964.

BETTELHEIM, B. "The Commitment Required of a Woman Entering a Scientific Profession in Present Day American Society." In J. A. Mattfeld and C. E. Van Aken (Eds.), *Woman and the Scientific Professions Proceedings.* MIT symposium on American Women in Science and Engineering. Cambridge: MIT Press, 1965.

BRALOVE, M. "Running Scared: Costly Lawsuits Spur Companies to Step Up Efforts to End Bias." *Wall Street Journal,* Aug. 2, 1974.

Carnegie Commission on Higher Education. *Opportunities for Women in Higher Education.* New York: McGraw-Hill, 1973.

Carnegie Quarterly. "Make Haste Slowly; The Outlook for Women in Higher Education." Fall 1973.

CARY, E. "Pregnancy Without Penalty." *Civil Liberties Review,* Fall 1973, 31–48.

CHALT, R., AND FORD, A. "Can a College Have Tenure . . . and Affirmative Action, Too?" *Chronicle of Higher Education,* Oct. 1973.

CLEVELAND, H. "Seven Everyday Collisions in American Higher Education." International Council for Educational Development, Occasional Paper No. 9, 1973.

COLSON, E., AND OTHERS. *Report of the Subcommittee on the Status of Academic Women on the Berkeley Campus.* 1970. *Green Hearings,* pp. 1143–1221.

Commission on Academic Tenure in Higher Education. *Faulty Tenure.* San Francisco: Jossey-Bass, 1973.

Commission on Discrimination. "Affirmative Action in Higher Education: A Report by the Council Commission on Discrimination." *AAUP Bulletin,* 1973, 59(2), 178–183.

Computer. "The Compleat Executive Secretary." Nov. 1973, 7.

DENNY, B. C. "The Decline of Merit." *Science,* Dec. 6, 1974, 875.

EVINGER, J. "Why New College Died; One Man's View." *Honolulu Advertiser,* Aug. 11, 1973.

FARNSWORTH, M. W. *The Young Woman's Guide to the Academic Career.* New York: Richards Rosen Press, 1974.

FOOTLICK, J. K. "Racism in Reverse." *Newsweek,* Mar. 11, 1974, 61–62.

FREEMAN, J. "The Building of the Guilded Cage." Pittsburgh, Pa.: KNOW, 1969a. *Green Hearings,* pp. 273–285.

FREEMAN, J. "Women on the Social Science Faculties since 1892, University of Chicago." 1969b. Speech reprinted in *Green Hearings,* pp. 994–1003.

GALBRAITH, J. K. *Economics and the Public Purpose.* Boston: Houghton Mifflin, 1973.

GOLDBERG, P. "Are Women Prejudiced Against Women?" *TRANSaction,* 1968, 5(5), 28–30.

GREEN, E., AND OTHERS. *Discrimination Against Women:* Hearings before the Special Subcommittee on Education of the Committee on Education and Labor, House of Representatives, Ninety-First Congress, Second Session, on Section 805 of HR 16098. Washington, D.C.: U.S. Government Printing Office, 1970.

HARRIS, A. S. "Statement of Ann Sutherland Harris, Assistant Professor of Art History, Columbia University." *Green Hearings,* pp. 242–260.

HECHINGER, F. M. "The Case Against Preferential Racial Quotas: Justice Douglas's Dissent in the DeFunis Case." *Saturday Review/World,* July 27, 1974, 51–56.

HOFFMANN, N. J. "Sexism in Letters of Recommendation: A Case for Consciousness-Raising." Modern Language Association *Newsletter,* Sept. 1972, 5–6.

HOLDEN, C. "NASA: Sacking of Top Black Woman Stirs Concern for Equal Employment." *Science,* Nov. 23, 1973, 804–807.

HOLE, J., AND LEVINE, E. *Rebirth of Feminism.* New York: Quadrangle, 1971.

HOLMES, P. "Affirmative Action, Myth and Reality." Speech prepared for the 1973 Annual Meeting of the American Political Science Association, New Orleans, Sept. 4–8, 1973. Text available from HEW, Office for Civil Rights, Washington, D.C.

Honolulu Advertiser. "Affirmative Actions." Apr. 24, 1974.

Honolulu Star Bulletin. "Steel Firms Sign Discrimination Settlement." Apr. 15, 1974.

HUBER, J. "Editor's Introduction." *American Journal of Sociology,* 1973, *78*(4), 763–766.

HUGHES, H. M., ed. *The Status of Women in Sociology, 1968–1972.* Washington, D.C.: American Sociological Association, 1973.

JOUGHIN, L., ed. *Academic Freedom and Tenure.* Madison: University of Wisconsin, 1969.

KILGORE, W. J. "Reviewing Tenure." *AAUP Bulletin,* 1973, *59*(3), 339–345.

KREPS, J. *Sex in the Marketplace: American Women at Work.* Baltimore: Johns Hopkins Press, 1971.

LEVY, C. "Release of Contracts to Berkeley Leaves Civil Rights Groups Wary." *Washington Post,* Mar. 24, 1974.

LOEB, J., AND FERBER, M. "Sex as Predictive of Salary and Status on a University Faculty." *Journal of Educational Measurements,* Winter 1971, *8,* 235–244.

MACHLUP, F. "On Some Misconceptions Concerning Academic Tenure." *AAUP Bulletin,* 1955, *41*(4). Reprinted in *Academic Freedom and Tenure,* Joughin, ed., pp. 177–209.

MC KINSEY, P. W. "Watchdog of Job Discrimination Snaps Its Leash." *Christian Science Monitor,* Sept. 25, 1973.

Manpower Information Service. "The Equal Employment Opportunity Act of 1972: Title VIII of the Civil Rights Act with 1972 Amendments." Washington, D.C.: Bureau of National Affairs, 1972, *3*(14).

MASLOW, J. E. "Is Title VII Sinking?" *Juris Doctor,* Sept. 1974, 28–36.

MATHEWS, L. "High Court Sidesteps Ruling in Crucial Rights Case." *Honolulu Advertiser,* Apr. 24, 1974.

NEIER, A. "Protest Movements Among the Disenfranchised." *Civil Liberties Review,* Fall 1973, 49–74.

NEUGARTEN, B. L., AND OTHERS. "Women in the University of Chicago, Report of the Committee on University Women." May 1970. *Green Hearings,* pp. 753–884.

Newsweek. "The New Campus Rebels: Women." Dec. 10, 1973, 120–126.

PAPANEK, H. "Men, Women, and Work: Reflections on the Two-Person Career." *American Journal of Sociology,* Jan. 1973, *78*(4), 852–872.

PETERSON, K. 1974a. "Faculty Question Teaching, Research Priorities." *UCLA Daily Bruin,* Apr. 10, 1974.

PETERSON, K. 1974b. "Professors Charge Nonacademic Criteria Employed in Department Tenure Decisions." *UCLA Daily Bruin,* Apr. 9, 1974.

Project on the Status and Education of Women. "Flint Feminists Win Admission to 'Men Only' Class." *On Campus With Women,* Dec. 1973, 7.

ROCHE, G. C., III. "Affirmative Action Revisited." *Private Higher Education—The Job Ahead.* Vol. 2. American Association of Presidents of Independent Colleges and Universities, 1973 Annual Meeting Speeches, pp. 11–13.

ROSSI, A. "Discrimination and Demography Restrict Opportunities for Academic Women." *College and University Business,* Feb. 1970. *Green Hearings,* pp. 923–926.

RUDOLPH, F. *The American College and University.* New York: Vintage, 1965.

SANDLER, B. "Statement of Bernice Sandler, Chairman, Action Committee for Federal Contract Compliance in Education, WEAL." *Green Hearings,* pp. 298–308.

SEABURY, P. 1972a. "HEW and the Universities." *Commentary,* 1972, *53*(2), 38–44.

SEABURY, P. 1972b. "The Idea of Merit." *Commentary,* 1972, *54*(6), 41–45.

SIMON, R., CLARK, S., AND GALWAY, K. "The Woman Ph.D.: A Recent Profile." *Social Problems,* 1967, *15*(2), 221–236.

STAINES, G., TAVRIS, C., AND JAYARATNE, T. E. "The Queen Bee Syndrome." *Psychology Today,* Jan. 1974, *7*(8), 55–60.

Stanford Observer. "Faculty Professoriate Committee, Study Rejects 'Rolling Tenure,' Rigid Quotas for Appointments." Mar. 1974.

Stanford Observer. "Marcuse on Women's Lib; Most Important, Most Radical Movement." Mar. 1974.

Time. "Begone You Rogues." Nov. 5, 1973, 109–111.

Time. "Founding Father." Nov. 5, 1973, 109.

TROMBLEY, W. 1974a. "Goals versus Quotas." *Honolulu Advertiser,* Apr. 2, 1974.

TROMBLEY, W. 1974b. "New UC Minority Plan Called Weaker than Original." *Los Angeles Times,* Feb. 8, 1974.

TROMBLEY, W. 1974c. "U.S. and UC Reach Job Bias Accord; Pact Embargo Ends." *Los Angeles Times,* Feb. 24, 1974.

U.S. Commission on Civil Rights. *Statement of Affirmative Action for Equal Employment.* Washington, D.C.: Government Printing Office, 1972.

U.S. Department of Health, Education, and Welfare. *Bulletin, Ad-*

vanced Statistics for Management, No. 14. Washington, D.C.: HEW Office of Education, Mar. 1, 1973.

U.S. Department of Health, Education, and Welfare. *Higher Education Guidelines, Executive Order 11246.* Washington, D.C.: HEW Office for Civil Rights, 1972.

U.S. Department of Labor. "Annual Average Salary, by Sex and Proportion of Women in Institutions of Higher Education, 1972–73." Washington, D.C.: Employment Standard Administration, Women's Bureau.

U.S. Department of Labor. "Equal Pay for Equal Work under the Fair Labor Standards Act." *Interpretive Bulletin.* Washington, D.C., 1971.

U.S. Equal Employment Opportunity Commission. *Fifth Annual Report.* Washington, D.C., 1971.

U.S. Equal Employment Opportunity Commission. *Sixth Annual Report.* Washington, D.C., 1972.

U.S. Equal Employment Opportunity Commission. *Seventh Annual Report.* Washington, D.C., 1973.

U.S. Equal Employment Opportunity Commission. "What Is Litigation Services?" *Mission,* Jan. 1974, 2(1), 3.

U.S. News and World Report. "Newest Campus Crusade: Equal Rights for Women." Dec. 13, 1971, 79–81.

U.S. News and World Report. "Now 'Men's Lib' Is the Trend." Mar. 18, 1974, 47.

U.S. News and World Report. " 'The Situation Has Worsened' For Women in Colleges." Dec. 13, 1971, 82.

University of Iowa. "Statement on Tenure and Academic Vitality." Ames, Iowa, Feb. 1, 1974.

WEAL. "Fact Sheet on Sex Discrimination in Universities and Colleges." *Green Hearings,* pp. 310–312.

WEISSMAN, M., NELSON, K., HACKMAN, J., PINCUS, C., PRUSOFF, B. "The Faculty Wife: Her Academic Interests and Qualifications." *AAUP Bulletin,* 1972, *58*(3), 287–292.

WEISSTEIN, N. "Kinder, Kuche, Kirche as Scientific Law: Psychology Constructs the Female." *Green Hearings,* pp. 286–292.

WOLFE, J. "Women Are More Predictable than Men." *Datamation,* Feb. 1970, 67–70.

Index